NIGHT
STUDIO

NIGHT STUDIO

A MEMOIR OF

PHILIP
GUSTON

BY

HIS DAUGHTER

Musa Mayer

ALFRED A. KNOPF

NEW YORK 1988

This Is a Borzoi Book
Published by Alfred A. Knopf, Inc.
Copyright © 1988 by Musa Mayer
All rights reserved under International and Pan-American
Copyright Conventions.
Published in the United States by Alfred A. Knopf, Inc.,
New York, and simultaneously in Canada by Random House
of Canada Limited, Toronto. Distributed by Random
House, Inc., New York.

Owing to limitations of space, all acknowledgments
for permission to reprint previously published
material may be found on page 257.

Library of Congress Cataloging-in-Publication Data
Mayer, Musa.
Philip Guston: a memoir.
Bibliography: p.
1. Guston, Philip, 1913-1980. 2. Painters—United States
—Bibiography. 3. Mayer, Musa. 4. Daughters—United
States—Biography. I. Title.
ND237.G8M38   1988   759.13   [B]   88-45208
ISBN 0-394-56377-8

Manufactured in the United States of America
First Edition

For my mother,
Musa McKim Guston

CONTENTS

ACKNOWLEDGMENTS

This memoir owes its existence to all those who have offered encouragement and help along the way. So many of my parents' friends responded warmly by digging out old letters and giving generously of their time to talk with me. Among them are Philip Roth, Herman Cherry, Clark Coolidge, Bill Berkson, Robert Phelps, Rosemarie Beck, Reuben Kadish, Stephen Greene, Jim Brooks, Charlotte Park, Josephine McKim Chalmers, Mercedes Matter, Elaine de Kooning, Karl Fortess, and especially Dore Ashton, whose critical biography of my father proved invaluable. A particular thank-you goes to my cousin Fan Weisbart, and her husband, Irving, of Los Angeles, for making it possible for me to find my father's childhood again.

I'm indebted to my longtime writing group from the New School for their patience and suggestions, and to the Columbia University Writing Division students and faculty who helped with early drafts of this manuscript, in particular Joyce Johnson, Stephen Koch, and Richard Locke. Ross Feld helped me to see what was missing. Maureen Howard's sensitive reading, her exhortation of my voice and process, were crucial. Robert Storr has been unusually generous with his time and the materials he used in preparation of his own Philip Guston book in the Abbeville Press Modern Masters series. Thanks go, as well, to Gloria Loomis, for believing in the book and in me; to Vicky Wilson, for asking the tough questions; and to Bill Farhood, for offering the necessary safe space to answer them. Every writer needs a loving best friend for whom no explanations or proofs are needed; Tom Mayer is mine. I hope that he knows how grateful I am.

LIST OF ILLUSTRATIONS

CHAPTER HEADINGS

NIGHT
STUDIO

ONE

Retrospective

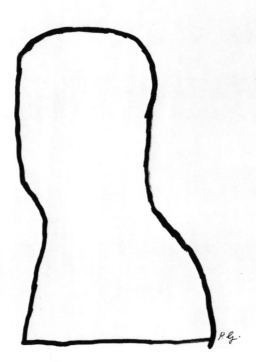

Stranger, 1970.

Those masterful images because complete
Grew in pure mind, but out of what began?
A mound of refuse or the sweepings of a street,
Old kettles, old bottles, and a broken can,
Old iron, old bones, old rags, that raving slut
Who keeps the till. Now that my ladder's gone,
I must lie down where all the ladders start,
In the foul rag-and-bone shop of the heart.
—WILLIAM BUTLER YEATS
"The Circus Animals' Desertion"

The summer my father died, I wanted to go home.

Not to my real home in Ohio, where my life and work and family were, but home to Woodstock, home to my childhood.

Picture it. It is the summer of 1980, July. My father has been dead a month. The funeral and phone calls are long over. Every afternoon a thunderstorm threatens, yet there has been no rain for weeks. It is quiet now at my parents' home, so quiet that one day my mother opens the school clock over the kitchen table and stops its pendulum. Its tick, which has been measuring their lives for so many years, is suddenly too loud.

My mother and I are alone with my father. There is no other way to say this: his absence seems as palpable and large as he was. Each night, in sleep, I somehow forget he has died; each morning, in the fragile moment of coming back to the world, I remember. I am staying in my old room, now the guest room, sleeping next to my father's empty studio, the resinous, acrid smell of turpentine and oil paint permeating my days and nights, as it had during all the years I was growing up.

I sink easily into the long Woodstock summer, breaking its surface with barely a ripple. Everything feels familiar. As if I have found the current again after a long, circuitous digression—through two marriages and two children, a move to Connecticut, then Ohio, a career as a counselor in community mental health—picking up again where I left off almost exactly twenty years ago, that first time I left home, for college, at seventeen. I wasn't ready to leave then, either.

But I am not seventeen, I am thirty-seven. And the ease of this return troubles me. I am supposed to be moving forward, upward—along some evolutionary, clearly liberated path. This slipping back can't be good, can it?

A month passes, then two. And still, I am here, in Woodstock. I don't know what to expect from my grief. But I have to stay. For reasons that are far from clear, I am not ready to leave my father at the bottom of the hill in the artists' cemetery and go on with my own life.

There are other, more practical concerns. A strange monument has sprung up where my father used to be; an edifice known as the Estate of Philip Guston now dominates our landscape, with its profusion of legal and tax matters to be handled, its concerns with storage and posterity and sales and proper exposure of the paintings and drawings. My mother, worn down by grief and the lingering effects of a stroke three years before, can't be expected to deal with all this by herself. I tell this to my husband and sons, my friends, my employer at the hospital where I work in Dayton. All this is perfectly true, and reasonable. Everyone understands. But I know there is more to it.

At night, when I can't sleep, I prowl around in my father's studio. Sometimes my mother joins me. Her heart leaps when she sees the light on late at night, she tells me; she half believes it is my father, working, and has to come out to determine that no, it's only me. We both wander around in our nightgowns, touching things, opening drawers, looking at paintings, dusting.

It is impossible to alter anything in the studio. My father's notes stay tacked up on the Homosote walls beside his desk—memos to himself, and lists of the paintings to be shipped to the retrospective of his work that has opened, only weeks before, at the San Francisco Museum of Modern Art. Pots of dirty paintbrushes stand on the drying palettes. Turpentine hardens into brown, gluey masses. His work shirts hang on the hook by the door, bespattered and torn at the elbow; his paint-daubed sneakers hold the shape of his feet. A heavily carved wood and leather chair with claw feet sits facing a wall where his latest paintings—small acrylics on paper—are hung patchwork style, with pushpins. An ashtray on a brass pedestal is still filled with his cigarette butts. Even this goes unemptied.

The accounting demanded by the IRS gives form to our days. We fill the hours with inventories, with lists of paintings and drawings. We work morning to night recording, measuring, photographing, discovering a sort of comfort in the images spread out around us.

Scores of photographs in glassine envelopes are stuffed into a four-drawer file; another contains articles, reviews, correspondence. A tower of carousel trays is packed with slides. Bookshelves hold catalogues and announcements. His huge rolltop oak desk bulges with letters. And there are his supplies, too, and the question of what to do with cupboards filled with hundreds of tubes of cadmium red medium, mars black, titanium white, the drawers of brushes, the rolls of canvas and reams of paper.

All this stuff. Forbidding in its sheer quantity, yet fascinating to me, it represents the fifty years of an artist's life—a huge, undigested mass. My father's memory was extraordinary; he would have known exactly where each catalogue and slide was. But if there's any organization to this chaos, I can't make it out.

Finally, one night in August, in an effort to bring chronological order to the volume of materials I have been sorting through, I lay out fifty different piles on the gray linoleum studio floor, one for each year of his career, from 1930 to 1980, a private retrospective.

Walking among the piles, dropping this review here, that catalogue or announcement there, I am possessed by a confusion of feelings. First, the familiar, upwelling pride that so much acclaim should attach itself to his work, that my father should be able to make from paint and canvas something so many people would care to look at and write about and own. And with this, that simple—by now habitual—transfer of worth from father to daughter, that seductive fool's gold of borrowed importance I've known and traded on all my life.

It feels strange to me—sad, really, and diminishing—that his life can be laid out like this, so neatly, on the floor—and that I should be the one to do it, to reduce him in this way. Standing there, among these piles, I become aware that our relative stature has altered in some fundamental manner. That there is a new equity I do not yet understand. In death, my father has become somehow smaller, while I, in turn, have grown. There's a feeling of power, of control on my part, as if through my efforts I could master my father, possess and contain him—and even perhaps, finally, temper in some way his overpowering influence on my life.

I look at the piles before me on the linoleum. Ranging along the upper left, near the storage racks, are the early years, the thirties and forties. This time seems alien to me, remote and mysterious. Involved as I am with my father's life, I am ignorant of his beginnings.

A copy of *Life* catches my attention. On the cover, an Ozark farmer leans on his hoe. May 27, 1946. Crouching, I leaf through the old magazine, looking for the article on Philip Guston. "You've got to *know* your stuff . . . to get ahead today," claims an ad for the "new, peacetime Regular Army." On the other side of that page is a photo of my father in his studio, hands clasped around elbows, moodily regarding one of his canvases. Behind him are two large paintings which he later destroyed. "Carnegie winner's art is abstract and symbolic," the caption reads. The painter, the article goes on to explain, no longer liked the portrait that won him the prize. *Sentimental Moment* was "too literal" a painting, he told the reporters from *Life*. I can't help smiling at the image they have fashioned of my father: the romantic, brooding artist, forever dissatisfied and contentious. It is so like him.

If This Be Not I, from 1945, is reproduced in color on the last page of the article (see plate 45). With its masks and riddles, its stagy Venetian mysteries, this painting has always served as my touchstone. I look immediately for the small portrait of me in the center of the dreamy, moonlit masquerade. A pensive, round-faced little girl with a silver paper crown on her head seems lost in the debris of the broken-down street. On either side are the figures of half-concealed sad punchinellos, older boys, wearing paper bags, blindfolds, dominoes. Of all the faces, hers alone is unmasked. She seems smaller than I remember her, less crucial, that child who was me.

From another pile, I pick up a newspaper clipping. It is 1948, three years later, but the same theme of children at play is noted by the critic Emily Genauer in the New York *World-Telegram*. "But what sort of childhood," she asks, "could the artist have had, for its memory to evoke such a tense, mysterious, even anguished picture?"

I wonder that too. Of my father's early years, I know nothing at all. I have never met his family. There are no boxes of photographs, no albums. I can't even imagine him as a child; in my fantasy, he has sprung full grown into adult genius, into the complex and probing melancholy I always knew. No childhood, no past.

It wasn't important to my father that I understand about his life. He had neither the time nor the inclination to pass on the sort of generational legends that families usually share. And I always sensed that there was something he wished to forget, a barrier posted, an injunction against my even asking. Mixed in with my grieving for my father is a keen sense of that loss. My loss. For they are my family, too, these nameless, faceless people, whoever they are.

I think of my own childhood. In 1948, I was five years old. That was the year my father won the Prix de Rome, and went away to Italy for a year. My only consolations during his long absence had been infrequent postcards illustrated with drawings. On one of them, I remember, each letter of the word "love" was transformed into a tumbling acrobat. I used to take those postcards out again and again to look at them, until their edges became frayed.

So many people—biographers, art critics and historians, even librarians preparing chronologies for catalogues—know more than I do about my father's life. I should be grateful that so much has been preserved and recorded, and I suppose I am; yet I am jealous, too.

These writers have asked him so many things, personal questions I hadn't thought of or wouldn't have dared to ask. The notion that I could have interrupted his complicated thoughts simply to satisfy my curiosity was inconceivable.

So I am forced to look elsewhere, aware that there is something more than a little pathetic about my turning to these secondary sources—like some doctoral student researching her dissertation—to learn about my own father's life. Nevertheless, it is what I have to work with. Perhaps then, through reading all this, I will know him at last.

Seven years later, I am still unraveling, still discovering. From interviews with his family and friends, from books and articles, letters, chronological notes and grant applications, anecdotes and fragments of memories, sketches and paintings, family photos and stories and trips to old neighborhoods—from all these sources a coherent past has begun to take form.

It has taken me all this time, and the demands of writing this book, to overcome my father's silent injunction, his dismissal of his past, and to make the necessary pilgrimage to California. Once there, I find I have waited too long. When I am finally ready to reconnect, it is too late. Two of my father's brothers survived his death, but both of my uncles have died since, without my ever having met them. The only living member of that generation is a niece, the same age as my father, who grew up with him.

A feeling of rightness grows in me as we sit around the kitchen table of my cousin Fan's comfortable home in Los Angeles, as she displays the family photo albums and begins to tell the family stories. We have had a long flight, my husband and I, and it is far past midnight, New York time. We really should wait until morning, we tell one another. But we don't get up. Fan and I smile at each other—first cousins, imagine that! After all these years, we can't stop talking.

M y father was born on June 27, 1913, the youngest of seven children, in the Jewish section of Montreal, in the wretchedly poor French-Canadian quarter.

"The morning light could not free itself from gloom and frost," wrote Saul Bellow of the Montreal ghetto of his own boyhood. "And wagons, sledges, drays, the horses shuddering, the air drowned in leaden green. The dung-stained ice, trails of ashes . . ." My cousin Fan has more benign memories, of ice-skating in the narrow streets, and of Philip at four and five, running into her family's dry goods store for a cookie.

In 1905, Philip's mother and father, Rachel and Leib Goldstein, had left Russia with Rachel's two children by her first husband. Jenny, the eldest daughter and Fan's mother, told her children about the family's flight from the terrible pogroms in Odessa. There were scary stories of crouching in cellars, in fear for their lives, hiding from the violent attacks against Jews that raged through the city. They had barely survived the difficult and turbulent ocean crossing.

Fan tells me that her mother Jenny was as straitlaced and superstitious as Rachel was easygoing and tolerant. Izzy, the first-born son, was a troublemaker who gambled and fought. I pick up the picture of my grandmother, squinting at the tiny woman with the foxtails round her neck, to find evidence of her strength. But all I see is a stolid, middle-aged lady, not particularly pretty, with the same jowls my father had, that are beginning to show themselves as a faint puffiness around my own jaw.

What became of her first husband, a stern, beetle-browed man, and the father of Rachel's first two children, is no longer known. The father of the five younger children, Rose, Harry, Nat, Irving, and Philip—all of whom were born in Canada—was a man named Leib Goldstein—known to my cousin as Wolf—also from Odessa. Of this man, who was my grandfather, there are no photographs, but a few phone calls and some digging manage to unearth his Canadian naturalization. Dated June 24, 1910, the creased and yellow paper states that Leib Goldstein—he later took the name of Louis—had come from Russia five and a half years before that, and was a blacksmith. An official has signed the document for him. All that remains of my grandfather is the wavering cross—"his mark," it says—on the tattered parchment.

Philip's father was able to find work as a machinist for the Canadian Railway, but when the family, seeking a friendlier climate, moved to Los Angeles in 1919, he had great difficulty finding a job. Yiddish yielded to English as the family language soon after they moved to California. Russian was never spoken; the immigrants were only too eager to leave the bad memories of the old country behind.

My grandfather ended up working as a junkman, driving a horse-drawn wagon through the streets, collecting refuse, a job he found humiliating. Fan describes him as a loner, a gloomy recluse who never came to the Sunday family suppers. He was a huge, brooding man, a grimy and menacing figure to her in his big black coat and slouch hat. She tells of running from him as a little girl, and of being mystified at the union of two such opposite people as Rachel and Wolf.

My grandfather, a junkman. I can't help but think of my father's last paintings, made in the years before his death. Of those terrible, loony wastelands, the piled-up images of junk, a life's debris, animate and inanimate, the legs and wheels and shoes and garbage-can lids.

"A pile of junk between two telephone poles; the urge is to kick it, disperse it." My father's hastily scribbled notes suddenly take on new meaning. "Another painting: I really only love strangeness, but here is another pile of old shoes and rags, in a corner of a brick wall—in front, a sidewalk. I've been there. I've seen it before, but I forgot."

It only confirms the picture I already have of my father doubling back, coming to terms, more than a half century later, with his beginnings. "Oh, it is all so *circular*, isn't it?" he wrote Dore Ashton in 1974 when she was working on a biography of him. "The recent work makes me feel free to use whatever formal and plastic imagery and capabilities I may possess. I mean from my own past too—all the memories. Please forgive my immodest comparison, but like Babel, I want to 'paint' of things long forgotten."

My attention is brought back to the immaculate kitchen in Los Angeles, to the photographs spread out before me, the wedding pictures, the portraits of Rachel and her children. "Babu—our grandmother—raised her children practically on her own. She took everything in her stride," my cousin says. "She had a wonderful philosophy of life: 'Don't take everything to heart,' she'd say. 'It'll kill you.' "

My grandmother was the spirited and enthusiastic center of the family. A small, spunky woman, she was thirty-four, with six other children, when my father was born. Rachel was independent and broad-minded, as fiercely affectionate and supportive of her children as her husband was remote. She kept a kosher household and enrolled her children in a *cheder*, but Leib, an agnostic, was opposed to any religious instruction.

My grandfather's despair worsened until finally, in 1923 or 1924 (the exact date isn't certain), he took his own life. It was my father, then ten or eleven, who found his father, the body hanging from a rope thrown over the rafter of a shed.

Sometimes, decades later, when Philip was deeply depressed or drunk, or both, he would mention his father's suicide to close friends. "Can you imagine how it feels to find your father like that?" he would ask.

After his death, Rachel lived alone with her younger children; a few years after my father had finally left California, she married again.

My cousin remembers my father as outgoing, full of life, affectionate, even during that painful time. "Philip always had a pencil in his hand," she says. He had often sketched as a boy, displaying an early aptitude for drawing. But it was after his father's death that his interest intensified and he began, at age twelve, to draw seriously. He was, as his friend Ross

Feld observed later, drawing "a distance for himself away from the family's shock and grief." His mother encouraged him, as she did her other children in their endeavors. Nat, seven years older but obviously fond of his youngest brother, was very close to Philip. Nat played the banjo; by his late teens, he was playing professionally in a dance band.

As a boy, my father loved the newspaper serials and comic strips. Particular favorites were George Herriman's *Krazy Kat* and Budd Fisher's *Mutt and Jeff.* For his thirteenth birthday, his mother gave Philip a year's correspondence course at the Cleveland School of Cartooning. "After the initial excitement of the different crow quill pen points, Higgins black India ink, and several-ply Strathmore paper, my interest subsided," my father explained later. "I became bored with lessons in cross-hatching, 'how to draw,' etc., and gave up the course after about three lessons."

At fourteen, Philip entered Manual Arts High School, where he finally discovered a friend whose interest in art equaled his own—Jackson Pollock. And the world began to open outward. One of their teachers, a man with the improbable name of Frederick John de St. Vrain Schwankovsky, provided their first real exposure to modern European painting and to the teachings of Oriental philosophy and mysticism. Schwankovsky took his students on trips to Ojai, to hear Krishnamurti urge his followers to challenge authority. "Revolt is essential," the Hindu master said, "in order to escape from the narrowness of tradition, from the binding influence of belief, of theories." (See Notes.)

At fifteen, Philip won a cartooning contest for teenagers in the Los Angeles *Times*, and his winning cartoon was reproduced. The following year, my father and Jackson Pollock were expelled for distributing satirical pamphlets attacking the English department at Manual Arts, and for protesting support for athletics and ROTC. Pollock went back, but my father never did return to high school. The only academic degree he was ever to receive was an honorary doctorate, from Boston University, some fifty years later.

Thinking of my father as a high school dropout pleases me. Although it is alien to me—or perhaps *because* it is alien—I take a perverse pride in my father's defiant spirit. I have always been such a good girl. Doggedly pursuing a graduate degree—my second—I am amused at myself for finding such pleasure in my father's plucky adolescent rebellion. And, of course, in its ultimate vindication.

In 1930, my father was awarded a year's scholarship to Otis Art Institute in Los Angeles. It was there that he first met a beautiful young art student named Musa McKim, whom he was later to marry. A small, soft-spoken woman, my mother was twenty-two when they met; my father was seventeen. Having spent most of her girlhood in Panama, where her father worked as a civil servant in the Canal Zone, she had followed her sister Josephine to Los Angeles, where she planned to study to become a painter.

"There was always something about Janie that was irresistible," my aunt Jo says. (Janie is her middle name; my mother was named after my grandmother, Musa Hunter.) "She didn't have to lift an eyebrow, smile, or anything. The men just *flocked* to her. Janie had all kinds of proposals. I've never seen anybody so effortlessly reap such a benefit." After picking her up at the boat in San Pedro, Jo took her sister, who was very reluctant, to see a fortune-teller in Hollywood. "You've come a long way, over a large body of water," the psychic said. "You think it is to study, but it is not. You've come to meet the man you will marry." My mother was furious.

Philip fared no better at Otis than he had at Manual Arts. The curriculum was strict and traditional. Only in the second year were students permitted to draw from the model; the first year, they were to draw only from casts. On one occasion, my mother remembers, Philip piled up every plaster cast he could find in one big mound and began to draw them. He and a new friend, Reuben Kadish, would sneak into the life drawing classes; without permission, they set up a small studio of their own in an unused space behind the school locker room.

My father was becoming increasingly discouraged at the pedantry of the instruction. "There I was," he said later, "thinking about Michelangelo and Picasso, and I had to study anatomy and build clay models of torsos." After a warning from a faculty member, the two young men were called into the dean's office and told they didn't belong there. The faculty member who had warned them was sculptor George Stanley, designer of the Oscar and the elephant symbol of the Republican Party. "That gives you some idea of the kind of art that surrounded us in Hollywood," Reuben Kadish points out. My father determined to teach himself.

At Otis, my mother had been impressed by the handsome young painter's intensity, although she found him a bit ungainly, and very unlike the men she was used to. "But Philip was just a boy then," she says. A sophisticated older man, a French writer in his thirties who'd come up on the boat with her father for a visit to California, soon captured her attention.

In the daytime, Philip worked briefly as stock boy in his brother Irving's fur business, drove a delivery truck for a dry cleaning store, and worked a machine that punched numbers on vests. He drew the line, however, at his sister-in-law Bee's attempts to find work for him as an artist at Walt Disney Studios, or at an advertising agency. Sometimes my father was able to get hired as an extra at the movie studios. In a 1931 John Barrymore film, *Trilby*, he appeared in the background as a young painter, complete with beard and beret. "I stormed the Bastille, participated in the fall of Babylon," my father recalled later. These early experiences fed a lifelong interest in film, as well as an obvious flair for the dramatic in his bearing and his talk.

Through Reuben Kadish, Philip met Los Angeles artist Lorser Feitelson, and began to frequent his studio. Feitelson introduced them to the Arensberg collection of modern European art—now at the Philadelphia Museum of Art—where he first saw the paintings of Giorgio de Chirico. *The Soothsayer's Recompense*, painted in 1913, the year of my father's birth, was in that collection. With its mysterious arcade and stopped clock, its deserted piazza slashed by harsh shadows, and its forever departing train, the world of this de Chirico painting hovers in a terrible silence, caught between enigma and clarity. But it was a later de Chirico in the collection, *The Poet and His Muse*, c. 1925, that haunted my father, for he spoke of it often, and quoted its ambiguous interior in his last paintings—the floor's wide boards, the open door, the mute torment of the faceless mannequins.

At night, Philip pored over borrowed art books, particularly those that contained reproductions of the Renaissance masters. The majesty and otherworldly stillness of the work of the Italian quattrocento painter Piero della Francesca in particular fascinated him. "They don't demand love," Philip said of the mysterious fascination that Piero della Francesca and Giorgio de Chirico still had for him almost fifty years later. "They stand and hold you off."

During this time, Philip painted and drew constantly, avidly. My mother still has some of his finely detailed and modeled colored pencil copies of Masaccio and Michelangelo frescoes.

Mother and Child, a massive, stylized maternal presence in a de Chirico–like landscape, was painted over the course of that year, 1930 (see plate 44). My father was fond of this picture all his life. He was proud enough of this precocious work to show it fifty years later in his retrospective. "I painted this when I was only seventeen," he would say. "In a closet, with Dutch Boy house paints."

It was through a photographer friend, Leonard Stark, that Philip met the photographer Edward Weston, who took my father's photograph. It is a striking portrait, revealing an intense young man, mature beyond his years, staring directly at the camera with dark, brooding eyes (see the front-of-jacket photograph).

A few years later, Feitelson severed his connection with the young painters, tagging them as Communist sympathizers. Reuben Kadish despised him for the public red-baiting tactics he used on his weekly radio program—"Lorser anticipated McCarthy by years," Kadish says— but my father never denounced his mentor. "Feitelson showed me Piero della Francesca for the first time," he said by way of explanation. "He opened up the Renaissance for me."

By this time, Philip was living with his mother, the only son still at home, in an apartment hotel near Venice, California. Now a tawdry beach scene of sidewalk performers and skateboarders, of drug dealers and beach bums, Venice was then a quiet, run-down community, but with a freedom to it, a relaxation of social mores that beach towns often have.

My cousin Fan's husband, Irving, offers to drive us out to Ocean Beach, near Venice, for a look. We stop to watch a limbo dancer who says he will walk on broken glass, but don't stay to see if he actually does. After some searching, some strolling up and down the cement walkway along the sand, we find the white brick apartment building Rachel and her son lived in, unremarkable, plain. I feel a vague sense of disappointment. What is it I expected to see?

With her children grown, Rachel no longer kept a kosher home. And, by the standards of the day, her behavior was not at all fitting for an elderly widow. Or so said the neighborhood gossips. In her fifties by this time, Rachel still loved to dance, and didn't mind asking the younger men, or taking an occasional drink or smoke.

Every week, this tiny, energetic woman would climb on the streetcar with her shopping bags to visit her children. "Come," she'd say. "Let's go have a dance. Let's have a dip in the ocean." Rachel encouraged her youngest son's independence, was proud of his growing talents. "She approved of everything he did," my cousin Fan tells me.

In a snapshot taken on the beach around this time, Philip sits on the shoulders of his brother Nat, who was by then playing in his own jazz band (see plate 3). Both brothers were tall and good-looking, sharp dressers, popular with the girls.

One evening, parked on a side street near Hollywood Boulevard, Nat crossed behind his car, perhaps to open the door for his date. They'd been out to the theater and were going dancing. But the brake wasn't set, and the car rolled down the slope, crushing his legs. Hospitalized, and in terrible pain, Nat died of gangrene.

Although my father was not to leave Los Angeles permanently until 1935, and though he continued, now and again, to live with his mother until then, he always spoke of leaving home at seventeen, which must have been close to the time of Nat's death. Whether it was this second, awful shock or Philip's increasing involvement with the world of radical politics and art that ultimately provided the springboard he needed to separate himself from his family, it's quite clear that after he left Los Angeles for New York, the break became all but complete.

There were a few visits, but they were very few. Rachel brought her new husband to St. Louis once in the mid-forties when my father was teaching at Washington University. It was the one time I met my grandmother, but I have no memory of seeing her. Philip went back to Los Angeles for her funeral in 1949, and for his sister Jenny's funeral ten years later. Apart from these visits and occasional letters from Fan, and from Harry or Irving, my father did not keep in touch.

In 1933, my father was given his first exhibition, at the Stanley Rose Gallery, in a bookstore in Hollywood that had become a gathering place for artists and intellectuals. Painter Herman Cherry, who organized the show, remembers that Philip, needing some pocket money, sold an important early work to Stanley Rose, owner of the bookstore, for twenty-five dollars. Only a photograph remains of the painting, *Conspirators*, a powerful image of Ku Klux Klan members plotting, with whips and ropes and a waiting wooden cross. The painting is still lost. Forty years later, when he was again painting Klansmen, my father was unable to track it down.

"Philip always wore a necktie," Cherry recalls. "He was nattily dressed, not like an artist. Making forty dollars a week, working for his brothers, he was considered very rich. The rest of us were all starving to death. That was always true, you know. Later, during the WPA and the forties, he made a lot of money. Phil had an early career. Made a big name for himself." He looks at me, cocking his head, a wry smile on his face. "Your dad always had a little of the bourgeois in him."

At first, my reaction is defensive. My father, bourgeois? Surely not. No, this is mere envy, distaste on the part of one painter for another's early successes. I think I recognize that old, perverse logic. Aesthetic virtue can be fashioned from privation, just as it is from rebellion. It softens failure. Money corrupts, and those who succeed are the sellouts.

But that's too easy. Haven't I just been listening as my cousin Fan talks about working day and night with her parents in their dry goods store? Haven't I been hearing about Irving's successful fur business? Long hours, hard work, complete dedication. The stakes are different, certainly. These were solid, conservative, upwardly mobile merchants and businessmen. Bourgeois. But they must have left some mark on my father.

Forged in that odd smithy of New World opportunity that was California during the twenties and thirties, the family dreams can only have been sharpened by a father's failure and suicide, a brother's tragic death. Perhaps this was the edge that honed in Philip and his surviving brothers some profound need to make something of themselves, no matter what the cost.

But whatever its genesis, it was in these boyhood years that my father formed a demanding and enduring image of what an artist should be. His biographer and friend, Dore Ashton, describes his early credo: "An artist worked assiduously, learned the entire history of his art, experimented, and above all, aspired to greatness. This romantic aspiration was evident to all who knew Guston during his late adolescence. Tall, slender, with a serious mien, he already carried himself like an artist. His energies were marshaled and he knew his direction."

America was deep in the Depression by then. Philip's work had already brought him in contact with strikes and brutal labor conditions. He heard stories of union busting and use of goon squads reportedly by the American Legion and the Ku Klux Klan. By the early thirties, the social and intellectual climate in the arts had begun to alter dramatically

1. My father, Philip Guston, age 10, in Los Angeles, 1923.

2. Philip *(left)* with his mother, Rachel Goldstein, his brothers, Nat and Irving, and his sister, Rose.

3. Philip and his brother Nat on the beach in Venice, California, c. 1929.

4. My mother, Musa, age 10, as a snake charmer, in Panama, 1918.

5. Musa with her parents and sister, Josephine,
at their house in Panama, c. 1916.

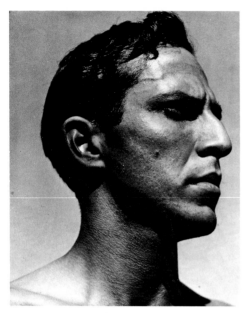

6. Philip at 16.

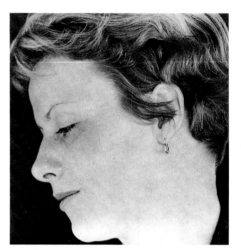

7. Musa at 21. Both portraits were taken by their
friend Leonard Stark in Los Angeles, 1929.

8. Musa with Cuna Indian women on a trip with her
father to the San Blas Islands off the coast of
Panama, 1933.

9. The Struggle Against War and Fascism, 1934. Philip *(left)* and Reuben Kadish stand in front of their finished fresco (with a poet friend, Jules Langsner), in Maximilian's Summer Palace, Morelia, Mexico. The photograph illustrated an article in *Time.*

10. Philip working on his WPA building mural, at the 1939 World's Fair in New York.

11. *Work the American Way*, 1939.
This is the completed mural.

12. My mother and father, photographed by my grandfather
shortly before their marriage in 1937.

13. Musa's Post Office mural in Waverly, New York, 1939.
The family group portrays my mother with her parents.

14. *Bombardment*, 1937–38.

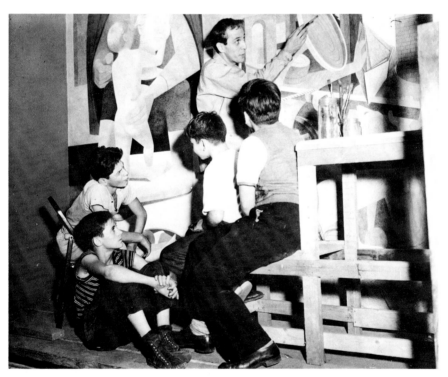

15. Philip explaining his mural for the Queensbridge
Housing Project to curious local children, 1939.

16. Philip's panel.

My parents collaborated on these two murals in Laconia, New Hampshire, for the U.S. Forestry Department, in 1941. The peaceful forest scene *(below)* is my mother's; my father depicted the lumberjacks at work.

17. Musa's panel.

18. My parents in Woodstock, summer, 1940.

19. My mother and I.

20. Philip's pencil drawing of me asleep, 1943.

21. My father holding me, Iowa City, 1943.

22. My mother and I, St. Louis, 1946.

23. *Martial Memory*, 1941.

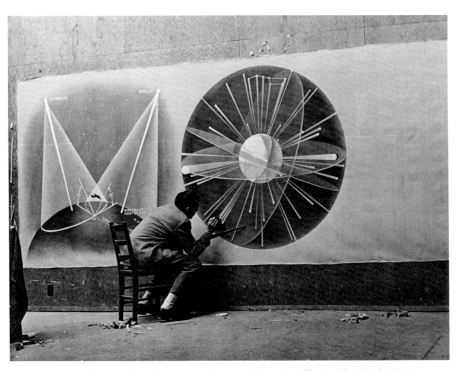

24. Philip working on the celestial navigation murals he painted for the Navy during the war.

25. Some of our Woodstock friends, c. 1947. I'm sitting in Fletcher Martin's lap, beside Herman Cherry. Behind my father is Helen Martin, and next to him is Jane Jones and her son, Wendell, Jr.

26. Glens Falls, 1947.

27. *Porch II*, 1947.

from the apolitical high style of the 1920s. Communism was in the air. The revolutionary spirit and imagery of Diego Rivera, David Alfaro Siqueiros, and José Clemente Orozco—three muralists who had led the renaissance of Mexican painting during the 1920s—was very strong in California, and was perhaps the most decisive influence on New Deal art in the years to come. To the Mexican painters, the mural was a people's art, accessible to all, a secular extension of Giotto and Masaccio.

The Marxist philosophy of the John Reed Club, a branch of which had newly opened in Los Angeles—which urged artists to "abandon decisively the treacherous illusion that art can exist for art's sake" —interested my father greatly. With his friend from Otis, Reuben Kadish, Philip painted portable murals for the walls of the club on the plight of the American Negro, specifically the famous case of the Scottsboro Boys. On one occasion, the so-called Red Squad of the L.A. Police Department broke into the club and shot out the eyes and genitals of a fresco he'd painted depicting a black man being flogged by Ku Klux Klansmen. That same year, the National Legion of Decency was formed to rid Hollywood of its leftist influences.

Together with Reuben Kadish and a poet friend, Jules Langsner, my father went to Mexico in 1934 to see the work of the muralists. "Originally," my father wrote later, "Reuben and I wanted to go to Italy to see the old frescoes firsthand. It was when we went to the San Pedro docks and found out how much it cost to go to Europe on a merchant ship, or even on a tanker, that we decided that above all we wanted to get out of Los Angeles. The only possibility within our means was to go to Mexico."

The trip did not begin auspiciously; somewhere in Texas, Langsner fell asleep at the wheel. Their car was wrecked and my father's knee was injured. By the time they arrived in Mexico City, they were broke. True to his promise to Kadish, who had written the muralist before they left, Siqueiros helped secure the two painters a wall of their own. The enormous space, a 1,024-square-foot wall in Maximilian's former Summer Palace, in Morelia, was given to them on the condition that they finish it in six months, working in true fresco style, completing large sections on wet plaster each day. The huge forty-foot-high mural depicts *The Struggle Against War and Fascism* (see plate 9).

When my father and Kadish returned to Los Angeles, *Time* magazine ran an article characterizing them as "parlor pinks" and describing their monumental frescoed figures of the medieval and modern Inquisitions. "Rising through a trapdoor are two hooded figures representing the Ku Klux Klan and Nazism. In the extreme right, Communists with sickle & hammer are rushing to the rescue. Crowed Patron-Discoverer David Alfaro Siqueiros last week, 'It is my honest belief that Goldstein and Kadish are the most promising young painters in either the U.S. or Mexico.' "

One day, at the Stanley Rose Bookstore, Herman Cherry received a letter from Panama, from someone he didn't know named Musa McKim. In the letter, she explained that she had attended Otis Art Institute and asked for Phillip Goldstein's address. "I gave the letter to Phil," Cherry says. "And he must have gotten in touch with her, because it wasn't long after that she came to live with him."

My mother had grown tired of art school herself and returned to Panama, to stay with her parents. Engaged for a time to an American tobacco merchant, she had become restless. She longed to study in Paris, but her father opposed it. She began thinking of the intense young painter she had met at Otis, wondering what had happened to him. "I simply couldn't get Philip out of my mind," my mother says.

She had just returned from a visit to the San Blas Islands with her father, who was making an anthropological study of the Cuna Indians there. Her letter to Philip was uncharacteristically daring. With it, she sent two photos taken by her father, one of her paddling a canoe with a Cuna Indian woman beside her (see plate 8), the other of her lying in her bunk on the *Imco*. "I was terribly seasick," she tells me; perhaps this explains her languorous loveliness in the snapshot.

My father wrote back immediately, enclosing photographs of his adventure—pictures of the murals in Mexico—and inviting her to come and live with him in Los Angeles. And she went. "I can still see Philip standing there in Hollywood, when he came to meet me," she says. "So tall, so beautiful, with that wonderful look of his."

At twenty-one, my father began applying for and winning commissions for mural projects under Roosevelt's New Deal. The first, also with Reuben Kadish, was in Duarte, California, at the City of Hope Medical Center, a tuberculosis sanatorium run by the International Ladies' Garment Workers Union. A cousin of Reuben Kadish's helped them get this job. "We by-passed the local government art bureaucrats—mostly because they were afraid to take on the union," Kadish remembers. Otherwise, he believes, "Neither Phil nor I would ever have gotten another job in L.A." My mother came along, and lived with Philip in the cramped little house he and Kadish had rented. What she remembers of that mural project, she tells me, is mixing the plaster. "The subject was lighter in tone," my father wrote in one of his chronologies, "depicting birth, youth, middle age, and death." Perhaps, beside the Morelia mural, it does seem less weighty, but one could hardly call it light in tone. Some thirty-five nude and partially draped figures gesture and pose in a highly symbolic and elaborate spatial frame. Complex and ambitious, it clearly derives from Italian Renaissance fresco.

The notion of government-sponsored work for artists was becoming established, particularly in New York. Public buildings all over the United States were to be decorated with works of art celebrating fundamental American values. "Hell! They've got to eat, just like other people," said Harry Hopkins, FDR's emergency relief administrator, defending a new program that would permit artists and writers to use their unique skills. The Civil Works Administration, which funded the Public Works of Art Project, was succeeded in 1934 by the Section of Fine Arts of the Treasury Department and later by other agencies, which became the Fine Arts Project—all of these commissions later referred to under the general rubric of Works Project Administration, or WPA, or "the Project." For the next eight years, my father's income came almost exclusively from mural commissions.

During the winter of 1935–36, at the urging of his high school friend Jackson Pollock, who had gone east in 1930 to study with Thomas Hart Benton but came back to L.A. for frequent visits, my father decided to make the move to New York City. The WPA was just getting started there, and plenty of work would be available. There were great collections to see, artists to meet. New York was already the center of American art.

As if to underscore this move, to separate his life before from whatever would be after, my father, in 1935, when he was twenty-two, started using the name Guston and spelling his first name with one "*l*." Though his complete motives are unclear, the changing of his name apparently began with a desire to impress my mother's parents. Later, deeply ashamed of his act, my father concealed his name change, and asked his biographer Dore Ashton to avoid any reference to it in her book. He even went so far as to repaint the signatures on some of his early paintings.

I didn't know about this change of name until I was in college. More shocked by his concealment than I was by the change itself, I remember turning the family name over on my tongue when I first found out what it was. Goldstein. I had a flash, a full, textured feeling of belonging to something, to someone, a tradition. Goldstein was a name that connected with other people, not a name to set a person apart, as Guston was. It was a common enough name, and I was tired, after a childhood of school teasings, of my two unusual names.

Many of his generation had changed their names. I knew that. But had my parents really been that afraid of anti-Semitism? Was my father— heroic figure that he was to me then—in some way ashamed of being Jewish? Had he wanted that badly to leave his family behind? Or was he after something else entirely, a sort of assumed identity, like the masked children in his paintings of the forties? All of the possible explanations were disturbing. While I became more curious about my father's past, I was still afraid to ask. Something, some buried unhappiness I sensed in him, warned me, as it always had, not to show my curiosity.

Now, twenty-five years later, I am still mystified as I sit in my cousin Fan's sunny kitchen in Los Angeles, drinking coffee and poring over old family photographs. A large painting from 1947 hangs in the place of honor in the living room. Five of my father's early watercolors decorate the bedroom and hall. In one of them, a still life of fruits on a tabletop, a blackbird is perched on a curtain, about to fly out the open window with a cluster of cherries in his beak. It is dated 1935, the year that Philip was about to make his own escape.

Fan's face is still girlish and soft at seventy-three; she is the age my father would have been, had he lived. They were born a month apart, she tells me. Looking at her eyes moisten as she talks about Philip, hearing the obvious love in her voice, I am sad that I waited so long to visit. And that the others, his brothers and sisters, my aunts and uncles—and Babu, the name they called Rachel, my grandmother—are all gone now, too, and I will never know them. I find myself sinking into a cozy dream of what it would have been like, belonging to a big family. The Goldsteins.

And yet a distance separates us, still. My father's reticence about his family, that deep sense of privacy my parents shared, is in me, too. All the years I haven't known these people prevail, and bring me back to the task at hand. I am researching a book, I remind myself; it's foolish, sentimental, to feel more than this simple connection.

For my father, though, the connection was anything but simple. How could it have been otherwise? Filled with obligation and ambivalent love and what could only have been an enormous grief, he must have longed to start fresh, to create a new life for himself.

Butthis is only a guess, a daughter's speculation. My own life has hardly equipped me to understand. My father's death when I was thirty-seven was the first real loss of my life. Can I even begin to know what it was like for him to lose so much, so early, or to fashion from these losses a life of such promise and focus? Or to free himself from his past—or *seem* to—so thoroughly, when I myself am so bound to mine?

When I look at my father, I think that I can now see my grandmother's resilience, my grandfather's despair. And in this duality, the riddle of the man exposed. For one moment, this seems to explain everything. In the next, nothing. Any such simple knowledge is hopelessly reductive. We are more than the joining of our parents, after all. It is not, I remind myself, the things that happen to us, but the meaning we bring to them, that matters, after all. Events suggest, but they do not explain.

I press on with my questions. With some apprehension, I ask my cousin how the family reacted when they found out that my father had changed his name.

But I have forgotten that these were the children of immigrants—pragmatic, eager for chances, for a new beginning. Not like me, in the next generation, longing for origins. My father, and his brothers and sisters, were the offspring of people who left their language, their homeland, everything. In the face of that, what was a name?

Besides, this is California, Hollywood dreamland. I have not reckoned with my cousin's deep pleasure at my father's success, felt no less keenly for all the coastal distance. Success is the great justifier. I can decipher that from the extent of her display—Guston paintings, Guston books, Guston stories. She has kept the letters, all the cards sent on birthdays. How many friends, over the years, have been shown these artifacts, and with what swelling of pride?

Oh, yes, I understand this sort of display only too well, how it seems to compensate, to fill in the absences.

So what *was* the family's reaction when Philip changed his name?
"None whatsoever," Fan says. "None. We felt as an artist that was what
he needed to do—nobody questioned it. When you get into that business
—well, it's like show business, you know."

"I have never been able to escape my family," my father wrote in an
unpublished autobiographical piece in 1978, two years before his
death. "As a boy I would hide in the closet when the older brothers and
sisters came with their families to Mama's apartment for the Sunday
afternoon dinner visit. I felt safe. Hearing their talk about illnesses,
marriages, and the problems of making a living, I felt my remoteness in
the closet with the single light bulb. I read and drew in this private box.
Some Sundays I even painted. I had given my dear Mama passionate
instructions to lie. 'Where is Philip?' I could hear them ask. 'Oh, he is
away—with friends,' she would manage, in a trembling voice. It was so
good to be away. I was happy in my sanctuary.

"When I was seventeen, I left home and went to the other side of the
continent.

"After a lifetime, I still have never been able to escape my family. It is
true that I paint now in a larger closet; much, much larger, with many
lights. Yet nothing has changed in all this time. It is still a struggle to be
hidden and feel strange—my favorite mood. Or to put it more precisely,
to live my life as a stranger or to be vacuumed up by family. Such a choice.
To breathe or not to breathe.

"So it is true that nothing changes. Friends, artists, poets, critics and
intellectuals, professors in universities. They are still the family coming
for Mama's Sunday afternoon chicken dinner. Art dealers and museum
directors, collectors of art, the world I have lived in for fifty years
remains the family. Now it is I who must lie and say that I am away in
order to hide. The talk is still about making a living, how to live, what to
do. Do not think I pride myself that I have not been infected. All that I
can truly say is that I am still struggling, like a drowning man, to be
unrecognizable, unknowable, to myself. The stranger.

"There has been only one gain since that innocent boyhood closet.
Now I know that it is a losing contest. As Kafka says, 'Bet on the
world.' "

Women Are Learners

Drawing for *Bombardment*, 1936.

My parents were married on February 4, 1937, a year after they moved to New York. The only witness to the perfunctory City Hall ceremony was Jackson Pollock's brother, Sande McCoy. Immediately after the wedding, my mother recalls, the happy couple went off, not for some romantic interlude, but to look at a subway station with some of the other painters in the WPA mural division. "Wouldn't it be great if we could get that wall for a mural?" Philip said. Later, he did some studies for the Penn Station subways, but the project was never completed.

By the late 1930s, half the artists in the United States were living in New York City. After the collapse of the art market in the early years of the Depression, the government subsidies of the WPA provided a lively milieu, a sense of artistic community, as well as a meal ticket.

"We'd work like hell," painter James Brooks remembers. "All day we'd work on cartoons [full-scale drawings] or murals, and at night we worked from a model."

They attended meetings at the Artists' Union, but steered clear of the incessant political bickering between the Stalinists and Trotskyites, and between the Marxist theorists and art-for-art's-sake advocates. Often, they'd go out to the movies or to the Federal Theater, another important gathering place. My father retained vivid memories of the ILGWU's famous musical *Pins and Needles,* Orson Welles's *Doctor Faustus,* performed in street clothes, and especially Marc Blitzstein's *The Cradle Will Rock*—an unorthodox and controversial opera about a steel strike. At the First American Artists' Congress in 1936, Lewis Mumford and others spoke of the impending war, the rise of fascism and racism, and the tenuous position of government programs in support of the arts. Government programs to subsidize the arts had been under constant attack from the right, the Hearst press referring to artists on the Project as "Hobohemian chiselers" and "ingrates." By 1936, more than six thousand artists were employed by the WPA, and by 1939, over a million works of art had been placed in public institutions in more than forty states.

When the Spanish Civil War broke out, my father painted *Bombard-*

ment, a tondo (round painting) showing the horrors of the Fascist air raids against civilians (see plate 14). When the painting was exhibited in New York at the first Whitney Museum Annual in 1938, Philip rolled it all the way from his studio on 22nd Street to the museum on 8th Street. *Look* magazine gave *Bombardment* a full page, reproducing it in a lurid orangy brown.

At the center of the painting the violent concussion of a bomb explodes a group of highly foreshortened, brilliantly colored figures toward the viewer. A mother clasps her screaming child; one man is knocked to the ground, while another catapults through the air with the force of the explosion. An ominous red-cloaked figure wearing a gas mask seems to fly out of the painting. Arrayed in formation across the bilious sky above are line after line of bombers.

It is a powerful work, perhaps the most overtly political of all my father's easel paintings. But it must have seemed terribly conventional to him in 1939, when he saw Picasso's depiction of Guernica, the first Spanish town to be devastated by saturation bombing.

During these years, my mother continued to paint as well, competing for several mural commissions. With Philip, she worked on panels for the Maritime Commission, to be installed in the S.S. *Hayes, Jackson,* and *Monroe,* three steamships later converted to troopships during the war. In 1939, she completed a mural for the post office in Waverly, New York, and in 1941, my parents worked on two companion pieces for the Department of Forestry in Laconia, New Hampshire.

From photographs she keeps hidden away, I can see that my mother's painting, too, had developed in the years since Otis Art Institute. There's a stillness in her painting, a sense of balance and order; people and animals and landscapes are expertly and lovingly rendered. But I look in vain among the newspaper clippings, the magazine articles, for anything that mentions her work.

When I ask my mother about this, she acts as if I am questioning the obvious. "But Philip's murals were wonderful," she says. "Mine were nothing!"

Immediately, I raise objections. How can she summarily dismiss her gifts as a painter? It seems so unfounded, so harsh. But there's no arguing with her; she is adamant. We go on to talk of other things, but her self-effacement continues to trouble me. I have to remind myself that my mother has made her choices, and is at peace with them. It is I who am still struggling to resolve what can't be resolved. To be her. Or to be my father. My two models, miles apart. And always this dumb need to *choose*—to be the artist's wife, or the artist.

Finally, I insist on a drive to Waverly, a small town not far from Binghamton, New York. Though we have traveled to Europe and across the United States several times to see my father's paintings, this is the first time I have thought to bring my mother here.

In the Waverly post office, over the postmaster's office door and the bulletin boards with their WANTED posters, is a mural depicting the early settlers and Indians in the area (see plate 13). The name at the lower right is Musa McKim, the date is 1939. My mother's mural was one of sixty-eight commissioned in New York State by the Section of Fine Arts.

The pioneer family grouping on the right, my mother explains, is a portrait of her own family. I recognize the features of my grandfather, Frederick McKim, in the father, sawing a board for the siding of his house. At the lower right, facing her father, a self-portrait of a demure girl seated in a white cap and dress, her eyes modestly averted. The ball of wool in her hand attracts the attention of a cat, whose tail is slyly curled around a clump of wild flowers. Behind the butter churn and the family cow stands the almost featureless mother, a portrait of my grandmother, Musa Hunter McKim, the first Musa. She is a tall, hefty woman, with strong shoulders and a short waist, a physique that has skipped a generation and is recognizably my own. Turned half away, partitioned from her husband and daughter by the placid cow, she hardly seems part of the family grouping. My mother's sister, Josephine, makes no appearance at all, unless it is symbolically, as the spirited black horse their mother struggles to control.

I walk around the post office, admiring the mural, taking pictures. The postmaster, excited to have the artist there in the flesh, is trying unsuccessfully—it's Saturday morning—to reach a photographer from the local newspaper. My mother seems distinctly uncomfortable. Later she tells me she doesn't really like the painting; reluctant to come in the first place, she thinks we are silly for making such a fuss.

Despite the growing recognition his murals received in the late 1930s, my father was beginning to have misgivings about his own direction, doubts over what his biographer Dore Ashton termed "the increasingly tendentious tone in contemporary American art." One caustic jibe of the late thirties—attributed to Arshile Gorky—described the painting of the times as "poor art for poor people." But if social realism was no longer viable for my father, a return to the Italian masters was equally problematic. At twenty-five, he began questioning his commitment to the Renaissance vision.

Philip discussed his own dilemma and modern art in general with Burgoyne Diller, his supervisor on the Federal Arts Project. "Well," the older artist would say, "you're good in the ancient manner." Diller, as well as other painters on the Project—Willem de Kooning, Arshile Gorky, Stuart Davis, to name a few—was deeply influenced by European abstraction. Alfred Barr's Cubism and Abstract Art exhibition at the Museum of Modern Art in 1936 had a profound impact on young painters. Picasso, Mondrian, and Miró were much discussed. Yet art historian Meyer Schapiro, foremost among those trying to reconcile Marxism and modernism at the time and much respected as an art historian by my father, rejected the notion of a purely abstract art, "finding little justification for the 'absolute' painting divested of 'content.' "

It was a difficult and crucial time for American artists. Social realism was dead, or dying, and a legitimate native form of abstraction had yet to take hold. War was imminent and the Left was collapsing. "The social crisis was to have no closing date and had to be accepted as the condition of the era," wrote critic Harold Rosenberg. "Thus art consisted only of the will to paint and the memory of paintings, and society so far as art was concerned consisted of the man who stood in front of the canvas." It is a resolution that seems, from our vantage point, quite inevitable. But Rosenberg's analysis, which points to the beginnings of abstract expressionism as an existential response to the turmoil of the late 1930s, was undertaken many years later, and from a secure position of retrospective wisdom. At the time, such a stance would probably have seemed suspect.

Jackson Pollock was now involved with Mexican muralist Siqueiros' experimental workshop on Union Square—a laboratory of political and cultural ferment, where Pollock and others were investigating the spontaneous use of materials, "controlled accidents," with the newest synthetic paints, spray guns, and airbrushes. This spontaneity was the obvious precursor to Pollock's famous "drip" paintings of the early fifties.

Philip used to watch Stuart Davis at work through a crack in the partition that separated their two studios. "He would mount his scaffold," my father recalled, "lavishly spread paint on large areas with a palette knife, step down, and look at the results for a while in his suspenders smoking his cigar. Then he would mount his ladder again and scrape the whole thing off onto the floor. I remember how impressed I was by this lavish use of paint, and by his willingness to change in the process while I, in my bay, still under the spell of the Renaissance, was laboriously working on my big cartoon."

In 1939, my father received his first important mural commission, an outdoor painting for the facade of the Works Progress Administration building at the 1939 World's Fair (see plate 11). His subject was "Maintaining America's Skills," and the work that he did on the large concave surface was quite different from any of his previous murals. The four figures—mason, scientist, surveyor, laborer—were simplified, stylized, abstract. In part, this was due to the difficulties of working on a curved surface. Gone was the elaborate modeling, the sinuous line; even his color scheme was reduced. "In a clear, positive statement," the *New York Times* reviewer wrote, "Guston has given visual form to a strongly felt abstract idea." Visitors voted his painting the best outdoor mural among the more than four hundred at the Fair.

In 1940, he completed work on a mural for the Queensbridge Housing Project in New York (see plate 15), from which, twenty years later, he attempted to have his name removed after a sign painter had "restored" it. *Work and Play* contained his first image of children playing, a mock street battle which, as Dore Ashton points out, was "seminal for Guston's future work." Always alert for the Communist menace, government inspectors imagined they saw a hammer and sickle in the curve of a dog's tail against a child's leg. My father was ordered off the scaffold until his background could be investigated.

Far-fetched as this story may seem now, there were, apparently, a number of other examples of extreme anti-Communist vigilance. One was related to me recently by my father's old friend James Brooks. During the McCarthy era, Brooks' mural *Flight* in the rotunda of the Marine Air Terminal at LaGuardia was painted over with gray enamel. The shadowed edge of the circular opening through which the shoulders and head of a Promethean figure protrude was suspected of representing the Communist symbol of the sickle. Only in recent years has the

mural—and the terminal itself, a wonderful Art Deco structure—finally
been restored.

After the Queensbridge mural was completed, my father resigned
from the Project to move to the small artists' colony of Woodstock, New
York, and concentrate on easel painting. "I was weary of mural painting,
municipal art commissions and officialdom altogether," he wrote later.
"I wanted to work independently on personal imagery." But to support
himself, he continued to work on several commissions for the Section of
Fine Arts. Over the next two years, he finished murals for buildings in
Georgia, in New Hampshire, for the President Lines, and for the Social
Security Building in Washington, D.C.

My father later referred to his time on the Project as a "training
ground," not only for him, but for the best painters of his generation.
"Everybody was given an opportunity to prove himself," he said. "The
project kept me alive and working. It was my education."

During that summer of 1941, Philip completed what he always spoke of
as his first mature work, *Martial Memory,* a street scene of boys at play
(see plate 23). With its uptilted, fragmented, and planar space, its images
of trash-can lids and kettles and paper hats, the painting clearly prefig-
ures work that was to come some thirty years later.

My parents moved to Iowa City that fall, where my father had been
offered a position as artist in residence at the university. An old friend
from Los Angeles, Fletcher Martin, was leaving the Iowa art department
and had recommended him. After the partial retreat of Woodstock,
Philip must have felt quite remote from the turmoil and controversy of
the New York art world, away from the days and nights of arguing
politics and aesthetics. For they were all there in New York by then—
Mark Rothko, de Kooning and Franz Kline, Pollock and Barnett Newman and all the others—that loosely knit and contentious group of
painters who were, in the late forties and fifties, to become the New York
School, the so-called abstract expressionists or action painters. Great
things were beginning. "What the hell are you going out there for?"
Pollock raged at Philip one night at the Minetta Tavern.

In fact, my father deliberately chose to seclude himself at a critical
juncture in his work. He was to do this repeatedly during his career,
particularly at those moments when external pressures were mounting
and internal confusion was at its highest. Though he was often claimed

by this or that "movement" in art, my father was never a joiner. No manifesto ever expressed his beliefs. He bristled at labels. "Rebels seldom make good revolutionaries," Lillian Hellman wrote, in *An Unfinished Woman*, "perhaps because organized action, even union with other people, is not possible for them." But he cared what his contemporaries thought, of course; he cared deeply. He was far from immune to their criticism. At an artists' party during the late forties, Philip was attacked for his reactionary stance, his staunch refusal to "go abstract." According to a friend who was there, he broke down in tears. Seclusion allowed him to work, to develop in his own way. Eventually, it became his only defense.

It was in Iowa City, a year and a half later, that I was born. It has become my habit to look myself up in books on Philip Guston, as if to reassure myself that, yes, I *was* part of my father's life. And sure enough, there I am, making my first and only appearance, not in the text but in the catalogue chronologies, between the entries for 1942 and 1944: "1943   Birth of daughter, Musa Jane."

My father was thirty at the time; my mother, thirty-five. They had been married six years. Though my mother was heavily drugged and barely conscious, my father had wanted to be present at my birth. Hungry for images and experiences of all kinds, he told me once, he'd simply wanted to see what a birth looked like.

My mother still has his letter to her parents in Panama, which she retrieves from one of her many files. I turn the letter over in my hands and peer at it. Though the hand is recognizably my father's, the ink has faded to a pale, almost illegible sepia on the brittle, tissue-thin sheets. My mother tells me that wartime censorship is responsible for the small rectangular hole where a phrase describing the weather has been cut out.

"The little Musa with brown hair and green-slate eyes arrived 8:30 P.M. Mon nite, Jan 18!" my father writes in his energetic scrawl. "I am so happy it is a girl because I want a little replica of Musa. She weighed seven lbs. and was the color of Indian red mixed with white when she came, but is nice and pink now."

"A little replica of Musa." That was what my father wanted. And that was precisely what I tried for so long, and so unsuccessfully, to become. It's an injunction made more powerful for having remained unspoken all these years. Strange that I should feel this giddy sense of confirmation, reading it now. So I'm not crazy. I didn't make all this up to justify my own fears and weaknesses.

My name, like my mother's, is Musa Jane. But to my parents, and their friends, I am Ingie. I have never liked my nickname, which apparently derived from my babblings as a baby. Names were always a sore point with me. All during my childhood, I secretly envied the special and universal names other children called their parents. I never called my parents Mom and Dad, or Mommy and Daddy, or even Mother and Father. I called them Musa and Philip, like everyone else. I have always called my parents by their given names. They wanted it that way. Sweet and bitter, like so many aspects of my childhood, this was as much a recognition of me as an individual as it was a painful denial of who we were to one another.

The University of Iowa Museum of Art owns a portrait entitled *Young Mother* that my father painted in 1944, of my mother with me on her lap. I am standing half naked, clad only in a shirt and cap, my outstretched hands loosely held by my mother, a ring of wooden spools and beads around one ankle, a blue stuffed cat on a small table to one side. My mother's face is strangely remote, ethereal. A certain tenderness is clear in the rendering of her features, but the painting also betrays the cool detachment of a Bellini Madonna.

It wasn't until I was twenty-three and pregnant with my second child that my mother confided the other circumstances surrounding my birth. My oldest son, David, had just turned two when I called my mother from New York to tell her I was pregnant again.

"Oh, dear," she said, sounding worried. "Well, don't tell Philip, whatever you do. Let me break it to him."

He was afraid, my mother told me when I saw her a month or two later in Woodstock, that with two babies, living in the near poverty that accompanied my husband's teaching job, I'd be unable to do anything with my life. "What do you mean?" I protested. "Isn't raising children doing something?"

She only shrugged and smiled.

"How did Philip feel about you having me?" I asked.

My mother paused for what seemed like a long time before answering. "He didn't want children," she finally said. "His work, well—you know. It was everything."

"But you did?" I persisted.

Musa nodded. "I suppose it was the war. All the men were leaving and I was terrified of being left alone. At least I would have that much of him, I thought. But Philip was terribly upset. He was simply beside himself, saying I had ruined his life. I thought I had done something quite dreadful." My mother stopped and looked at me as if suddenly concerned that what she was revealing might disturb me, then went on hurriedly to say, "Of course, when you arrived it was entirely different. Once he saw you."

My mother was right—I did feel my father's affection for me. But it wasn't that simple. Nothing ever was, with him.

Talking with my parents' old friends now, I still hear echoes of his ambivalence. I hear, "Oh, your father loved you dearly," and, "Philip was terribly proud of you." And I hear that one day, during her pregnancy, my mother came home with some baby clothes. At the sight of them, my father felt nauseated, he told a friend. In a fit of disgust, he gathered up the baby clothes and threw them in the back of a closet.

It was a simple equation: more time spent working to support his family meant less time in his studio. My very existence meant an abridgment of his freedom.

And yet, early photographs show me as a happy, curly-haired toddler in corduroy overalls, playing in our big white frame house in Iowa City. My father looks on with the bemused delight of any new father for his daughter. His lovingly detailed portrait in pencil of me sleeping when I was a baby still hangs over my mother's dresser (see plate 20). Though I remember little, those years spent in Iowa—and later in St. Louis, where my father was head of the painting department at Washington University —were apparently idyllic and untroubled for me.

Without any question, it was my mother who made them so. It seems ironic—terribly unbalanced and counter to my own feminist leanings— that my father should have captured so much of my attention. Nevertheless, that's how it was. And still is, I suppose. He was the one I longed for; it was his approval that I craved. Like any child in my predicament, I became attached to the depriving parent. Sadly, in the economy of my emotions, my mother didn't count—or didn't *seem* to at the time.

But it was clearly my mother who was with me during all the years of my childhood. She was so immediate a loving presence from the beginning that she became largely invisible. In the act of embracing, the loved one disappears; such devotion seems almost to preclude knowing. My mother's keen sense of her own relative unimportance was also incorporated by me, swallowed without question as an article of faith—as the obverse, perhaps, of my father's genius.

I didn't have to long for her; she was there. Available as my father was never to be. Eager to play, to teach, to feed, to read to me or warm my clothes beside the wood stove, and to be delighted by some small thing I said or did, she possessed that rarest of qualities in a woman: she was a natural mother.

But for my father, the responsibilities of wife and daughter only added to a growing sense of crisis. The radical young painter, living a nomad's life as he worked on his mural projects, yielded uneasily to the family man. Here he was, a high school dropout and political activist from Los Angeles, invited to be a professor of art on the faculty of a midwestern university that had been, for years, the center of a well-established school of regional painting. This was Grant Wood country; the master himself had left the faculty the year before. Small-town life must have seemed to my father—as it did to me in 1969 when I moved with my first husband and young sons to a little town in Ohio—rather exotic and interesting.

In some ways it suited my father's mood perfectly. In removing himself physically, he'd left behind, for the time being, at least, the ongoing dialectic with abstraction, the conflict between modernism and history and social responsibility. "I would rather be a poet than a pamphleteer," he is quoted as saying in an issue of *Art News* published two months after my birth.

My father's paintings of the early forties, especially works like *Sentimental Moment* and *Musa McKim*, recall Camille Corot's portraits of peasant women, which he loved for their melancholy, solid beauty. The French painter's landscapes, for which he is best known, were of little interest to Philip, but I remember him once taking me to see Corot's portraits at the Metropolitan Museum when I was in high school. Philip's paintings of this period are saturated with the loneliness, if not the surreal quality, of Giorgio de Chirico. In them, the masquerades of late Venetian painting with their staged, theatrical blue lighting are given a melancholy turn on deserted streets of city slums. In a letter to a friend, he wrote about the Midwest, of the "lonely, empty squares, 'Gothic' city halls, armories, big clocks illuminated at night. Railroad stations. Trains. Soldiers moving around—the war years . . ."

One of his students, the painter Stephen Greene—who posed for *Sanctuary* in 1944—remembers Philip as looking as if "he had stepped out of a Piero painting." There they were, in what Greene describes as "a small, shabby-looking, tasteless, isolated, midwestern town," not at all the "Athens of America" that *Life* magazine had described. But my father impressed Greene deeply: "This was a man of stature by personality, and by his obvious desire to be a great painter."

My father's contributions to the war effort took the form of commissioned murals on celestial navigation (see plate 24) and illustrations for naval air training, published in *Fortune* magazine. His first one-man exhibition at Iowa, in 1944, shows the two directions his work had taken during those years—the complex, poetic, and intensely private moments of his portraits and paintings of children, and the more illustrative drawings and watercolors, clear remnants of his mural days, but informed by a new painterliness and sense of composition he'd learned from easel painting.

Nineteen forty-five brought many successes. In that year, he was given his first one-man exhibition in New York at Midtown Galleries—which was critically well received. Only Jackson Pollock, who had come to be a "nagging conscience figure for Philip," according to Stephen Greene, did not like the show. After the opening, when they were celebrating at a restaurant, "Pollock wandered in, ragingly drunk, and upbraided Philip for some form of aesthetic betrayal." That same year my father won the Carnegie Prize for his painting *Sentimental Moment*.

There was little satisfaction for him in this. In fact, he destroyed much of his work during this period. In what remains, the space has become flat, frontal, and increasingly abstract, the allegorical themes of unmasking and torture compressed into flat, cagelike claustrophobic spaces. Clear signs of the postwar revelations of the Holocaust are in these paintings, images of stacked-up limbs that reappear in his work some thirty years later.

"Outwardly, there was every reason for Guston to feel at ease in the world," writes Dore Ashton. "He had, by the age of thirty-four, won most of the major honors available to American artists of the time. He was deeply admired by students and colleagues . . . [but] Guston's sense of having completed a phase in his artistic life was profound enough to fill him with uneasiness. . . . He was already mentally preparing for a struggle with himself that would end, after two academic years in St. Louis, in what Guston has at various times called a kind of breakdown."

"I entered a very painful period when I'd lost what I had and had nowhere to go," my father said later. "I was in a state of gradual dismantling. I began to think, 'Well, maybe I don't really possess anything anyway, and maybe I'm not as good as I thought I was. Maybe I don't know what I think I know.' "

At two and three and four, I knew about my father's torments chiefly through his absences, his moody preoccupation with his own concerns. There were no scenes of anguish, no lashings out, no frightening moments—or none that I can remember. Occasionally, unpredictably, like sun breaking through overcast, he would suddenly become aware of me, would sweep me up in his arms and play with me for a few minutes, or kiss me affectionately.

Being a good father was certainly the least of his concerns. At the same time, being a good daughter was well on its way to becoming the greatest of mine.

In 1947, my father won a Guggenheim fellowship and was able to leave Washington University and return to Woodstock. At first we lived on the side of Overlook Mountain in Byrdcliffe, a former artist's colony of houses and studios, complete with theater and unused dining hall; it had been established in 1902 by the Utopian English philosopher Ralph Whitehead and his wife, Emily Byrd, as a formal colony like Yaddo or MacDowell, but had become, by that time, simply inexpensive rentals for artists in the area.

Later, we moved down to the rival settlement on the Maverick Road, built by a dissenting group of artists who established a community of their own—with its own concert hall and theater—and built a primitive, ragtag collection of houses and studios some three miles distant, in the valley. Over the years, we lived in several of these houses before my parents finally bought one and modernized it. At that time, they were little more than tarpaper cabins; faced with split pine logs, they boasted no plumbing or heating. On the Maverick, you stoked your own wood stove, pumped your own water, padded to the outhouse in the moonlight. Taking a shower meant remembering to fill a pail with water and set it out so the sun could warm it.

My kindergarten teacher at the Woodstock public school, a Mrs. Quick, forbade free-hand drawing. My mother, receiving my carefully traced Thanksgiving turkey, was outraged and complained to the school, an uncharacteristic act of assertion on her part. Not gregarious by nature, my mother rarely confronted anyone, and dreaded social and community activities. A year or so later, she was gratified when Mrs. Quick appeared at our door selling cheap encyclopedias.

That winter my father completed *The Tormentors*, an almost fully abstract painting (see plate 46). A dark, somber work, a "night" painting, *The Tormentors* is deeply depressive in tone. In it, a web of spidery whitish outlines—some of them recognizably nailed shoe soles—hovers over a black ground. Clearly, it represents an ending, a sinking of forms into despairing oblivion.

In the fall of 1948, my mother and I moved into the town of Woodstock. My father had won the Prix de Rome and was off to Italy for a year, to see firsthand and for the first time the frescoes he had loved since boyhood. His painting had come to an impasse. In Italy, he hoped to renew himself at the source.

Before then, my father had often been away for days, even weeks at a time, but for the first time in my life I remember feeling he had left us completely. My mother brought me to New York to see him off on the boat. She remembers looking up at him from the pier, seeing him standing with the other artists at the rail and sensing that he wouldn't be coming back to her. Characteristically, she had held herself at least partly responsible for his deepening depression.

"I wasn't good for him," she says when we talk about it.

"Why?" I ask, incredulous, but she only shakes her head.

When we got back to Woodstock, my mother collapsed, staying in bed for days. "I don't know who took care of you," she tells me, but a painter friend, Bradley Walker Tomlin, came to talk with her, she remembers. That house on Orchard Lane was small and cluttered, yet it seemed very empty to me. I associate that time with being sick, with ether nightmares, a tonsillectomy. At school, for the first time, I felt remote from other children. The bright spot of that year was at Christmas, when my father sent me a band of toy soldiers, carabinieri—Italian police, each playing a different musical instrument—as well as a small wooden Pinocchio and marzipan fruit.

The following summer, when I was six, my mother left me in Woodstock so that she could spend four months in Italy with my father. It is only recently that my mother and I have begun to talk about this time.

"I shouldn't have left you," my mother tells me now, "but when Philip wrote and asked me to come, I didn't think of you. I thought only of being with him, that he wanted me with him."

"Couldn't you have taken me with you?" I ask.

My mother looks at me, aghast. "Taken you? Oh, I wouldn't have known how. Philip didn't want *you* there."

"But that's terrible," I say.

There is a silence. My feelings are hurt by the blunt evidence of my mother's loyalties. Still, it is I who have stirred up these waters, I remind myself, encouraged this new frankness between us. I try to keep my voice level. "I mean, it was terrible of him to make you choose like that."

Now it is my mother who seems irritated, defensive, as if I have attacked what is unassailable. "Terrible? But why? He was an *artist*. That was simply who he was."

And I've no answer to that, except for my own anger.

The first part of that long summer I spent up on the mountain, in Byrdcliffe, at a place called the French Camp, a sort of boarding school where no English was permitted. My memories of this place are of long corridors and blowing curtains, of bare white rooms, and being given pennies to spend for candy on infrequent trips into town.

Later in the summer, I was taken to St. George's, a church camp on the Hudson River, where I remember stepping on a hornet's nest and being terrorized by swimming—the river looked so huge and broad to me. I was sure I'd be swept away by the current. It was a strange fear, really. When I was older, I remember being proud of my mother for her effortless racing dives and smooth Australian crawl. Her sister was an expert swimmer; actually, my aunt Josephine had been quite an athlete as a girl, an all-around National Outdoor champion who competed on the U.S. swimming team in the 1928 Amsterdam Olympics, and again in Los Angeles in 1932, bringing home a gold medal.

With that sort of heritage, you'd think I would have learned to love the water. But during that summer my parents were away in Italy, I became afraid of it. To this day, I feel a certain dread of the water, a fear of drowning. Like all irrational fears, this one certainly bears more than its own weight.

I changed in other ways, too. "You were always so lively before," my mother says. "Curious about everything, and friendly. But when we came back, you were subdued, somehow."

I ask her what she means.

"Oh, I don't know," my mother says. "Serious. Quiet, I guess. Shy."

When they came home that fall, my parents brought me a beautiful Swiss china doll. I christened her Baseleia, after her birthplace. She had real human hair, fine ivory teeth just visible through her slightly parted lips, blue glass eyes that were fixed, and a delicate porcelain body that was soon cracked and broken. My mother took her to a doll hospital, to be repaired, but I never really played with her after that. She reminded me of a time I wanted to forget. Baseleia still lies, unstrung, in an old wooden box. Her porcelain limbs are wrapped in tissue paper; her green velvet dress with the embroidery of wild flowers has faded.

Shortly after I was born, my mother stopped painting. Not all at once. For a time, she painted small things—botanical illustrations of wild flowers, paintings of nests, of children and birds. In my parents' house, there are many paintings hanging, but only one of them is my mother's. Hidden behind the kitchen door, a garland of cupids, *en grisaille*, cavorts around the wooden frame of a mirror.

A scrapbook she made for me with pictures snipped from old *Life* magazines contains pages of great horned owls, of propellers and apples, armadillos and lighthouses. On one page Gulliver is besieged by Lilliputians; on another a Belgian countess lies in her white satin bed with a dozen or so of her thirty-five dogs. And there is picture after picture of mother animals and their babies—dogs, burros, flamingos, cats. One story, entitled "A Good Provider," shows a mother mouse dipping her tail in a bottle of salad oil, climbing down a rope to her nest, all the while carefully crooking her tail so it will not drip, then stretching it out for her children so they can lick off the oil. My father's valentines and notes to me were each carefully pasted in this scrapbook. It was my favorite book.

My father encouraged her whimsical forays, brought out my mother's marvelous little drawings—a tiny nest, a speckled shell—to show to friends. "It's a dangerous business to be married to a great painter," Rosemarie Beck—I know her as Becky from the years that she and her husband, Robert Phelps, were friends with my parents—tells me. Encouragement of what is merely charming can stunt an artist's development, she believes. "Too much praise for that which would not grow," is the way she puts it.

From somewhere, a bookcase, Becky retrieves one of my mother's paintings she's kept all these years, of a small, surreal bird with a shell in its beak. She hands it to me. It *is* charming. "Yes," Becky says, "but it's a terrible thing to be praised for something that is not the best you can do."

I nod, still not quite understanding.

"Oh, it's not a deliberate condescension," she hastens to reassure me, seeing my puzzled look, "but it is inevitable."

As I'm sitting with Becky, something my mother said not long before comes back to me, another piece of that same puzzle. One day up in Woodstock I'd been pushing her, pressing her to explain. But why *exactly* did she stop painting, I'd asked her, point blank. Hadn't my father encouraged her?

"Yes, of course he did," my mother said curtly, as if she were a little irritated at my denseness. "He was always very sweet about it. But how could anyone see Philip's work and want to go on painting?"

I nodded. Yes, I thought, I know. Of course. The deadening effect of that comparison seemed very familiar to me. Nothing she did as a painter would ever have seemed good enough.

Was it then, around the time that I was born, I find myself wondering, that my mother began collecting things, fossils and leaves and shells, and my childish sayings, my swing songs and jump-rope rhymes? When I look at her collections it seems clear now that there was some wistful compromise concealed within them, some sort of scaling down of larger ambitions. Some settling, between the needs of her husband and her child, for smaller aesthetic pleasures, more commensurate with what she mistakenly thought were her own limited capabilities.

And she began writing poetry.

ON WOMEN

Settle too far down with a beach image
of woman, work too hard for her,
and you both end up bitter and decrepit.
This need not happen. Women are learners.

They learn from their children.
They learn from their husbands—particularly
from their husbands. They learn from friends.
And from books. From books
they learn about their children, husbands
and friends. And about themselves.

They learn that they should be willing
to sacrifice a little comfort
for a little beauty. Many know this by instinct.
Some have to learn it each day all over again.
The latter are the more conscious
of their blessings, if not
the more attractive.

It is not surprising
that the most comfortable shoe in the world
is worn by the most uncomfortable woman.
It does not look like a shoe.

As for the woman tapped on the behind
by the rolled newspaper
of a man going to mass,
on the steps of St. Veronica's
on Christopher Street,
nothing has come in on that yet.

THREE

Stern Conditions

Untitled, 1951.

I hold my inventive capacity on the stern condition that it must master my whole life, often have complete possession of me, make its own demands on me, and sometimes for months together put everything else away from me.

. . . Whoever is devoted to an art must be content to deliver himself wholly up to it and to find his recompense in it.

—CHARLES DICKENS

It was my mother who found this quote. My father printed it in large letters and posted it on the studio wall over his desk, where it hung between reproductions of Giotto and Masaccio frescoes (see plate 70). How grateful my father must have felt that Dickens had so clearly articulated—and, I suppose, validated—the landscape of his renunciation. It was not my father's fault that he could not be a husband like other husbands, a father like other fathers. So the unspoken argument went. My mother tried in her gentle way to help me accept this, to know that it wasn't callousness or lack of love that was the problem. It was Art.

"It was thrilling to go to Arezzo or Orvieto for the first time," Philip said later of his Prix de Rome year. "Seeing the frescoes, the Uffizi in Florence, and Siena excited and exhausted me. After a month of painting in Rome, I found I did not feel like painting. I wanted to walk the streets, and feel free to think about what I was seeing. In a sense, I was searching for my own painting. . . . It was a trip to Venice, seeing Tintoretto and Titian, and to Paris, where I was very affected by Manet and Cézanne, and going later to Spain and seeing Goya and El Greco—it was seeing the 'painterly painters' that made me want to paint again. I canceled the remaining year of my two-year fellowship and returned to the U.S."

A photograph taken that year shows my father standing uneasily in his high-ceilinged, skylit studio at the American Academy in Rome, beside a painting he later destroyed, as he did all his work during that year, except for a few spidery drawings of hillsides in Ischia (see plate 28).

In the fall of 1949, my mother and father came back from Italy and settled again in Woodstock. He returned to the painting he'd been working on when he left, *Review,* and began struggling to resolve its conflicts. But the work was not going at all well that fall, and so Philip and a friend who had himself been "hiding out" in Woodstock, Bradley Walker Tomlin, decided to take a studio together in New York, an arrangement that lasted only a few weeks. Tomlin, a gentle and soft-spoken man whose calligraphic abstractions have since been widely acclaimed, died not long afterward, in 1953; his death affected my father deeply.

Philip easily found another studio on 10th Street, but it was some time, a difficult year of regaining bearings, before we settled. For some months, we stayed in Robert and Becky Phelps' tiny flat on Bedford Street, and then at the Albert Hotel. I was six years old that fall. My memories of this year are as fragmented and sketchy as our living arrangements must have been. Already thrown off by the summer apart from my parents, I withdrew even further.

That was the year we began shuttling between New York City and Woodstock. Those years during the early fifties were characterized by those trips back and forth, with me lying on the wide, criblike shelf behind the single seat of our blue 1942 Plymouth, looking out the rear window. In those pre-Thruway days the drive down 9W to the city took more than three hours.

My father immersed himself in the New York art world. His depression had lifted, and the notion of painting as process began to obsess him. He began painting the first completely abstract paintings of his career. At first they were very dark, dark reds and black; dense, subtle walls of flat, enigmatic forms, barely emerging from the void. But by 1951, the work had become spare and spacious, subtle markings in muted grays and ochers and pinks. Bare canvas began to appear, drips and impasto that attested to a new spontaneity. Increasingly, too, a sensuality asserted itself in the paint surface, a lushness of stroke that belied the arduous process of leaving familiar ground and striking out for the unknown. "Painting seems like an impossibility," my father wrote, "with only a sign now and then of its own light."

White Painting, 1951, was the pivotal work, the new beginning (see plate 29). "I wanted to see if I could paint a picture—have a run, so to speak—without stepping back and looking at the canvas," Philip said later about this painting, "and to be willing to accept what happened, to suspend criticism. Instead of walking back, pulling out a cigarette and thinking, to not suspend my own endeavors, but to test myself, to see if my sense of structure was inherent. I would stand in front of the surface and simply keep on painting for three or four hours. I began to see that when I did that, I didn't lose structure at all."

Finally, after his years of crisis in Iowa, St. Louis, and Woodstock, and his renewal in Italy, my father had found a new way to work.

The school year would begin for me at the public school in Woodstock, or, later, when we moved down to the Maverick Road, in West Hurley. When the weather became too cold for our primitive, uninsulated house, we would move into the city until spring made it possible to move back up again to Woodstock. In New York, I attended the old P.S. 41 on Bedford Street in the Village, then not the model public school it is now, but a drab, overcrowded place where children were crammed two to a desk.

Built in the late 1850s, 51 West 10th Street, where we lived for several years, had a venerable history. The Studio Building, designed by Richard Morris Hunt, was the first building of artists' studios in New York City. In the last years of the century, it became a "clubhouse of the Hudson River School," housing Winslow Homer, Frederick Church, and scores of others. We were among the last of its tenants, for it was demolished in 1954. Our apartment there was a small one-room cold water flat with high, slanted ceilings and a skylight. The toilet was down the hall, and the area where I slept was separated from the rest of the room by a tall bookcase. My father's studio was in the same building. I remember roller-skating around the block and down to Washington Square, wearing steel skates that clamped to the oxfords I hated to wear, and the skate key on the shoelace around my neck. I was so rattled by the rough, pebbly pavement that when I took the skates off, I seemed to be floating.

I was terribly lonely there, I remember. More at ease with adults than with children, I didn't make friends readily. The disconnection of each school year made it a hopeless proposition. I was always the new kid. Years later, I would sometimes catch myself bragging about how many different elementary schools I'd attended, as if that privation were something to be proud of. How tough I was, how smart I was, how I always managed to get good grades anyway. But it was nothing to brag about; it was simply my way of managing. Adversity as opportunity, transformed into a feat of endurance.

My father's needs always came first. I never thought to question this; it was axiomatic, an article of faith. My father *had* to be able to work in peace up in Woodstock for as long as the weather permitted; in New York, during the winters, he *had* to feel free and unencumbered to come and go as he chose. And this took precedence over any longing I might have had for stability or consistency. Not that I made a fuss about it; taking my cue from my mother, I specialized in flexibility.

It wasn't until I was much older, in high school, the same school for *four* whole years, all year long—familiar faces in the fall, a group of girlfriends for the first time—that I began to enjoy the time we spent in the city; until then, I felt rather like Persephone, condemned to spend six months in Hades. My real life was in Woodstock.

But in other ways, life with my parents was very full. I was exposed to so much, so early. My picture books were the volumes of art and architecture my father had brought home with him from Italy, and his great pleasure at my interest prepared the ground for my own love of painting. I was taken to galleries and museums and foreign movies, to concerts and dance recitals. I listened to chamber music and jazz and poetry. I read voraciously.

Most of all, I listened to the grown-ups talking, trying to follow those marvelous freewheeling, expansive conversations of the fifties that seemed to touch on everything. Talk about the newest Italian movie would lead into a discussion of nineteenth-century French poetry, and then move to some obscure point on the metaphysics of St. Augustine, or locate a corollary in the *scuola metafisica*. Someone would tell a joke about Joe McCarthy or HUAC. Someone else would be raving about a newly discovered restaurant in Chinatown, where the steamed bass with black bean sauce was beyond description. There would be explosions of laughter, another round of drinks; finally everyone would get up to dance to a Meade Lux Lewis record. Always, at the center of this pastiche, laughing and talking, dominating the evening, making the most cogent points and telling the best stories, was my father. And I loved knowing

28. Philip in his studio at the American Academy, Rome, 1948.

29. *White Painting*, 1951.

SUMMER 1953

Dead lacey insects.
Seams stitched with orange
Thread. The red button
Found. Goodnight, sweetly,
And thank you for the riddle.

30. One of my mother's early poems,
illustrated by Philip.

31. Practicing on the porch of
the house on Maverick Road.

32. Philip in his New York studio on Tenth Street, c. 1951.

33. *Drawing 1954.*

34. Philip with the art historian Sam Hunter, who organized his show in 1966 at the Jewish Museum, and the painter Franz Kline.

35. My father with the sculptor David Smith at a Sidney Janis Gallery opening, 1958.

36. In Rome, 1960.

37. The back porch in Woodstock.

38. *Celebration*, 1961.

39. Philip in his Woodstock studio in 1964.

40. With Morty Feldman at the New York studio on Twentieth Street, 1965.

41. The 1962 Philip Guston retrospective at the Guggenheim Museum.

42. With Dan Kadish at the Guggenheim opening.

43. At my wedding in 1962. Reuben Kadish and Philip
are standing behind Danny and me.

that, seeing the enormous attraction that he had for other people. Never a part of this myself, only half following the conversation, I was completely captivated. I'd lie in bed later, trying to remember what had been said, gorged with the thick pudding of talk that had been so richly studded with images and voices and ideas.

My daily life was dull by comparison. Third and fourth grades, I went to the West Hurley Elementary School, a white frame schoolhouse about two miles from the Maverick Road. First through fourth grades were in one classroom, fifth through eighth grades in the other. My entire fourth-grade class was left-handed—all four of us. Long hours and days were spent listening to the teacher working with the "little kids." It was at this school that I was mocked for the first—but by no means the last—time for my name, my vocabulary, my unflagging desire to please the teacher. "Mucilage," I was called, or "Moose," or even "Muss." And once they knew my nickname—Ingie, a name I didn't like well enough to defend—I was called "Inky" or "Stinky."

One Halloween, I went to the school party in West Hurley as a wizard, resplendent in a costume my father had decorated for me. I wore an old muslin sheet and a tall, conical hat, covered with arcane symbols my father had painted, staying up late the night before to complete the decoration. My mother, outraged that I didn't win any prizes, took me that same evening to the Woodstock party, where, she claims, I did win a prize. My memory of the evening is of having a terrific stomachache that kept me doubled over, more witch than wizard. And of wishing I had a store-bought costume, like the other kids.

I was a large child, not graceful or well coordinated, too timid to be friendly, acting a bit like a know-it-all in class. There are painful memories of being chosen last for softball, stumbling out of bounds at hopscotch, or waiting my turn to enter the slapping jump rope, and the humiliation of bringing it to a tangled halt each time I tried to jump in. I remember standing in a circle of kids at recess, the ringing, hollow bounce of the red dodgeball, the thrill of fear I felt each time it was aimed at me.

I was uneasy with other children. Their play was too rough, or required too much agility or skill. They were the initiated; they knew things I didn't. Far into adulthood, it seemed to me that others possessed knowledge I didn't have. And competition frightened me. Something in my classmates' ease with one another, their taunting and showing off and whispered confidences, always seemed foreign, beyond my reach. It was simpler to go off and play by myself.

Not surprisingly, I found my refuge in books. I was an avid and early reader, devouring seven or eight library books a week throughout my childhood. I read rapidly, carelessly, anything I could get my hands on. Of particular fascination, always, were stories of families, especially large families. *The Swiss Family Robinson. The Five Little Peppers and How They Grew.* Such domesticity seemed mysterious, even exotic, to me.

Television was still new then, in the early fifties, and exciting. Every day at school, the previous night's episode of "Howdy Doody" or "Gunsmoke" would be the topic of recess conversations. I was terribly envious. My parents refused to buy a television until my senior year of high school, thinking (with justification, if my own children are any proof) that I would stop reading and thinking for myself if I had a TV to watch. But I saw it differently then.

One day, in third grade, I finally got to do something that I imagined every other kid did all the time: I was invited to go to the home of one of the girls who lived in West Hurley—to watch TV after school! No one had ever asked me before. I have a clear memory of walking down that ordinary street of small tract houses behind my classmate, of entering her kitchen with its faint odor of garbage, of the dim, drab cave of a living room, the rounded eye of the television springing to life, and of the hour or two I spent in rapt contemplation of silly animals doing violence to one another. It wasn't only the cartoons that enthralled me, either. I was sunk in the vision of the family around the TV, her two brothers wrestling on the rug, teasing and poking at one another, her mother yelling at them to shut up from the kitchen where she was talking on the phone—all the give-and-take of normal domestic relations. True, the father wasn't home that afternoon. But I could imagine him coming home from work, sitting there in his recliner, proud of his kids, an arm around his daughter and the youngest boy climbing on his lap.

These people I barely knew seemed to be a real family in a way that my family was not. We were three related people—mother, father, daughter —living together, but not, somehow, a family. That afternoon, the children I was visiting pushed and shoved and teased and wrestled—acting up in all the ways that normal children do. How strange that they could be themselves, I thought—children, not careful replicas of their parents. I never felt that freedom.

For the few years that I was intensely interested in astronomy, I thought of families as constellations. My mother and father and I were like three distant stars, points on a triangle, far away but still connected to one another. Other families were more like star clusters, I thought, huddled close together like the Pleiades. But ours was a house of quiet separations, of closed doors, each of us retiring to work and think and read, alone. Beyond the enforcement of privacy, there were few rules.

To my parents, as far as I could tell, the very idea of family had always meant intrusion and interruption. Holiday celebrations were ordeals. It was impossible for me not to notice how my father reacted to such expectations, not to worry about becoming one of those obligations myself. When a car turned in the driveway, my father would run, calling out as he disappeared into his studio, "Tell them I'm not here! I'm not home!" When the telephone rang, he'd be there, in the background, shaking his head emphatically with his finger to his lips. "No," my mother would say. "Philip isn't here."

Toward the end of his life, my father's sense of the burden of family obligations came to extend far beyond his biological family, to encompass all demands the world outside made upon his time and energies. Often, during my visits in those later years, when I was working as a counselor in a community mental health agency in Ohio, he would take me into the studio, sit me down in the tall swivel chair at his drawing table.

"Ingie," he'd begin, "I know *you* understand how difficult it is for me. . . ." And I would sit there and listen to him, flattered that he was confiding in me, as he poured out his troubles. Invariably, they revolved around his despair at the encroachment of the world on his privacy. "They," the people out there—dealers, collectors, university and museum people, students—were consuming him; their demands were becoming unbearable.

But as I listened, an old, uneasy provisional feeling of being inside the charmed circle of my father's awareness rose up in me. I knew it was true. How long would I have his attention? (Not that I had it then; it was always *he* who had *my* attention.) It would last during that visit, no longer—that is, until the next trip east, six months or a year later. During the intervening months, my mother would intercept my calls. Philip was working, she'd say, or the phone would ring and ring—they would have unplugged it.

"Because of Philip's gift for intimacy," a friend of his commented recently, "you always thought you were the one person in his universe. But then, two minutes later, it was someone else." It was true. But the beam of his gaze, the warmth of the encounter, were all-enveloping at the time. He seemed so grateful to be understood. All I'd do was listen, maybe proffer a banal interpretation, some weak prop for his ego. And he would thank me profusely. "Ingie listened to me ranting for *hours*," he'd report later to my mother, shaking his head in wonder. "She's *so* terrific." And I'd sit there and smile, soaking it up. As my mother said not long ago, "Philip was friends with whoever would listen to him."

A pile of unanswered mail was always there, on his desk, haunting him. Too selfish and too generous at the same time, he couldn't bring himself to answer all the letters, and he couldn't bring himself *not* to. Overcome with guilt, he would finally sit down at his desk and answer a dozen or more at one time. In 1979, after his first heart attack, I helped him compose a form letter to respond to the many requests that continued to pour in by phone and by mail. "I am a painter," the draft began. "Were I to respond to every letter sent to me, I would never have time for my work . . ."

After he died, I found this neatly typed on my mother's old Smith Corona. He had kept the letter, but never used it.

During most of my childhood, my parents had two groups of friends: those who lived in Woodstock—year round or, as we did some years, late spring to early fall—and those who lived in New York City. A large group of artists made their home, temporary or permanent, in Woodstock, among them Fletcher Martin, a big, gruff Texan my father had known since early California WPA days, Herman Cherry, and a number of other painters, among them Wendell Jones, Karl Fortess, Yasuo Kuniyoshi, Eddie Millman, Arnold Blanch, and Doris Lee.

Raoul Hague, an irascible Armenian eccentric who has been a neighbor for over forty years, still lives year round in his wood stove–heated cabin next door with his collection of clocks of every kind, all ticking and chiming at once, and his 1911 edition of the *Encyclopaedia Britannica* bound in masonite. Raoul is a carver of large, sinuous torsos with names like *Ohayo Mountain Butternut* and *Bearsville Walnut* after the woods of their origin. Sometimes he and my father were on speaking terms; often they were not. When they weren't, six months or more could go by without a word passing between them. It was laughable, these two stubborn men stumping around their property, ignoring one another. Then, suddenly, there would be a reconciliation—why was never any more clear than the reasons for the rift in the first place—and to celebrate my father would cook dinner for Raoul. I remember dancing at night, to flute music, on the pine needles outside his house. When we visit Raoul now, he presents us with wooden spoons he has carved, or small toy birds set on odd pedestals of wood and broken wineglass stems. Stepping into his cabin has always been like entering one of Joseph Cornell's boxes.

For quite a number of years, my parents' best friends in Woodstock were the writer Robert Phelps and his wife, Rosemarie Beck, who later gave me violin lessons. After working all day, the two couples would get together in the evenings for food and drink and conversation. Beckett and Genet and Sartre. Rilke and Auden. The implications of existentialist thinking on the creative act, at least that's what I thought they were talking about, for it was far beyond my understanding. The conversation went on and on, far into the night. While the grown-ups talked, I would listen. Sometimes, I'd play quietly with their baby son, Roger, showing him a game I'd invented that involved throwing socks over a beam that crossed the high ceiling of their living room.

Robert Phelps is a slender, witty man with an infectious, helpless laugh that has always made me smile. The first Christmas they knew one another, 1947, Philip presented Robert with a drawing of a bird that had captured his attention in the St. Louis Zoo. Forever after, Robert was the "secretary bird," tall, elegant, but somehow a trifle silly. A lover of French literature, especially the obscure but prolific Marcel Jouhandeau, Phelps is best known for his commentary on and collections of Colette's writing. The two men went to movies all over the Hudson Valley. Becky, often more vocal than her husband, still expresses herself in passionate bursts of energy, jumping up from her chair, gesturing dramatically. I remember cozy evenings at their house, sitting by the wood stove, the murmur of voices and laughter, and the lovely feeling of being picked up in my father's arms, half asleep, and carried home from their little cabin in the woods.

When I visit them now, the stories that pour out are infused with the same warmth. Their memories of my parents, and of me, during the late forties and early fifties are still vivid, and obviously cherished.

"We were all so terribly poor then," Becky says. "Your mother had a gift for making one piece of bread seem like four. Philip would say, 'But Ingie's getting more than anyone else!' He was sometimes a terrible child."

"But Musa defended you marvelously against Philip," Robert remembers. "She would say, 'No, Philip, it's Ingie's turn.' 'That's Ingie's.' 'Ingie gets another slice of bread.'"

Listening to them, I can almost see my father's hand, reaching playfully toward my plate, my mother slapping it away.

"You had a very happy childhood, I think," Becky continues. "You were a lovable child. You always came in, saying exactly what you felt like. You weren't apologetic, you didn't cringe, you were interested in almost everything—"

Embarrassed, I interrupt. "Come on, Becky. You're idealizing me."

"But Philip had enormous pride in you," she exclaims, opening her hands as if to show the size of my father's feeling for me. "Couldn't you feel his pride in you?"

"No, not really," I reply.

We sit in silence for a moment. Robert looks at me, then down at his hands. What is she up to? I imagine they are thinking. Is she settling scores, harboring grudges? But I don't doubt the rosy image they paint. It's lively, and quite true, as far as it goes. This nostalgic re-creation of their friendship with my parents casts an irresistible glow; I can bask in it too. Surely we all have some such charming vision tucked away somewhere, a glossy picture of the past with the darker moments airbrushed out.

I try to explain. But when I speak of my loneliness, my sense of isolation, I feel that old, cautious drop in my stomach, a sinking feeling that I am revealing too much, betraying my parents by admitting to my own unhappiness. Robert and Becky listen, they nod; they seem to understand. They tell me about their son, now a psychologist, devoted to helping others, just as I used to be. Isn't that a coincidence? Becky remarks. It's not, but I keep this to myself.

Should I be surprised that my sense of how it was is so different from theirs? That inside, I wasn't that happy, forthright, creative child they knew? That my mother may have defended my plate, but was not able to exact from my father the kind of attention I wanted and needed?

"Well, of course," Becky says. "He wanted to work when he wanted to work. And he wanted to be a papa when he wanted to be a papa." She looks at me, smiles. "You now know that when you work, you don't want to be divided."

Yes, I do understand it now. Becky is right. I can summon up a certain rueful empathy. I know what it is to feel impatient at interruptions of my work. To resent the demands of others. I, too, have seen how the real world—yes, even the lives and feelings of the people closest to me—becomes thin and insubstantial, far less compelling than the world within.

One day, when I was very small, no more than three or four, my mother had made gingerbread cookie dough and rolled it out for my father to cut. Philip spent hours making a cookie for me, cutting up currants, marking the reins and the halter of a beautiful Greek horse. It was put in to bake with all the other cookies. When I saw it, I cried, "Oooh, my cookie!" and reached for it.

"But you couldn't touch your horse cookie, that Philip had made for you," Becky Phelps tells me now. "It was nailed on the wall, as a great sculpture."

It was through Robert and Becky that I met the van Rijns, the wealthy family who lived next door to them and who owned Rotron, a local factory that made airplane parts. I must have been nine or ten when I met them, just entering that magical age when little girls begin to dream of horses. The spaces between the roots of the big hemlock tree beside our house had become stables for my little model ponies; elaborate corrals were staked out and fenced with twigs. But the van Rijns had the real thing. In the middle of a rather primitive artists' colony, they lived like landed gentry, with a stable and several horses, and acres and acres of lovely rolling fields to ride them in. Their younger daughter, Vera, became my first real friend.

The van Rijns were Dutch, remote descendants of Rembrandt, and in their house there was always a feeling of Old World decorum. Once I remember a table knife's being used as a gentle prod against tall Vera's slumping shoulders—a young lady must sit straight at table! her mother, Tita, insisted. Vera was a lanky and freckled tomboy, with long straight brown hair that hung in her eyes. We were both in awe of her older sister, Eva, glamorous at eighteen, the very opposite, it seemed, of us.

Vera rode in all the local horse shows. I would watch her trot around the ring, envious of her smart velvet cap and black jacket and riding crop, admiring her firm control of the spirited animal she rode, the way horse and rider lifted effortlessly over the jumps. While Vera practiced her jumping on a beautiful sorrel mare, I was allowed to ride bareback on a gentle old gelding named Sonny, who stopped frequently to graze. Despite much clamping of knees and vigorous tugging on his scruffy mane, I would usually have to slide off his broad back and yank his head up out of the grass, whereupon he would look quizzically at me as he chewed, as if puzzled that I might actually want to go somewhere.

My mother was so captivated by my friendship with Vera—and her cousin Cosima who came to stay one summer—that she wrote a children's story about us. In it, three girls, friends, fall asleep in the shade of a giant willow tree beneath the nest of the mysterious Lightning Bird, "a legendary bird that turns somersaults and stores objects in its nest associated with magic and superstition." There is a rainstorm. During the night, certain magical substances drip down on one of the unsuspecting girls and the next morning Vera wakes up to find herself transformed into a centaur, half girl, half horse. "She appeared to be," my mother wrote, "half nine-year-old, going on ten, in a blue and white striped T-shirt, half colt. . . .

"Scattering the dew and the grasshoppers, Vera took off over the Turtle Pasture which was filled with several kinds of goldenrod, cobalt-blue Asiatic dayflowers, shell-pink beadlike lady's thumb, common blue asters, and the Punchinello pods of the milkweed, not yet ready to open and release their parachutes; plus many a specie of grass, insect and small animal. But it is also possible to sail through all this without seeing anything."

The first time Vera came over to my house to play, my father, who was working in his studio, overheard me say to her, "Well, come this way, this is where the outhouse is."

When we came back down the path from behind the house, a few minutes later, he heard Vera saying to me, "But you must be very poor, not to have an inside bathroom."

"Not at all," I replied. "We're just a hundred dollars short of being very, very rich."

My father told this story with pride to his friends. It's a testimony to him, and to my mother's resourcefulness, her capacity to make do, as well as her absolute belief in my father and his work, that I never thought of us as poor, even when we were. I never really wanted the things we didn't have. We were different, that was it. Our life was bohemian, romantic. An adventure.

In general, my father tried to stay away from the social scene in Woodstock. This was often difficult. After his successes of the fifties in the New York art world, Woodstock was eager to claim him as its own. It seemed the Woodstock Artists Association or Art Students League was always trying to get him to exhibit or teach or jury a show; he would hide in his studio, letting my mother act, as she always did, as the guardian of the gates.

When, in 1967, long after I'd left home, my parents again left New York City to live full time in Woodstock, they became even more reclusive, guarding their privacy with a mailbox with only a number on it and an unlisted telephone, usually rigged so it wouldn't ring.

It wasn't easy to maintain his privacy, those last dozen years of my father's life. Those were the same years, after the Woodstock festival (which occurred, actually, in Bethel, New York, some sixty miles away— the concert's promoters were from Woodstock), when Tinker Street came to resemble a bucolic extension of St. Mark's Place and Tompkins Square Park, when Joan Baez and Bob Dylan sang on the porch of the Expresso Cafe, when the sleepy little town of Woodstock exploded from the modest artists' colony it still was in the fifties to become the booming summer resort it is now, crowded with gift shops and boutiques. But for my father, Woodstock always remained a place where he could work, his sanctuary, his closet.

When he was finished with a painting, Philip would often cook one of his elaborate meals to celebrate. A Chinese dish with shrimp, or some Russian specialty his mother had taught him, like borscht or a pot roast with latkes, served with applesauce and sour cream. "Oh, those potato pancakes!" Robert Phelps recalls. My father often took me to movies. Together we would range far afield, to Kingston, Saugerties, Rosendale, even to New Paltz, searching for good films. With Philip, I saw all the fine Italian movies of the fifties, the best of them, like de Sica's *Bicycle Thief* and Fellini's *I Vitelloni* and *The White Sheik,* more than once.

But the New York art world of the fifties had an entirely different flavor. The social life there was faster, and more threatening—at least to me, probably because I was so much less a part of it. When we were in the city, I saw little of my father, especially when his studio was separate from where we lived. He never cooked, preferring instead to seek out new and undiscovered restaurants with his friends. And he worked at night, taking long walks through the deserted streets when the painting wasn't going anywhere, stopping off at the Cedar Street Tavern, the artists' hangout, to see who was there. Often, he would just be getting up when I came home from school. I'd find him sitting at the kitchen table, nursing a hangover with a cup of black coffee, coughing terribly from the cigarettes he smoked incessantly.

There was exhilarating company for Philip in New York—especially his closest friend of the fifties and sixties, Morton Feldman, the composer, whom he'd met through John Cage. Cage, an iconoclastic composer and foremost proponent of experimental minimalist music, was a man who, in Dore Ashton's words, was "a master at Rejection, a model. And Nothing was his special province." My father went with Cage and Feldman to hear D. T. Suzuki lecture and, for a time, became interested in Zen Buddhism and the significance of "the Void."

I didn't understand this at all. What I remember of John Cage were interminable concerts where the composer sat at his prepared piano for long periods of time while "Nothing" happened and the audience fidgeted restlessly. Cage came up to Woodstock once, for a visit, with the dancer Merce Cunningham, a marvelous elfin figure of a man. My father's friend, Mercedes Matter, recalls the performance of one of Cage's pieces at the Maverick Concert Hall on that occasion. "It was total silence," she says. "All that happened was that David Tudor opened the keyboard and closed it, but no sound." Mercedes throws back her head and laughs at the memory. That sexy, dramatic laugh of hers, like some special, evocative scent, carries me back to those days in the fifties; I can hear Mercedes still, clearly, over the voices and music at one of her many parties on MacDougal Alley. "In this half-outdoor theater," she continues, "it framed the most throbbing, saturated sounds of night. It was really quite marvelous. If it had been in a New York concert hall, with coughing and shuffling of feet, it would have been completely different."

Out of a scene from *A Midsummer Night's Dream*, John Cage, an amateur mycologist, led all of us in a procession through the Catskill pine woods hunting edible mushrooms. He gave them to my mother to cook, ignoring her dubious glance. "Trust me," he said, and we all had to taste the strange, discolored things fried up in butter. "Delicious!" my father proclaimed.

"During those years we all talked constantly about an imaginary art in which there existed almost nothing," Morty Feldman said. "In a sense it was a three-way conversation, though I never brought the ideas of one to the attention of the other . . . 'Nothing' is not a strange alternative in art. We are continually faced with it while working." He told this story about his two friends in his article "Philip Guston: The Last Painter," written for *Art News:* "I remember taking a long walk with John Cage along the East River. It was a gorgeous spring day. At some point he exclaimed, 'Look at those sea gulls. My, how free they are!' After watching the birds I remember saying, 'They're not free at all—every moment in search of food.'

"That is the basic difference between Cage and Guston," Feldman continued. "Cage sees the effect, he ignores its cause. Guston, obsessed solely with his own causality, destroys its effect. They are both right, of course, and so am I. We complement each other beautifully. Cage is deaf, I am dumb, Guston is blind."

My father also used to tell stories about the three of them. "Cage and Feldman were in my studio, in 1951 or 1952," my father wrote, "and I had done what were probably the sparest pictures of all. . . . I think one painting just had a few colored spots on it, and lots of erasures. John Cage was very enthusiastic about it, and he said, 'My God! Isn't it marvelous that one can paint a picture about nothing!' Feldman turned to him and said, 'But John, it's about *everything*!' "

Morty Feldman was a tall, heavyset man with a thick shock of almost black hair over an absent forehead, and eyes that were obscured by glasses with lenses like the bottom of a bottle (see plate 40). His morose, sardonic demeanor concealed a quick and biting critical intelligence. He was a man whose appetites more than rivaled my father's. They both loved to eat and drink and smoke, and they loved doing it together. The two men prowled the city for movies and good cheap restaurants. My memories of Morty have him stretched out and snoring on our wicker chaise, following some feast the two friends had shared.

During this time, my father was showing his new paintings at Peridot and Egan galleries. Mercedes Matter remembers Philip sitting in her living room for hours, entranced by a Mondrian drawing hanging beside her fireplace, one of the "Plus-Minus" series. My father's work, clusters of trembling, luminous brushstrokes hung in a cloudy, atmospheric space, seemed to confuse the critics. His paintings of this period possessed a strange, agitated stillness. Certainly they didn't have the bold expressionist gestures of de Kooning, Kline, or Pollock, or the inscrutability of Rothko or Newman.

A new term was coined: critics began calling Philip Guston an "abstract impressionist." They compared his work to the later Monet, to the famous paintings of water lilies at Giverny. Essays were written about a return to the natural world. In fact, this was not precisely the case. Nature was never a direct or conscious model for my father's painting; the influence was more formal, or even metaphysical, than it was impressionistic. "I recall a strong preoccupation with the forces of nature at work," my father said later. "Sky and earth, the inert and the moving, weights and gravities, the wind through the trees, resistances and flow."

Harold Rosenberg, for many years the art critic for *The New Yorker*, a huge, gruff man with a booming voice and an imposing manner that belied the sensitivity of his perceptions, became a good friend, and his daughter Patia my occasional playmate. Unlike other critics of the time, Rosenberg knew that the painting of the fifties had to be understood from the inside out. He used the term "Action Painting" to convey his belief that the painters of the New York School were linked not by a common style, but by a common involvement with process. "At a certain moment," he wrote in 1952, "the canvas began to appear to one American painter after another as an arena in which to act—rather than as a space in which to reproduce, re-design, analyze, or 'express' an object, actual or imagined. What was to go on the canvas was not a picture but an event."

"To paint is a possessing rather than a picturing," my father wrote in 1956. "Usually I am on a work for a long stretch, until a moment arrives when the air of the arbitrary vanishes, and the paint falls into positions that feel destined." What most of the critics failed to recognize was that these paintings were records of transcendent moments; they represented a poetry of process, the evidence of hundreds of erasures, working wet on wet. "Look at any inspired painting," my father told *Time* magazine. "It's like a gong sounding; it puts you in a state of reverberation."

The paintings of the fifties, with names like *Attar, Beggar's Joy, Dial,* and *Zone,* continue to be the most broadly appreciated of all of my father's work, probably because their shimmering, sensual surfaces are so lovely. Twenty years later, people were still coming up to him at openings, puzzled by new work, and telling him how much they loved the paintings of this period. Why had he changed, they always wanted to know. How he hated that question! It betrayed a profound misunderstanding of the creative process itself. Such people didn't realize that for him, nothing was as constant as the continual need for change. Never to be satisfied. Never to rest on one's accomplishments. But it was never change for the sake of change, but instead a painful process necessitated by a ruthless self-examination and criticism. "What made being with Philip such a pleasure," a poet friend, Bill Berkson, told me, "was that he was completely engaged with a pursuit of—well, truth. I mean, 'The Truth.'"

As the inevitable conflicts and doubts reentered his work, the forms became more emphatic and the colors darker. By 1955, the year he joined the Sidney Janis Gallery, with many of the other artists of the New York School, my father's work had already begun its next metamorphosis. "I began to feel the need for a more solid painting," Philip said later. "I began to look at my earlier work with a kind of renewed interest—the solidity of them. I found it a terrific, challenging problem, in my own terms, to create forms."

I rarely saw the inside of the Cedar Tavern or the Artists' Club, but at one time or another during my childhood I met most of the painters and poets and other luminaries of the fifties. It may have been a glamorous, thrilling time in the New York art world, but for me it was disquieting. The New York artists were a different breed, it seemed to me, less domesticated and more troubled than their Woodstock counterparts. I was aware of the powerful pull this world exerted on my father. Still, while his restlessness and appetites drew him away from us, an equal pull seemed always to bring him home.

Within a very few years, the painters of my father's generation had exploded into prominence. "The response to the painting had created a kind of euphoria," according to Elaine de Kooning. "Everyone was used to breadcrumbs, and suddenly here was all this attention in the press. It was all very stimulating. You felt you were not working in a vacuum anymore."

I still find it impossible to square my own memories with what I know to have been true of the New York art world during the early fifties. It is difficult to recapture this time. In 1955, Dore Ashton, returning from a long trip to Europe, recorded these thoughts in her journal: "New York as always breaks one. But it stimulates too. Painters talk about a 'new nature.' They also discuss business. Martha Jackson's revolution—she buys out whole studios. Ah, the market! More galleries. Ever more galleries. More painters, less craft and more schmaltz . . . "

To me, this journal entry is as telling, somehow, as any analysis by a formalist critic like Clement Greenberg or an art historian-chronicler like Irving Sandler. A unified view of that time in the New York art world stubbornly refuses to present itself. Perhaps there is none. Or perhaps the complexity and competitiveness of my father's relationships with his peers makes it impossible, the fact that he was and was not a part of them, at one and the same time.

"In the early days, we all went to each other's shows," Philip said many years later. "Barney Newman and Mark Rothko and Franz Kline and I, de Kooning too. Now, *there* was a group of people who worked *totally* differently. There was a great separation there. People talk about 'the New York School' as if it really was a school, but there were a great many differences."

Despite critical acclaim, Philip Guston is never included—even now —in that unassailable "inner circle" of abstract expressionism, with Pollock, de Kooning, Kline, and Rothko. Perhaps this is because he had missed the germinal experiments and revolutions of the late 1940s that signaled the emergence of his contemporaries. While they pioneered abstraction in New York, my father had been out in the Midwest, making a name of a different sort for himself. His success there—the grants and prizes and publicity—was something neither he nor the New York painters had particular respect for. His conversion to nonobjective painting had been late and difficult. As my father himself would eventually admit, the image maker in him, that demiurge that feared and longed to create "golems," probably never did feel entirely comfortable with abstraction. But was that really the problem? If so, if doctrinaire adherence to abstraction was the issue, then de Kooning's and Pollock's return to figuration during the fifties ought to have been seen as heresy, which, of course, it was not. In retrospect, it looks as if the picture of Guston as latecomer or misfit was painted not by his peers, but by critics. The real problem was, Philip Guston couldn't be classified.

"We used to talk about that all the time," Morty Feldman said. "What did he have in common with Kline, or de Kooning? I think that the reason Philip changed [to the late work, in 1968] is that the book was in and he wasn't included. And maybe he shouldn't have been. What the hell did he have to do with Jackson or de Kooning anyway?"

Jackson Pollock was a frightening figure to me, in serious decline during the last three years before his death in 1956. On one occasion, he terrified me by barging into our room at the Albert Hotel, raving drunk and belligerent, looking for my father. "With Jackson," Feldman recounted, "there was always sibling rivalry of a very horrendous nature, in every sense, including coming to blows in the Cedar bar."

Certainly, this had everything to do with the drinking they all were doing. "Philip drank a good deal," says Elaine de Kooning, "but never really got drunk, never went beyond the pale. He was charming when he drank, and charming when he was sober. Unlike Jackson, who was hostile when he drank and stricken mute when he was sober."

One night at a party, according to friends, Pollock actually tried to push my father out an upper-story window during a drunken fight over who was the greatest painter.

The Cedar Street Tavern was the hangout for the artists. During the years that we lived in Woodstock and my father was teaching once a week at NYU, he would come into the Cedar bar every week on the night he stayed over in the city. "There was a definite, regular cycle of his state of mind," Mercedes Matter recalls. "It would repeat over and over again. We'd see Philip for a few weeks and then he'd come in one night in an absolute gloom. He'd say, 'I just scraped off months of work on the floor. I'm not a painter. It's no use.' And he'd have everybody down. Everybody. He had this ability to project his mood onto the whole situation. Utter despair!" She laughs, remembering. "And it never failed that the following week he would float in, not touching the ground, and say, 'I've just finished the first painting I've ever done!' And he'd take everybody, like the Pied Piper, and we'd go off for the whole night and have a terrific time, never stopping, close the bar and then go on for something to eat at Rappaport's. The whole night was just a great celebration."

The Artists' Club, which met on Friday nights, was the other center of the social scene. "We were concerned with the breakdown of the recognizable image, and the explanations by some of the artists of their changes, which were never satisfactory..." James Brooks said later of the Club. "We all really knew that there wasn't quite that much of a community anyhow. The commercialism, or the sales, rather, that came later separated a good many artists. Some artists sold and some didn't. They didn't like to embarrass each other by talking about their sales. . . . It split up that close group and artists became more and more on their own as the whole market opened up. When the Club disintegrated, it was expected, I think, but it was sad."

To get into the Club, you had to be sponsored by one of the members. It was my father who first brought Herman Cherry there. "There were two groups," Cherry tells me. "There was Barnett Newman, Clyfford Still, Bob Motherwell, Adolf Gottlieb, and Ad Reinhardt. They were the 'rabbis,' a closed group of intellectuals. The others were just bummy artists—they were slipshod, wore old clothes, drank a lot. They would buy a bottle and dance on Friday nights."

Among the "bummy artists" was Bill de Kooning, a short, sturdy Dutchman, who would arrive at the Cedar bar with a new "girl" on his arm—they were universally called "girls" in those days—tall and invariably gorgeous. His primacy among the painters after Pollock's death always seemed strange to me; he wasn't a grand, articulate talker, nor was his appearance particularly striking. All artists were like my father, I must have assumed; their physical presence reflected their personality.

Mark Rothko, a solemn figure in round wire-rimmed glasses, was temperamentally more like my father. Their work, however, could not have been more different. Though my father was fond of Rothko, he was not in sympathy with the spiritual bent of his painting, nor with its aspirations toward "the sublime." Like Philip, Rothko was Russian in origin, and given to morose introspection—*razdirat' dushu,* which means, literally, to "tear out" or "bare" one's soul, referring to the practice of Russian men who sit up all night drinking vodka and brooding, reciting their grievances, real and imagined.

"The mutual attraction between Rothko and me," my father said later, "had to do with the fact that I go all the way in whatever it is I do, and he certainly went all the way in whatever it was he was doing." After they had visited one another's studios, Rothko once said to my father, "Philip, you are the best storyteller around, and I am the best organ player." Two years before his death, my father was still puzzling over this comment. "That was in 1957," Philip said, "and I still wonder what he meant."

I remember Franz Kline as a squat, muscular man with powerful arms, a thin mustache, and expressive, sloping eyebrows gathered at the center of his forehead that gave him an expression both fierce and mournful. "Painters seldom spoke to each other about art," my father said, "but once in an easy and light bar conversation with Franz Kline, he offered this: 'The real thing about creating,' he said, 'is to have the capacity to be embarrassed.' And he gave one of the better definitions of painting I know of. 'Painting,' Franz said, 'is like hand-stuffing a mattress.' "

Until I was old enough to stay at home alone—eleven or twelve, I think—my parents took me with them to parties in New York. I was more at ease with adults than with children, certainly, but I disliked these crowded artists' parties just as I did gallery openings. All that smoke and noise. The changes that occurred in people when they'd had too much to drink. They were unpredictable and emotional, sometimes even violent.

Heavy drinking had, according to Elaine de Kooning, become epidemic by then. "None of us had any experience with drinking, and then the liquor began to flow, free liquor at openings. Getting drunk was exhilarating." She shakes her head, remembering, and tells me about the time at the Cedar bar when Franz Kline had called her over one midnight, just as she was trying to leave. "A waiter came over and Franz said, 'We'll have twelve Scotch and sodas.' The waiter said, 'Are you expecting more people?' And Franz said, 'No, for *us.* Six for her and six for me.' Franz liked that sense of security.

"The whole art world became alcoholic," Elaine continues. "Everyone drank that way so you felt totally normal. We thought it was social drinking because everyone else did it. Everyone was hung over every single day. Everyone would have blackouts and repeat themselves and get so smashed they'd be staggering around. Everyone was a stand-up comic. It was like a ten-year party."

But they didn't think of themselves as alcoholics, Elaine says; like most people, they thought alcoholics were Bowery derelicts. She remembers Philip's studio on 10th Street, a couple of doors down from her husband Bill de Kooning's studio. "The first day he came home," she tells me, "there was a bum on the steps. Philip said, 'You'll have to move.' The bum looked up at him and said, 'You must be new on this block. This is my stoop.' Philip was rather taken with that, actually. Each of the artists had his own bum."

There would be wild poker games and dancing, extravagant costumes. Sometimes I would try to follow the grown-ups' conversation; more often than not, though, I would try to find a place in the apartment or loft where I could read or be by myself. Consigned to the bedroom, I would hungrily watch TV, if there was one.

But what I searched for, incessantly, was evidence of family life among my parents' friends. At most of these parties, I was the only child. With few exceptions, artists didn't seem to have children; or if they did, they'd been left behind long before, with their failed marriages. Seeking shared experience, I always wanted to find another artist's child to be friends with, and never really did.

Artists. Except for my father, I didn't think much of them. The interchangeable pretty women who came and went with them confused me. But I don't ever remember associating my father with these women. Or wondering why my mother stayed home with me so much of the time. Vaguely, even when I was young, I would hear of divorces and separations, of this or that painter's "girl." But my mother's devotion was so pure, and my father's affection for her so evident, that it simply didn't occur to me.

"Phil was handsome, he was tall, he was successful. The girls just absolutely adored him," says Herman Cherry. "He was terribly attractive to women. And Phil was terribly attracted to people who were attracted to him. It was irresistible for him."

Hearing about it now, encouraging his friends to talk about my father's affairs, his drinking, his ambitions and self-indulgence, is an oddly sobering experience. Their responses to my inquiries are tentative, at first. I can see the question forming on their faces: how does she feel hearing this? Indeed. I stop to take my temperature, and find it surprisingly cool. Shouldn't I feel more disillusioned and angry than I do? Somehow, there's less shock and anger in the hearing of these revelations than I would have expected. The prevailing feeling is one of sadness for my mother. But, strangely, no real sense of surprise. It's as if the details are new, but the knowledge is not.

Louis Bernstein, my father's accountant and trusted friend, asked me recently how my interviewing was going. Fine, I told him, except that people seemed uneasy talking to me, the daughter, about my father's affairs. He nodded, then pointed to a Guston drawing of a nude my father gave him that was hanging beside his desk. "You know, I asked Philip about that drawing once," Lou said. "I said, 'How could you just draw a lovely, naked woman like that, without wanting to make love to her?' And Philip said, 'What makes you think that I didn't?'"

But certainly I had no direct knowledge as a child of my father's affairs, or of his sporadic problems with drinking, except, perhaps, in the intuitive way children always seem to sense such things. No, what I feared had something to do with my father's unpredictable dark moods, his need for the freedom and isolation of his studio—the whole topsy-turvy nature of the man. It was the uncertainty of that whole world and the people in it that frightened me.

There were exceptions. Mark and Mel Rothko were noted for their holiday gatherings. I remember taking comfort in the Rothko family, in their apparent stability. Their daughter Kate was too young to be a playmate for me, but they were still a family, a real family. They made a big deal out of Christmas, which my parents always celebrated reluctantly, and only for my sake. At a certain age, I was no longer supposed to "need" Christmas or birthday parties or gifts anymore. At Christmas, the Rothkos' East Side town house seemed like an island of domesticity, full of good food and cheer, a sort of haven for people who missed their own families.

My last Christmas at the Rothkos' was in 1963, when my son David was only two months old. Their son, Christopher, was three months old at the time. That day I remember leaving David upstairs in the nursery in the hands of their large, scrubbed-looking and efficient Irish baby nurse. To me, living on a teacher's salary in a forty-two-dollar-a-month tenement on the Lower East Side, this was inconceivable luxury.

They seemed to have everything, I remember thinking at the time. Having a baby late in life seemed so romantic, so ultimately domestic and cozy. So it could happen. Artists could make others happy without making themselves miserable. And vice versa. Such a thing was possible.

But then, seven years later, Mark Rothko killed himself, and I decided I didn't understand any of it, after all.

FOUR

So Much Preparation

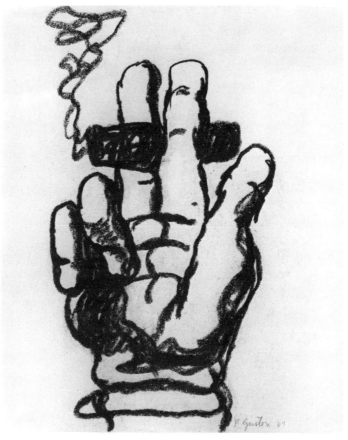

Untitled, 1967.

"Everyone carries a room about inside him," wrote Franz Kafka. "This fact can even be proved by means of the sense of hearing. If someone walks fast and one pricks up one's ears and listens, say in the night, when everything round about is quiet, one hears, for instance, the rattling of a mirror not quite firmly fastened to the wall."

When I was twelve, my parents decided that I could spend the summer in my father's old studio, across the driveway from the house. My room, the room I carry inside me, is that studio in Woodstock.

Seeking more space and privacy, my father had moved to the "stone studio," a building on the back of our property that had been constructed by a potter in the thirties entirely of fieldstone and mortar. It boasted a fine portico with columns turned on the potter's wheel, a heavy wooden Dutch door, on which I loved to swing, and, on the north exposure, three arched windows that faced into the woods. It was always cool and damp inside, even in the dog days of August. Outside was a large, freestanding kiln of brick with a high chimney that was yielding even then to the encroaching vines. Like many of the buildings on the Maverick Road in Woodstock, the stone studio had no plumbing, electricity, or heating. A new floor was laid, and, because my father liked to paint at night, an electric line was put in, thick metal cables that snaked along the stone walls. An oil heater was installed; my parents liked to delay our return to New York City as long as possible each fall, waiting until the cold weather outweighed their desire for quiet and privacy.

The result of my father's move was my chance to have a space all to myself—his former studio. Nothing was more attractive to me than the idea of living alone. On my own, I thought, feeling grown-up and independent.

A single large room with a high, sloping ceiling, my studio had a tall square window also on the north exposure, which began at eye height and extended up perhaps eight feet to the point where the pitch of the roof cut it off. On the side opposite the window, a wooden loft had been constructed which created, beneath it, a cozy nook into which my bed and dresser fit. Above it was stored a collection of painting stretchers, old furnishings, trunks. It, too, had been built in the thirties as an artist's studio. The place had history—a raw, workmanlike smell of paint and turpentine, my father's legacy. It was more than just a room: it was a studio, a place for creative work. I took this idea very seriously.

That summer, I began riding my new three-speed Raleigh bicycle the three miles to the Art Students League near Woodstock, taking a class in life drawing with Arnold Blanch. I covered the fiberboard wall my father had painted on with my clumsy charcoal sketches of the nude model—Arnold believed in short poses. Sometime that summer, I decided that this quick, spontaneous sketching was not enough. I wanted to learn anatomy, what was under the surface, making those lumps and bulges in the model's skin. Dimly, I knew that my father had taught himself to draw. I set about painstakingly reproducing from my father's Michelangelo book a sibyl or two from the Sistine Chapel ceiling with my Faber 2H pencil and gum eraser.

My drawings became more meticulous. I was getting better at it; anyone could see that. But Arnold Blanch would look over my shoulder and shake his head at my last drawing of the morning, the model's "long" pose, a forty-five-minute reclining position. I'd blush, feeling him standing there, pleased and proud at my careful shading, my delicate line. "No, no, no," Arnold would invariably say. "Much too tight." He'd take the pencil from my hand and make a few bold, suggestive strokes on the paper to illustrate what he meant. "You see?" I would bite my lip, nodding, trying not to reveal my disappointment. "Good girl. Just try to be spontaneous. Free." He'd move on to the next student.

Free? But I wanted a classic academic training, the kind where you learned perspective and proportion. I wanted to be able to reproduce reality perfectly. Then I could be free. I decided I'd teach myself, as my father had done. I borrowed the copy of Gray's *Anatomy* my father had acquired during his student days, got a long sheet of brown butcher paper, and drew a skeleton to scale, life size, which I then placed proudly in the center of my wall. Using different colored pencils, I began to attach muscles to bones, seeing where they were articulated and how they combined to produce the visible human form. An icon, this drawing stayed on my wall for years, representing the dead seriousness of my intentions.

I wanted to be an artist. When I was accepted as an art major at the High School of Music and Art in New York City, I felt that I was on my way. My heritage and circumstances would overcome what was lacking. Besides, I had my own studio, when all my friends at school were crammed into stuffy New York apartments with their brothers and sisters. How lucky I was!

I don't think I ever admitted to myself what seemed so obvious only a few years later when I quit painting—that my work, while gaining in technical competence, had never had much substance or feeling. I remember going up to the attic one hot summer day when I was visiting my parents right after I was married, looking through old toys my mother had wrapped in tissue paper and packed carefully away in shoeboxes. Under the eaves were a few dusty portfolios and small oils, my mother's and my own. I stood there for a long time, stooped over my scuffed black portfolio, looking ruefully through those early drawings. It seemed to me that some were missing. Where were my studies of the nude that had seemed so expert to me at fourteen? Surely they couldn't be these amateurish efforts. Whether it was the stifling, still air of the attic, or the clumsiness of my drawings that depressed me, all at once I couldn't breathe. I had to get out of that confining space. I scrambled back downstairs, and the attic stair sprung shut again, folding invisibly into the ceiling.

My father—wisely, perhaps—never commented on these early efforts, though I longed for a word from him, just a smile or a look of encouragement to let me know I was on the right track. It must have been the summer after my freshman year in high school that I finally screwed up my nerve and asked him to come into my studio to look at the painting I was working on. It was a still life, apples and a bottle on a tabletop, the most mundane of subjects, an exercise. But it was the best thing I had done. He stood there, surveying it for a long while. "That's . . . interesting," he said finally. He walked over to the easel and ran his thumb over a passage of blue behind the table. "Look at this," he said. I went and stood by his side. "Don't you see?" he asked.

"See what?"

"This background here. Just look how it's painted. Now, what was going on inside you when you painted that?"

I looked carefully. I couldn't remember what I'd been thinking. It looked perfectly OK to me. "What's wrong with it?" I asked.

Suddenly, he seemed irritated, almost angry. "There's no feeling in it, that's what's wrong. It's flat. Filling in. Like painting a house. You can't just—" He must have noticed my disheartened expression, because he stopped. His voice softened. "I'm sorry," he said. "I don't mean to hurt you, darling, but you have to understand—that's simply not painting."

I looked at the floor.

"You did ask me."

I nodded and he left. After that, though we often talked about art, about his painting and the work of other artists, I never again asked for my father's opinion about my own work. And he never offered.

MEMBER OF AUDIENCE: In relation to Piero [della Francesca], do you think you're more conscious about his work than he was?

PHILIP GUSTON: Do you mean that he didn't think about all the things that I think about him? Yeah, that question always comes up. I don't think I could be one millionth conscious about what he was doing as he was. We talk about past masters and the question always comes up did they think of all these things. I wonder why. (Pause) Well, first of all, how did the painting come into existence?

MEMBER OF AUDIENCE: He liked to do it and so he did it.

PHILIP GUSTON: Oh, yeah? *(Laughter)* You know, if you'll forgive my saying so, that's the pure Hollywood idea about artists. The most expressionist of painters, like van Gogh, who was supposed to be this mad genius, cut off his ear—he was compulsive. Did you ever read his letters to his brother Theo? He was the most conscious of artists, the most conscious of what he was doing. He goes on for pages about Rembrandt, Giotto. The reason I say it's a Hollywood idea is that everybody would like to believe that the average man could, he too, be van Gogh, or leave his wife, like Gauguin. It's a fantasy. Someone asked Jean Renoir if it wouldn't be nice to make a movie about his father. He asked, What about? He came in, he hit us over the face, he ate, he left, then four hours later he came in again. Nothing happened to poor Renoir. He just painted. Of course painters know what they're doing. There's no such thing as an unintelligent painter. It's an anomaly.

During the years of my childhood, my father taught for a living. He was a wonderful teacher, by all accounts, and yet he dreaded and resented the time he spent teaching. Like most artists, what he most fervently wished for was to be able to work, undisturbed. Despite critical success at points in his career, my father was, for the most part, unable to support us from the modest sales of his paintings and drawings.

It was not in him to go through the motions; he put all of himself into his teaching. As a result, it exhausted him. "Philip had such a splendid enthusiasm about him," Stephen Greene, an early student of his from the University of Iowa, says. He remarks on my father's commitment, even at twenty-nine, to "the romance of the artist, highly sensitized, romantic, giving but finally leaving you as well as himself alone."

But the romance of the artist did not encompass teaching. "I tried to impart to the students what I knew about what had excited me," my father said later. "But it was as if the energy or concentration drained out of me into them." Those years at Iowa and at Washington University in St. Louis left him confused and demoralized about his own work.

"Teaching is a way to lose interest in what you thought you were interested in," my father told an interviewer at Brandeis in 1966. "You can't just believe something and teach it and continue believing it." He had found it difficult to work with graduate students. "They're like your disciples," he said. "You eat with them. You go drinking beer with them. They come to your studio and you go to theirs. It's not just a class situation. And while this is good for them, you have to be more alone to paint. Besides, you can only teach what you know. How can you teach what you don't know? But when you paint, you have to deal with what you don't know."

When he began teaching again during the 1950s at New York University and Pratt Institute, my father was adamant about not wanting to work with painting students, preferring instead to teach beginning drawing. It didn't interfere in the same way with his own work, he felt.

After receiving a Ford Foundation grant in 1959, he didn't teach again on a regular basis until he was appointed University Professor of Art in 1973 at Boston University's School of Visual Arts, a position that permitted him sufficient distance and time between visits so that his own work was undisturbed.

"His monthly visits . . . were exhilarating and exhausting experiences for both the students and the faculty," said a colleague, Joe Ablow. "Guston, as he confessed with pride, was a 'zealot.' He was a man possessed by art. Even after long hours in the studios he went on like a

Talmudist, discussing in his excited, imaginative, often outrageous way every aspect of our common calling. It took days for us to sort through all that he had offered during his three day assault on the school."

My father was a great teacher because he was a great talker. He loved a freewheeling exchange. When an idea excited him, he would often hold forth, dominating conversation. Personal revelations, speculations on art and literature, or on any field of human inquiry—science, metaphysics, politics, psychology—all of it interested him. He wore out his friends, keeping them up until all hours in marathon dialogues that would eventually become monologues as their stamina failed to match his.

It did not seem to matter one whit whether he was in a lecture hall or a restaurant, a classroom or a living room or a taxicab. Because of his intense need to articulate his own experience as a painter, he was a natural teacher. He taught, as most great teachers do, by example.

When he spoke, he gestured broadly and eloquently with his strong hands, a Camel perpetually between tobacco-stained index and middle fingers of his left hand—a gesture so characteristic of him that he used it repeatedly as an emblem of himself in his later drawings and paintings.

Until his death, my father gave slide talks and seminars several times a year at Yale and Columbia universities, the New York Studio School, the University of Minneapolis, Cooper Union, Brandeis University, Skidmore College, New College in Sarasota, the Detroit Institute of Fine Arts, and a number of other schools.

"He was a marvelous speaker," says Herman Cherry. "I was in awe sometimes when he spoke. He could create a persona that was quite remarkable. He was very exciting, like a movie star, in a way."

"Students are very hungry," Elaine de Kooning says, remembering a whirlwind visit my father made once to the University of Georgia, where she was teaching. "They'll take as much as they can get. And they ate him alive." She describes a punishing day of studio "crits," of breakfast, lunch, and dinner with faculty and students, and a slide talk in the evening, winding up at three in the morning in a local hangout. "Philip just talked on and on, tremendously entertaining, smoking all the while, never repeating himself. The students were completely enraptured. The whole time Philip was just giving and giving. It was absolutely incredible," Elaine continues. "This was 1976, and I'd known Philip twenty-five years, but it was still kind of amazing to me, this wild generosity and vitality."

My father's gifts as a teacher did not go unremarked in the academic community, as his several awards and honorary degrees testify. He was much in demand as a lecturer and juror; students, past and present, were always citing his influence, sending him their slides, and asking for his recommendations. Until the day my father died—and even afterwards, for a while—the mail daily brought requests of this kind at an increasing —and what had been to him an alarming—rate.

During my childhood and adolescence, what I remember of my father's teaching were his groans and complaints as he tore himself away from the stillness of his Woodstock studio to go into the city to teach at NYU or Pratt. It seems to me that I was working too—working to make myself quiet and charming enough to merit this sacrifice. I always knew he'd far rather be at work in his studio.

My father's teaching mystified and excluded me, as well as making me feel guilty. It was the mysterious place he went to when he left us each week to go down to the city. Only once can I remember actually being present when my father was teaching; that was one summer, while I was still in high school, when my father went to lecture and critique student work at the Yale Summer Art School at Norfolk. I remember a beautiful estate with croquet lawns and big barnlike studios, and a mixture of feelings I could not untangle at the time. My father spoke informally, in a very relaxed yet intensely personal way. The students, initially shy, seemed to absorb his enthusiasm as the afternoon wore on, and the session ended with laughter and a barrage of questions. Clearly, they had found his talk stimulating. I had, too. But I felt a little petulant. Never had I heard my father speak so immediately and vividly about his experience —he was telling them things he had never told me. And I sensed in these students, a few years older than I was, some of the same mixture of diffidence and excitement that I felt, too, on those evenings my father and I sat up late at the kitchen table in Woodstock and talked about ideas.

That evening, at his slide talk, I sat there in the darkened lecture hall, looking at slides of his paintings I had seen and not seen before, and felt as if I knew my father very little. It seemed to me that I wasn't really an only child, after all, but only a favored one—and somehow a lesser one as well, because I was younger, less focused. For the first time, I realized that I had dozens of older and more accomplished brothers and sisters, each of them competing for my father's attention.

"As long as the possibility existed that I would see Philip and he in turn would see my work," one student wrote my mother after my father's death, "I felt connected to a great force."

"One day," another student wrote, "while Philip was looking over some of my work, I confided my feelings of hopelessness at my future as a painter. Philip quoted a line from one of Kafka's diaries, which I carry in my spirit and mind to this day. When he saw how despondent I'd become, he told me that Kafka had written, 'Art is the axe that breaks the frozen sea within us.' I sort of stood there, speechless (he always seemed to have a great flair for the dramatic word). I thought that just about summed up in ten words what I'd been feeling for the past 23 years."

"It feels like I am a child, struggling with a sentence only half said—faced with never being able to finish that sentence to the one person who matters." The student who wrote this note also sent my mother an opening announcement for his first one-man show in New York four years later, in 1984. "Philip remains the most inspiring of my teachers," he wrote then, "in his commitment to painting and as a role model in his self-trust and courage. It saddens me that I can't share my enthusiasm with him. . . . The day I won a Fulbright to Italy, I ran up to B.U.'s office and found Philip. His reaction was revealing as well as endearing. Philip's face lit up with his crooked grin and high eyebrows. He then gently patted my cheek with his hand. I expect I'll remember Philip's visits to my studio for a long time, but his tenderness and warmth at my 'success' is my most vivid memory."

During the difficult times of the 1970s, when the art world was still busy being shocked and offended by my father's late, figurative work, his shows at the David McKee Gallery were always well attended by young painters and painting students. After the long-standing disappointment of no sales and negative reviews—which persisted for a decade, until shortly before his death—it was heartening for him to see the interest of the younger generation in these strange new images.

Some powerful force had moved through him, he often told these young painters. That was how he had come to see it in those last years. My father refused to claim ownership of this force; he approached it with great humility and trepidation. What he had learned by the end of his life was how to position himself, he told his students, how to make of himself a vessel for what moved through him. "I never feel myself to be more than a trusting accomplice," he said.

Despite his earlier doubts about teaching graduate students, my father came to enjoy his monthly visits to Boston University during those final years. After the solitude of Woodstock, there were people to talk to. And his sojourns were infrequent enough not to interfere with his own work.

Within the circumscribed relationship of teacher and student, with its inherent and easily enforced limits, my father could afford to be generous. Knowing he would not be called upon more than once a month to look at a student's painting, he must have felt free to extend his help. From all reports, his critique of student work was never doctrinaire or mean-spirited. He spent time with each student, taking care to discover and address the real concerns.

For me, there's an obvious irony in all of this. How is it that such a man, a remarkable teacher for so many, should have had so dampening an effect on the creative life of his own daughter? Apparently, the young painters who studied with him were able to absorb what he offered without themselves feeling diminished. I was not.

"Philip had the one quality which is most important for a teacher in any field at any level," one of them wrote my mother, "the ability to make the individual feel that his or her ideas, feelings, etc. were *worth* expressing, that honesty with oneself and the joyous continual attempts at self-expression are what painting is all about—not that we should be seeking the 'right formula' or watching to see what the 'others' are doing."

With such a man for a father, why was it, then, that I spent so much of my life looking for formulas, craving approval, and thinking my own "ideas, feelings, etc." were *not* worthy of expression?

There is, of course, no simple answer to that question. My father's relationships with students were straightforward; the terms of the transaction were clear. But with his daughter, of course, things were much more complex. His generosity was compromised. Evidently, he feared my expectations. Guilt and obligation and resentment were always there to muddy the water.

For my part, there was the clear sense that my talents, such as they were, seemed puny next to his. It felt impossible to muster sufficient conviction to do anything with them. I was not alone in this; my mother held herself back, too. Perhaps it was her influence on me—her fears and feelings of inadequacy—that prevailed.

But it's easy to cast blame. Too easy. And we all labor under such influences, after all. Sadly, I didn't receive the same messages my father's students received from him. After years of bitterness, I think now that this was as much my doing as it was his, perhaps more. To avoid being wounded by my father's judgments, I concealed myself, offered him as seamless and polished a persona as I could manage. Because I expressed no anguish, I was given no quotes from Kafka. Because I didn't run to him in my moments of triumph, I received no tender pats on the cheek. The fact is, I didn't feel the same encouragement because I didn't take the same chances. Whatever my creative gifts might have been, I learned to hide them from my father, and from myself.

There was something else, too, some refusal on my part to accept or even to perceive the terms of the creative struggle itself. My father used to say that creation was an act of monstrous egotism, of utmost conceit. Now I see he was right. For years it seemed that my father's legacy in me had generated only the need to create, without the means. But then I thought the means had to do with something higher, something God-given, not with something as base as egotism or conceit, the simple will to see what one could do, how far one could go. I couldn't see, couldn't let myself see, his passionate self-involvement for what it was.

Instead, I entertained a high-minded and unreachable notion of Art. Not for me the messy struggle, the fears, the doubts. I wanted guarantees. At one moment feeling woefully inadequate, at the next hopelessly grandiose, I wanted assurances of greatness—from the outset. And though the urge in me remained, painfully unexpressed, for almost twenty years, it seemed better to me not to try than to try and be judged mediocre. Better to do other things, I told myself, better to play it safe.

"I cherish the memory of the time Philip said, 'This is your *first* painting,' " a student wrote, "and remember always the excitement of having this person whose opinion I so much respected look at my work and really *see* it and feed back to me such acute perceptions about myself and the work."

How could I not feel cheated, reading this letter? I've lost out on something I will never have. I've been cheated by my father's egotism, by his self-involvement, of course, but also by my own timidity. It was as much my failure of courage as it was his failure to reach me, to offer approval and attention, early in my life, when I most needed him.

A final irony: it is only now, when he is gone—and perhaps because he is gone—that I have begun to understand what he was telling his students all those years.

"To know and yet how not to know is the greatest puzzle of all," my father told an audience at Harvard in 1977. "We are primitives in spite of our knowing. So much preparation for a few moments of innocence—of desperate play. To learn how to unlearn."

FIVE

In the Studio

The Painter, 1969.

S ometime during the fall of 1980, a few months after my father's death, I received an invitation to a first screening of Michael Blackwood's hour-long documentary *Philip Guston: A Life Lived*. Much of the film had been shot in San Francisco, only weeks before he died, but it also contained footage taken in his studio during the early 1970s that I had never seen.

I was eager to see the film, and excited at the prospect of its being shown nationally on PBS. My mother had declined to see the film for the time being; it would have been too upsetting for her, we agreed. I hadn't given a thought to my own response. Now that the time had come, sitting there in the tiny editing room at Blackwood Productions, I began to feel overwhelmed. The room was close and cramped. There were too many of us packed in. Roberta Smith, an art critic who admired the late work, was there, and Ross Feld, a close friend of Philip's in his last years, as well as Blackwood and his assistants.

The film began. Struggling against sudden tears, I concentrated on taking deep breaths and kept my eyes locked on the small editing console. It was such a shock, seeing him again. Alive, but not alive. Talking, smoking, laughing. My God, I thought, this is gruesome, ghoulish. Photographs are bad enough. But at least they are static; they don't create this awful illusion of life. I couldn't look away from the image of my father shambling around the galleries of the San Francisco Museum of Modern Art, looking so terribly tired and ill. His eyes were black marbles of pain, bloodshot and haunted, his face unnaturally florid, a ruddy false health that made me wonder all over again how he had gotten through that week. In my emotional state, I barely registered what was being said. It was painful to hear the sound of his voice, not only that it was *his* voice—so familiar and so absent now—but the awful halting slowness of his speech. Garrulous, but always eloquent, Philip had been such a great talker. Would the people who saw this film realize that? With his failing heart, my father struggled so to articulate his thoughts that last year. Would they notice this, as I did?

Relief filled me as the film moved into the earlier segment of Philip at work in his studio. He began tacking a large piece of canvas to his painting wall with a staple gun. This incarnation of my father was eight years younger, healthier, still graying and heavy, but undeniably closer to the vigorous man I wanted to remember. But there was something about this scene that bothered me, too. Philip was frowning, his eyes fierce with concentration; that particular furrow of his forehead and the tight set of his mouth were unfamiliar to me. I watched his moves, the precise stirring of the gesso, the slap of his wide brush against the canvas. And then came the understanding, in an aftershock no less jolting, in its way, than the initial tremor—though it didn't bring tears, but instead a sensation of emptiness, an old, musty feeling of exclusion. What I was becoming aware of, sitting there, was really quite obvious. How was it I had never realized it before? In almost forty years, I had never seen my father paint.

The images of him on film, squeezing paint on the big glass tops of the rolling tables he used for palettes, taking brushes from cans and mixing his pigments, stepping up to the canvas tacked on the beaverboard wall in the center of his studio, the sinuous way the paint flowed from his brush to create those familiar forms, and then his stepping back to look at what he'd done—all these were revelations to me. Watching him at work was peculiarly embarrassing. Like eavesdropping on an intimate conversation, it seemed to be a violation of some profoundly private act.

And it had been. After the film crew left on the day they filmed that sequence, my father destroyed the painting. Later that night, seeing some passages that didn't satisfy him, he began making changes. "And before I knew it, the whole painting had vanished," he told Blackwood. "The painting I had almost finished here wasn't bad. But it looked almost too good. It was as if I hadn't experienced anything with it. I don't mean that I always have to struggle with it, but it looked too pat. It felt to me like additions—this, and that, and that, and that—whereas what I'm always seeking is a great simplicity, where things can't be separated."

I wasn't invited to my father's studio very often. I didn't ask, nor did he volunteer. Not, at least, until I was much older, in my twenties, and coming to Woodstock for infrequent visits. Often my father would say no, that he was in the middle of something. Next time, perhaps. Did I mind, terribly? And I would feel relieved. It was safer somehow to see his paintings in museums and galleries—where they were already public property. Here, in his studio, they seemed so personal, so connected with him.

When I did go into the studio, he'd spread his most recent work around the walls, then sit back in his big, carved armchair and light a cigarette. I'd walk around from painting to painting, feeling his eyes on me. The silence would seem to resonate with expectancy. There was always an awkwardness between us at these times. I think we both felt it. Perhaps he didn't like putting me on the spot; for my part, I'd be busy worrying about finding something to say that would seem perceptive to him—some breathless sentence or two that would invariably come out sounding pandering or inflated. Often, I didn't know what to say. The changes in his work caught me unprepared; I, too, needed time to understand. The notion that I was probably free to say anything, that what I thought might not matter very much to him, simply didn't occur to me.

My mother was always the first to see his completed work. When he finished a painting, in the middle of the night, he'd often wake her, too exhilarated to sleep or wait for the morning to share it with her. But my mother never minded this. After the long hours and days of separation from Philip while he was working, she was eager to be with him, and gratified by his need for her. Her opinion was crucial to him; he'd watch her face to see if it registered enthusiasm. "What shall we call it?" my father would ask. But when my mother gave him suggestions, she tells me, he would invariably find a title of his own.

"You know, I can't stand to look at this one," my mother said the summer after my father died. We were photographing *Ceremony*, a painting of the middle forties. Apparently, he'd made some changes in the painting after she'd commented on its composition. She sounded angry; she had not forgiven herself for meddling. "You see that," she said, "the upside-down figure on the left? I should *never* have said anything. It was *perfect* before."

During those quiet Woodstock summers while I was in high school, my mother was working in her studio too—a little den off the living room where she set up her desk and typewriter. All of us, my mother, my father, and I, each off in our separate building, spent the long, lazy days in our studios working. It was a good, companionable feeling. The drowsy afternoons seemed to stretch on and on, everything falling still and silent in the heat except for the buzzing cicadas; I'd try to work or read until I'd finally fall into a stuporous sleep. Sometimes we'd all go to find a place to swim. Near the Art Students League, a walk through a pine woods would bring you to a rocky basin known as the Big Deep. On really hot days, we'd drive past the Ashokan Reservoir spillway to swim in the icy, clear rock pools of a place we called the Gorge.

I had begun writing poetry, too—the usual tortured adolescent ramblings. One of my favorites was "Buttermilk Falls." In it, I described a hike I took up a creek on Peekamoose Mountain, where I came across a dead fawn lying in a clear pool of water, apparently fallen from the rocks above. Using great clusters of adjectives, I described the scene—the green of the forest above, the filtered beams of sunlight, the single black butterfly (Death!) which had alighted on the fawn, my own feelings of transcendence.

My father, pleased with my intellectual development, had started giving me books to read. I became a convert to existentialism, reading Kafka, Kierkegaard, Camus, Sartre. In the evenings, after dinner, we started talking about art, about ideas. The French symbolist poets, the Russian novelists. There was something so romantic, so tantalizing for me about all that darkness; the intensity and isolation matched my own—or so I fancied—and gave me a way of understanding my father. "I seem destined to have to suffer every possible mood, to acquire experience in every direction," I read in Kierkegaard's *Either/Or.* "Every moment I lie like a child, who must learn to swim, out in the middle of the sea. I scream; for I have indeed a harness about my waist, but the pole that holds me up I do not see. It is a fearful way in which to get experience."

By this time, we were living in New York City except in the summertime. We had moved to the top two floors of a loft building on 18th Street, between Irving Place and what was then Fourth Avenue. Between 1948 and 1956, my father had sold only two paintings. We depended on his teaching income. But now, we had some money, finally. With de Kooning, Rothko, Kline, and others, my father had joined the Sidney

Janis Gallery in 1955 and was finally selling his work with some regularity—the major paintings for as much as $2,500, which seemed like a lot at the time—most of them to Janis himself, who provided a steady, dependable income for his artists in return for buying their work directly. Sidney Janis could afford to wait for sales; his artists could not.

Our main living quarters at the 18th Street loft were on the third floor, as was my bedroom, half partitioned from the rest by a large freestanding cabinet. Everything in that loft was stark white, and built in, from the piano and couches and tables to the wall after wall of cupboards. Harry Holtzman, the loft's previous tenant, had helped Piet Mondrian when he'd first emigrated to the United States. Apparently, the influence of the great Dutch painter on Holtzman had been profound; living among all those white cupboards was rather like living inside Mondrian's *Broadway Boogie Woogie*.

My father's new studio, on the top floor, had been Walt Kuhn's studio before his death. That space was undivided, a single huge, skylit room with an alcove in which my parents slept. It was there that my father's work again began changing. While still abstract, the paintings of these years were darkening, coalescing, increasingly assuming form and conflict. "The poise, the isolation, of the image containing the memory of its past and promise of change is neither a possession nor is it frustrating," my father wrote in a statement for *It Is*, a journal of abstract expressionist art in 1958. "The forms, having known each other differently before, advance yet again, their gravity marked by their escape from inertia."

The delicate colors of the early fifties deepened; black began to appear with increasing regularity, and harsh permanent greens and cobalt blues, as well as undiluted passages of the cadmium red medium which was later to become his signature color—together with mars black and titanium white. By the late fifties, that shimmering, atmospheric quality the critics had erroneously likened to impressionism, really the product of layer upon layer of strokes and erasures, of rose madder and soft grays, painted wet on wet, the lovely record of an anguished process, was completely gone, replaced by a boldness and gestural authority previously unknown in my father's work.

Though they were still painterly, these canvases were no longer as pretty to look at. Restless, their anxiety overt, they were, instead, directly disturbing. There is a feeling of a motive power gathering, the beginnings of an ominous sense. During the last three years of the decade, Philip painted dozens of small gouaches and oils. When his work was changing rapidly, my father often worked small—as he did again, a decade later, producing a flood of small panels of shoes and books— as if gathering momentum for the statement of larger work. The titles of the late fifties are significant: *Actor, Traveler, Painter, Sleeper*—self-reflective names he used many times, adding a roman numeral for each variation.

For me, this was an exciting time. I had had best friends before—Vera in Woodstock, Molly at Grace Church School, a private school in New York where I'd spent my eighth-grade year. Now, for the first time, at thirteen, I was part of a group. Together, my girlfriends from the High School of Music and Art and I discovered Greenwich Village and the Beat Generation. We were a few years too late to feel like pioneers—the Village was touristy now; the counterculture had, as usual, been co-opted. Everyone, it seemed, was a beatnik. You could buy "Howl" and *On the Road* anywhere. We adopted the new uniform. Gone were the frilly crinolines, the saddle shoes, and Daddy's white shirts of the early fifties. We were dressing head to toe in black—tights, turtleneck, straight skirt with a kick pleat, black ballet slippers—the romantic severity relieved only by long dangly silver earrings or perhaps a free-form pendant on a rawhide thong. I wore my hair long and loose, wishing it was straight rather than curly.

We roamed 8th Street, MacDougal and Bleecker, Washington Square —especially on Sundays, when there would be folk music in the Circle. We saved our money to buy cappuccino at Figaro's or Rienzi's; we casually leaned against the cars on MacDougal Street, affecting a jaded world-weariness we didn't feel, watching the passing crowd. Too young for the hipster scene at the jazz clubs, too cautious yet for reefer madness, we gravitated instead toward the more wholesome side of the Village— folk music. Edging into the inner circle around the performers on Sundays in the Square, we sang along, learned all the words to all the songs, folk-danced barefoot.

My father wept when Adlai Stevenson lost for the second time in 1956; he told me he felt as if he himself had been defeated. But I was young; Joe McCarthy and HUAC were only names to me. World Wars, the Great Depression, Hiroshima, and the Holocaust were events to read about in

books. In my first surge of youthful idealism, I was convinced that the
tides of social change were turning. After all, wasn't Pete Seeger singing
about the bomb? Weren't he and other people from SANE sailing out
into the Pacific to block atomic tests? One night, I sat in Carnegie Hall
and cheered with thousands of others, convinced that the peaceful vision
the Weavers were singing about could come to pass. Great things were
coming, breaking us loose from the placid complacency of the Eisen-
hower years, I told my father. He regarded me gloomily. "I hope you're
right," he said, and sighed.

"Oh, what a beautiful city!" Dave Van Ronk sang the gospel song in
his whiskey voice. "Twelve gates to the city, Hallelujah!" It could have
been New York he was singing about. Those days, the city seemed spread
out for us like a wonderful playground. We rode the subway at any hour
to each other's houses in all the boroughs. Music and Art was a public
high school for gifted students, started by Fiorello LaGuardia, New
York's visionary mayor from the New Deal days. Our school song took
its melody from the last movement of Beethoven's Ninth. Students came
from all over the city. One girl I knew even made the long trip from
Staten Island—first bus and ferryboat, then subway to 135th Street, then
that long, long flight of steps up St. Nicholas Terrace to an ugly neo-
Gothic building that looked as if it belonged to the CCNY campus.

My first real boyfriend, Josh Rifkin, was something of a musical
prodigy. Known later for his recording of Scott Joplin's piano rags, he
was a talented pianist and composer in high school, and interested in
electronic music at a time when it was barely known in the United States.
Josh impressed my mother by writing a fugue for recorders—I had, after
many years of struggling, given up the violin for this less daunting
instrument—in the baroque style on the spot one afternoon, then picking
up my alto and playing all three parts, transposing when needed. It was
Josh who showed me how to sneak into Carnegie Hall through the
Recital Hall next door, where he would invariably find us an empty box
in the Dress Circle. Once we were seated, with the Philharmonic tuning
up below us, he would open one of the scores he'd borrowed from the
library for that evening's performance, whip a baton from his pocket, and
proceed to conduct the entire concert from his pilfered seat.

Our 18th Street loft building was torn down and we moved farther
uptown, to an apartment on 34th Street between Ninth and Tenth

avenues. Tired of empty, echoing spaces, and the absence of privacy of loft living, I was thrilled to be living in an ordinary two-bedroom prewar New York apartment. At last I had a room of my own, with a real door that actually closed; there was even an elevator, with an elevator man who called me "little lady." I thought it was very classy. Of course, it was an odd neighborhood—hardly posh, not really an area where many people lived—made noisy by an exit for the Lincoln Tunnel across the street. Still, I loved it.

My friends and I would sit and talk for hours at the all-night Bickford's cafeteria on the corner of Ninth Avenue and 34th Street. Or we would lie on my bedroom carpet until late at night listening on my new hi-fi to Ella Fitzgerald and Vivaldi, Beethoven and Miles Davis and the Modern Jazz Quartet.

Philip rented a studio in Chelsea, on West 20th Street, a huge, dirty cave of a space over a firehouse, where the perennial gloom was punctuated by a few deep wells of light beneath the skylights. I visited there only once or twice. Absorbed in my own social life, I was less and less aware of what my father was doing.

In the late thirties and early forties, Philip and his boyhood friend Reuben Kadish gradually lost touch. The Duarte mural in 1935 had ended the years of their collaboration. My father had come to New York and gone to work for the WPA. For years after that Reuben had tried and failed to win mural commissions. During the war, he had gone to China as a civilian artist with the American troops. After the war ended, disillusioned about his chances in the art world, Reuben bought a good-sized farm in northern New Jersey and settled there as a dairy farmer with his wife, Barbara, and their two young sons. Another son was born a year or two later. By then, Reuben had stopped painting completely. It was a hard life for a young family, working that farm. Not until the late fifties, when Reuben had finally returned to the New York art world— this time as a sculptor—and was doing large terra-cotta and bronze figures and teaching at Cooper Union in New York, did he and my father reestablish contact.

It was sometime during the summer of 1958, between my sophomore and junior years in high school, when I was fifteen, that I was taken to the Kadish family farm one weekend for a visit. The two older boys, Danny, who was nineteen, and Ken, a year younger, showed me the place. Their brother Julian, too young to be interested in squiring me around, stayed in his room that day, working on some science project. In the barn, Danny tried to show me how to milk a cow, shooting streams of milk from a cow's full udder into the open mouths of a litter of kittens lying in the hay nearby, and letting me try some too. I can still taste the rich, warm flavor on my tongue. I stood by the shed that served as a stable, admiring the horses, as Ken vaulted on the back of the pony, Buster, who bucked and kicked around the pasture.

The family no longer farmed the land themselves. By that time the two smaller farmhouses and their barns and outbuildings had been leased to tenants, immigrant Dutch Calvinist farming families with lots of blond, stolid sons to help with the milking and haying. The Kadish family lived in the big old main house, which was always, in the fourteen years that I knew it, being repaired and improved, projects often begun with great enthusiasm but left unfinished.

It was so different from Woodstock. Living in the country had meant the undisturbed summer silence to me, the quiet of pine woods, where there wasn't even a lawn to mow. My mother liked leaving the land around our house in its natural state, and my father couldn't have cared less. Barbara Kadish, on the other hand, spent days on end in her terraced flower gardens. Late spring was breathtaking with dozens of varieties of iris she had bred in a rainbow of colors. In a quarter-acre vegetable garden, they grew all their own produce, canning and freezing everything. Even though they themselves weren't farming anymore, there was always work to be done. Fences to be mended, post holes to be dug, siding to be replaced and painted, horses to be groomed, chickens to be fed. The list went on and on.

All the outside work besides gardening was done by Reuben and his sons. Their ability to fix things was impressive. Danny and Ken had both rebuilt junked cars. I was taken for a ride in an old black Model-T Ford that Ken had lovingly restored. By the end of the afternoon, I was as completely charmed by these two tanned, muscular young men, one curly-headed and dark, the other straight-haired and fair, as I was by the place itself. It was beautiful land, that farm, hundreds of acres of lush, rolling green fields and woods and ponds, of hillsides dotted with grazing cows, of pigs and horses and chickens.

Danny—the older one, the one with the dark, curly hair and hazel eyes—was everything the skinny, intense boys I'd been used to at school were not. He seemed so mature, so competent. He wanted to be a painter. Besides, he went to NYU, and what high school girl could resist the thrill of dating a college man? He wasn't just a country boy, either; he seemed to know the city too, that seamier side of things I'd been too young to explore before, the jazz clubs. He took me to the original Five Spot, on the Bowery and 2nd Street, to hear Thelonious Monk and Ornette Coleman, and to the White Horse Tavern over on Hudson Street, Dylan Thomas' old hangout, he told me. I was impressed. Before long, we were going steady—though we were too hip to call it that.

At my twenty-fifth high school reunion in 1985, they gave us copies of our high school yearbook pictures to wear as name tags. In mine, I am serious, unsmiling, long ponytail slung over one shoulder. Plastic glasses of wine firmly in hand, bored spouses in tow, we sidled around the big room, eyeing the strangers, making tentative approaches, looking at the yearbook pictures they had pinned on us, at the aging faces, then at the pictures again, finally breaking into smiles of recognition. "You haven't changed at all," we reassured one other. "You're just the way you were."

For my high school graduation, my parents took me to Europe. I remember sitting by the airplane window, somewhere out over the Atlantic, unable to sleep from the excitement of it all—the trip to come, my graduation that afternoon, and college ahead of me. As the sun rose peach and gold outside my window, I looked out at the hazy pink line that separated light from dark and told myself that my life, my real life, was only now beginning.

Since my father's Prix de Rome twelve years before, he'd been dreaming of returning to Italy to revisit his pantheon of Italian masters. Now, he wanted to show them to me. In high school, I'd become interested in art history; this trip confirmed my interest. First we would go to Venice, for the Biennale, where thirteen of his paintings, with those of three other artists, were to hang in the American pavilion. Then it was on to Florence and Rome. We'd end up in London, after short visits to Paris, Belgium, and Holland, but spend most of the summer in Italy, traveling around Umbria and Tuscany to see all the Piero della Francescas.

Sitting on the balcony of the Pensione Seguso in Venice, looking out at the Giudecca glittering in the misty sunlight, hearing the slap of water against stone, the clunk and creak of wood on wood of the gondola oars, seeing the golden bubbles of San Marco's domes rise across the enormous expanse of pavement and pigeons—I wanted it never to end. That summer was filled with such moments.

In Florence, we met up with Peter Janson—H. W. Janson, the art historian—his wife, Dora, and twin sons, Tony and Peter, just my age, with whom I had played in St. Louis when I was a little girl. I sat out on our balcony with Tony, admiring his fencing scars from prep school, and talked about going away to college. We discovered Florence on long walks in the first light of dawn, when the streets were empty of tourists and the only places open were the coffee bars, where, standing beside laborers going early to work, we drank cups of the blackest espresso.

In Rome, we stayed at the American Academy up on the Gianicolo, one of the city's seven hills, and took our meals with the Fellows. I felt very grown-up, sitting on the terrace at breakfast with all the artists and classicists, soaking up the conversation, delicately cutting a ripe fig with a knife and fork. My father escaped for two weeks to Sicily, which he had never visited, leaving my mother and me alone to wander the city. One of the Fellows, a classics scholar, insisted on taking me to the Villa Giulia and the Forum, and on long romantic walks along the belvederes, with all the lights of Rome spread out beneath us, twinkling through the pines.

It was on that trip that I learned to love Renaissance painting. There, in the dank recesses of Italian churches, lit up for a few lire slipped to the caretaker, were the pictures I'd seen in books all my life. My father took delight in my enthusiasm. It was no pretense on my part; the frescoes *were* wonderful. "Look at the line, how alive it is!" my father would exclaim, pointing at one of Paolo Uccello's battle scenes. "Just look at those magnificent heads!" Seeing it all with him, I couldn't help absorbing a part of his passion. "Look at how weighty those *putti* are," he'd say as we craned our necks at a Tiepolo ceiling, "how everything soars and is so heavy, too."

My father's Italian was fluent and enthusiastic; everywhere we went, he engaged people in conversation—waiters, guards, shopkeepers. "Did you see our Masaccio?" a newspaper vendor would ask him, launching a ten-minute conversation on art which had begun with a simple request for directions. *"Che colore! Che luce! È molto bello, eh?"* It was as if my father had come home again, as if now he was among his people. I'd never seen him so relaxed and happy. I listened and began to learn a few words of Italian here and there. *"Tre biglietti, per favore,"* I'd say proudly at the station. Local buses took us to tiny hill towns like Urbino and Assisi, where we'd hastily dump our things at the hotel and run off to find the Piero or Uccello we had come to see. Waiting for the town hall of Borgo San Sepolcro to open, coming out of the hot, bright noonday sun into that cool, bare, whitewashed cave of a room to see Christ, resurrected, unearthly, stepping over the sleeping bodies of the Roman soldiers as if for the first time. "As he emerges from the tomb," wrote Camus about this fresco, "the risen Christ of Piero della Francesca has no human expression on his face—only a fierce and soulless grandeur that I cannot help taking for a resolve to live. For the wise man, like the idiot, expresses little."

I kept a diary, recording every church and museum, every ferry and bus and train ride, pasting the tickets and forms in it each day, searching for a way to preserve my wonderful Italian summer. I bought postcards of all the paintings we saw. Somewhere, in my mother's attic, is a shoebox full of Titian and Raphael, of Masaccio and Piero and Tiepolo.

Though I continued to study painting and drawing that fall when I went off to Oberlin College, I felt that my real interests and talents lay in art history. I had begun to doubt my potential as a painter; if I couldn't create great art myself, at least I could study the works of others. During the two years I was at Oberlin, I took every course offered by Wolfgang Stechow, a noted scholar of Northern Renaissance Art.

The flat, bucolic countryside of north central Ohio made me a little restless; as in Dutch landscape painting, its enormous sky dominated everything. Though I often missed New York and my boyfriend Danny Kadish there, I was happy at Oberlin. I had my own life, finally, apart from my parents. My father had left me many times; this time, it was I who left him.

In May of 1962, as I was completing my sophomore year of college, I flew to New York for the opening of my father's retrospective at the Guggenheim Museum. It was a gala event, the crowning achievement of a life's work; yet there was something spooky about it, too. For one thing, my father seemed almost as disturbed by this exhibition as he was honored. I didn't understand it at the time. Now, of course, it seems obvious that any such summation of an artist's career, coming in mid-life, would be difficult. In my father's case, this looking backward only added to an already gathering sense of crisis, a sense that was not unlike what he had faced during the mid-forties, twenty years before.

"When the show was first hung, it was somewhat traumatic for me," my father admitted to an interviewer four years later. The previous year, he explained, following a "collapse about it," he'd actually canceled the retrospective. "As if I had to act out the fear of myself seeing it all together, because by not seeing it all together, I could still perpetuate certain hopes and myths about myself that I needed."

But then, characteristically, Philip changed his mind. "Then I wanted to have it. It would be a greater defeat not to have it than to have it. I thought I'd better face it . . . in exposing it to myself and in being willing to be judged on my production, my work—I thought that this might be a way I could get rid of it and move on."

The retrospective went off as scheduled (see plate 41). "After it was hung," he said, "my first response was shock. But after a few weeks, almost as one would feel after an operation of some kind, I recovered. It took me about a year to get started painting again, and stop brooding about the work. But it was of great value to me. I think I became more ruthless with myself in the work following."

Before the opening, my mother and father and I walked down the long spiral ramp. The Guggenheim is not a museum ideally suited for paintings; the architecture overshadows anything in it. But the show was impressive, nonetheless. Except for the Biennale in Venice—a crowded, carnival-like affair—I had seen Philip's paintings hung only in galleries. The cramped rooms of the Sidney Janis Gallery on 57th Street, with their low ceilings and intimate dimensions, never had been quite able to contain the paintings on their walls. In the vast open spaces of the Guggenheim, I felt as if I were seeing them for the first time, curling down that ramp, not flat on the walls but hovering a foot or so in front of them on struts, like a collection of jeweled butterflies on pins.

"I'm a goner," my father said that night before the opening. Half humorously, he drew his finger across his throat, tilted his head, and rolled up his eyes, mimicking a gruesome demise. "That's it," he groaned, "I'm finished now. I'm done for." He shuddered, as if the whole event chilled him. Somebody brought him a drink. My mother stood there, smiling nervously. She hated openings as much as he did—

more, perhaps, because of her diffidence. Just the usual opening night jitters, I thought, looking at them; having seen my father before many openings, I didn't take this self-dramatizing very seriously.

More was changing than I knew. Looking at it now, with the clarity of hindsight, I can see that everything was in flux for them. My parents were entering a time of real crisis in their marriage. The next year, when his retrospective was in Los Angeles, my father spent a full month in California, ostensibly to be there while the exhibition was hanging at the L.A. County Museum of Art, but staying longer than he had planned, to prolong an affair with a wealthy collector. My father was fifty years old. He was drinking too much, and smoking and eating too much. He wasn't sleeping. After years of this sort of punishment, his health had begun to suffer. His work was in decline. Implicitly, the message of the Guggenheim retrospective seemed to be that the best of his work—and his life—was behind him.

When Philip at last came home from California, he confessed to Musa about this affair, and all the others. "He told me everything," she says, ruefully, "but I had nothing to tell him." Days of talking and long walks in the woods, my mother remembers, were followed by a trip to Montreal, to see the house where Philip was born. It was like a second honeymoon.

As for me, I was lost in my own world, oblivious to all of this that night at the Guggenheim. I was busy being overwhelmed by my father's success, star-struck and impressed by the occasion, the elegant restaurant we went to afterwards—no Chinatown tonight! It seemed that my father had, at last, truly arrived. In a photograph someone took at the opening, I am wearing a new blue silk dress with shoes to match and long white evening gloves, working hard to reflect the glamour of the evening, to seem like my father's daughter, the very picture of cool, nineteen-year-old sophistication (see plate 42).

I wasn't cool inside, however. A few minutes earlier, just as everyone was leaving the plush office of Harvey Arnason, the director of the museum—beige carpeting and round porthole windows—Danny Kadish had stopped me and delivered what was intended as a proposal, though it had the insistent tone of an ultimatum. If I wouldn't come back to New York, we were through, he said. Being separated while I was at Oberlin was too hard on him. He wanted to get married.

Later that year, in September, right before classes were to start at NYU—they had a great art history department, I kept reassuring myself —Danny and I were married at the Kadish farm in New Jersey (see plate 43). It was a potluck affair; we'd given our families only two weeks' notice. We hired a bus to bring the wedding guests from the city. My parents brought the wedding cake, baked by a Hungarian couple they knew in Bearsville and decorated with suns and moons and flowers and hearts by my father, much as he had decorated my Halloween costume years before. I wore the same blue silk dress I had worn at my father's opening. At the time, this choice seemed merely practical; it was my one really nice dress, after all. It wasn't until years later that I understood the obvious symbolism.

It was at the farm, too, the summer following, when I was pregnant with my first child, that I gave up painting, finally, just as my mother had, around the time of my birth—though I did not make that connection then, either. In my mind, there was no link at all between my being Philip Guston's daughter and my marrying an artist, the son of my father's boyhood friend. My father had nothing to do with it. Danny and I had just met, fallen in love, gotten married; that was all. And there was certainly no connection between becoming an artist's wife and giving up my own creative work. I would have denied any such interpretation vehemently. All I knew at the time was that none of my painting was very good; it seemed flat and illustrative. I remember walking into the small, stuffy room adjacent to the bedroom upstairs, a room the Kadishes used for storage, to look at the canvas I'd been working on. The air was still; a fly buzzed against the window. I don't remember feeling much more than relief as I put the caps on the tubes of paint and turned my painting to the wall.

At that time, I knew very little about my father's increasing dissatisfaction with the art world. I knew he had left Janis that year, along with Rothko, de Kooning, and others. But I wasn't really sure why. Not until almost twenty years later, in 1981, when I was interviewing Sidney Janis in connection with the catalogue raisonné I was working on, did I put it together. "Why did they all leave me?" the old man asked rather plaintively, and I could almost believe he didn't remember. That was the year—1962—when across 57th Street, in a big, fancy store, Janis opened the first major exhibition of pop art. Overnight, it seemed, the art world changed. My father was in despair over the selling of art, over the slick, depersonalized gloss—not only of pop art, but of minimalism as well— that was taking center stage in New York. Art was no longer struggle; art had become marketing.

"Frustration is one of the great things in art," my father wrote, "satisfaction is nothing." His own work was increasingly focused on dark forms floating heavily in a luminous gray scumble, the overcast occasionally broken with pale pinks and blues. It is a strange, difficult kind of painting; few critics understood or liked it then or now. My father claimed not to care, but, of course, he did. His growing sense of personal crisis was clearly connected with what was happening in the art world. It was evident in his work.

H. H. Arnason, director of the Guggenheim, spoke of his ". . . sense of the canvas as a place, a stage on which dramas are enacted by living forms." In an introduction to a Guston show at the Jewish Museum that he organized, Sam Hunter wrote that ". . . his forms themselves changed into denser blocks, slabs, and wedges of paint, obtrusive individual presences striking uncertain dramatic attitudes like actors in a play who hadn't learned their parts."

By the year of the Jewish Museum show, 1966, the changes in the New York art world had crystallized into a decided reaction against abstract expressionism on the part of many critics. A mood of "irritation" prevailed, according to Dore Ashton. One of the more virulent attacks against this show came from Hilton Kramer, of the *New York Times,* who termed my father's style "genteel," and claimed that "a painter so limited in range of feeling, who restricts himself so severely to slender and much repeated vocabulary, is not an ideal candidate for an exhibition of the sort currently installed." The exhibition itself was, in Kramer's mind, "an attempt to re-inflate a reputation that has admittedly grown a little flat in the op-pop hurly-burly of the sixties."

In my living room hang several large paintings of different periods in my father's work, one of them from 1960. People rarely comment on it, and when they do, it is often to remark at how somber and depressive it seems, how strangely ominous the black, headlike form is. The painting's title is *Mirror—to S.K.*

In fact, Søren Kierkegaard was much on my father's mind during this period. "I have but one friend, Echo," Kierkegaard wrote, "and why is

Echo my friend? Because I love my sorrow, and Echo does not take it away from me. I have only one confidant, the silence of the night; and why is it my confidant? Because it is silent."

My father found another echo in Franz Kafka's writing. "March 13, 1915," one of Kafka's diary entries reads. "Occasionally I feel an unhappiness which almost dismembers me, and at the same time am convinced of its necessity and of the existence of a goal to which one makes one's way by undergoing every kind of unhappiness."

My father read a great deal of philosophy. His bookshelf is crammed with Kafka and Kierkegaard, Henri Bergson, Schopenhauer, Nietzsche, Martin Buber, St. Thomas Aquinas, Jung, and Spinoza. Select any one and let it fall open. Jean-Paul Sartre, for example, in his book on Baudelaire, quotes one of the poet's letters, written in 1857: ". . . what I feel is an immense discouragement, a sense of unbearable isolation . . ." That might have been my father speaking, during the mid-sixties.

But why glorify one man's personal torment, especially when it comes at the pinnacle of what had been, after all, a largely successful career? As Harold Rosenberg wrote in 1966 in the Foreword to his book *The Anxious Object*, "To mention anxiety is to arouse suspicion of nostalgia or of a vested interest in the past, if not of a reactionary reversion to the middle-class notion of genius suffering in a garret."

But Rosenberg goes on to put the forces operating at the time in context, discussing the "social isolation of art" that had confronted artists in the postwar period. "Must one remind budding art historians," he writes, "that the uneasiness of art in the face of its own situation was not adopted by artists as a manner, in the way that one adopts a leather jacket or a hair-do that covers the eyes? Anxiety was forced upon art as the experience that accompanies the rejection of shallow or fraudulent solutions."

In this view, anxiety is necessary process. The doubts, the questioning, even the self-flagellation, all have their rightful role to play in the act of creation. "The doubter is like a whipped top," wrote Kierkegaard. "He stands upright exactly as long as the lashes continue. He can no more stand erect by himself than can a top."

When my father returned from a week of tests at Johns Hopkins Hospital in Baltimore once, he wrote to Dore Ashton, "I thought my organs were rotting away, but no—all in fine shape. I'm supposed to lose weight, stop booze, stop smoking and have *no anxieties* about *life* and *art*. Imagine! I didn't bother explaining to him that my whole life is *based* on *anxiety*—where else does art come from, I ask you?"

"The anxiety of art is a philosophical quality," Harold Rosenberg concludes, "perceived by artists to be inherent in acts of creation in our time. It manifests itself, first of all, in the questioning of art itself. It places in issue the greatness of the art of the past (How really great was it? How great is it for us?) and the capacity of the contemporary spirit to match that greatness. Anxiety is thus the form in which modern art raises itself to the level of human history."

"I have a studio in the country—in the woods—but my paintings look more real to me than what is outdoors," my father wrote in 1967, when he, in a final gesture of disgust with the art world, gave up the New York studio on 20th Street, and moved to Woodstock permanently.

"I'm almost going into a kind of figuration," he told an interviewer at the time. "Heads, still life forms, solid as I can make them—although not recognizable. I don't feel the need for that. In the early sixties, the colors disappeared. I wanted to work with the simplest means possible. I didn't even stretch any canvas, just tacked it on the wall. Finally, I was just using white and black. Painting had become a crucial problem of location. I didn't stretch these canvases. I rigged up what looked like towel racks, just to hang them up. By the end of four years, the studio looked like Macy's rug department!" (see plate 39.)

He began to build a new studio in Woodstock, a big cinder block affair that looks like a factory building, connected to his first studio, the room I loved so much as a teenager. "You walk outside," he wrote, "the rocks are inert; even the clouds are inert. It makes me feel a little better. But I do have a faith that it is possible to make a living thing, not a diagram of what I have been thinking: to posit with paint something living, something that changes each day."

Because of this, because my father wanted to create living things, a fierce humility was necessary to counterbalance what he considered to be the enormous conceit of his creation, his shame at bringing yet another golem into a world already too full of living things. "I have the courage, I believe, to doubt everything," Kierkegaard wrote. "I have the courage,

I believe, to fight with everything; but I have not the courage to know anything; not the courage to possess, to own anything."

In an article for *Art News*, entitled "Faith, Hope and Impossibility," published in 1966, my father summarized the dilemmas he was facing in this way: "But you begin to feel, as you go on working, that unless painting proves its right to exist by being critical and self-judging, it has no reason to exist at all—or is not even possible.

"The canvas is a court where the artist is prosecutor, defendant, jury and judge. Art without a trial disappears at a glance: it is too primitive or hopeful, or mere notions, or simply startling, or just another means to make life bearable.

"You cannot settle out of court."

The pain of this labor, however excruciating, is essentially productive; therefore, it remains bearable.

"Many artists feel anguish and in crisis, especially the artists of my generation in N.Y.," my father wrote Dore Ashton after reading her first draft of *Yes, But . . .* in 1974. "Do you think the frequent use of 'crisis' and 'anxiety' gives the impression that I am in constant pain? Sure, there is plenty of trouble along the way—lots to cope with. But when the picture takes form, the new structure elates and calms me. I would hope that the looker does not feel he is looking at pain, trouble, and anguish, but at a new image which he can contemplate—get a real positive charge. . . . Discussing my work once with Clark [Coolidge, the poet] he told me a story that stays with me. Melville was writing to Hawthorne, after having finished *Moby Dick*. He wrote, 'I've written an evil book and feel spotless as a lamb.' "

SIX

Some Music

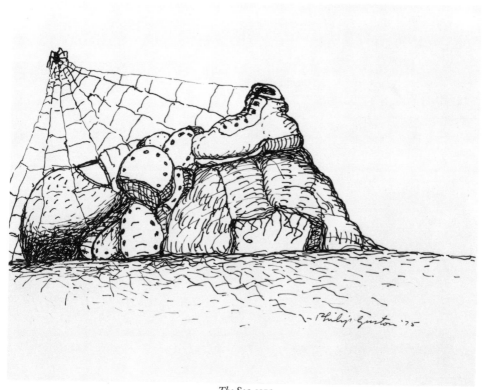

The Sea, 1975.

O n the way to a hiking trip in the White Mountains one recent summer, I decided to stop in the small town of Laconia, New Hampshire, where two murals, companion pieces, one painted by my mother, the other by my father, still hang. Commissioned by the Section of Fine Arts for the U.S. Forestry building in Laconia, they were completed in 1941, two years before I was born, at their studio in Woodstock (see plates 16, 17).

I have never seen the paintings before. After a long, hot drive from New York, and some difficulty finding the municipal building, Tom— my second husband—and I enter a small office with a Smokey the Bear poster and stacks of brochures on the White Mountain National Forest. Can the murals be in this drab place? "Is anyone here?" Tom calls. A uniformed ranger appears behind the counter. He brightens immediately when I mention the paintings. Oh, yes, he says, he knows the murals.

His smile fades. "They're in this big room downstairs, you know. That's where our offices were up until just last week. Social Security is moving in there now."

The wooden floor of the empty room downstairs shines in the late afternoon sunlight. As it happens, it has just been varnished the night before, the ranger explains. We'll have to take our shoes off. Tiptoeing across the slightly tacky floor, we turn around and there they are.

The yellowing black-and-white photographs in the file in Woodstock have not prepared me for this. The paintings are larger than I imagined. Each six by fifteen feet, flanking the doorway by which we just entered, the two murals cover an entire wall of the room.

The flora and fauna of the White Mountains are the subject of my mother's mural, on the right. A family of deer approach a stream to drink, the buck lifting his head, as if startled by a sudden movement. A snowy egret flaps gracefully to land beside a Muscovy duck, while in the background a beaver gnaws at the trunk of a tree. In the foreground, a mother bear sniffs at her cubs hiding in an old dead stump.

The lush gathering of wildlife is naturalistically rendered, but the plants and animals have been so profusely collected in one frame that the painting reminds me—in concept, not in execution—of the nature dioramas I saw as a child in the American Museum of Natural History in New York. Despite this staginess, the carefully observed and tenderly painted details are filled with a delight and reverence for the natural world that I instantly recognize as hers.

I am surprised at how good my mother's painting is, and then a bit ashamed by my surprise. Those self-deprecating remarks of hers about the smallness of her talent—which have so easily and imperceptibly been absorbed by me as gospel—have to be examined again, it seems.

I find myself remembering a time, two years before this, when she and I, in a fit of nostalgia, were up in the attic one day, sorting through old treasures. Under the dusty window, I lifted a sheet to uncover some small paintings of children and birds she had done when I was a baby. "Are these yours?" I asked.

"Oh, those old things," she exclaimed. "I'll have to get rid of them."

"Don't you dare," I said. "I want them, even if you don't."

But I forgot the paintings; they are still up there in the attic. At least I hope they are. Now, I remember, too, the wonderful cast bronze bell— modeled first in clay over a wineglass—of a full-skirted lady holding a shell to one ear, listening to the sea, just as I used to listen to a conch shell my mother had brought from Panama. The bell sits on my mantel now, but I barely managed to rescue it from a box of clothes and books she was giving away to the Library Fair, an annual Woodstock rummage sale.

That day she actually tried to take the bell away from me when I picked it out of the box. "Come on, Ingie," she said. "You don't really want that silly thing, do you? It makes an awful noise."

"But I like it," I said.

My mother made a dismissive, impatient gesture with her hand. "I don't see why."

"Is there something wrong with that?" I persisted. "Can't I like it?"

"I suppose so," she said.

She turned, then, and walked from the room, seeming almost angry at me, as if I'd displayed some lapse of taste in admiring her handiwork. As if I were obliged to devalue her, just as I was obliged to admire my father.

Tearing my eyes away from the pastoral mountain scene, I walk over to the other side of the large room. My father's painting, to the left of the door, could not be more different, and yet the two murals obviously belong to one another. A logging crew is at work with crosscut saws and awls. Stacks of sawn-off logs fill the foreground of the snowy landscape.

The pine woods in the background, the white birches, even the horse in harness, are bold and stylized rather than entirely naturalistic, with all the attention of the painting on the labor of the men. It is a powerful and dynamic composition, the work of an accomplished muralist.

There they are, side by side. Inviting comparison. How difficult that must have been, especially for my mother, working together in the same studio. And I have to admit it: I think his painting is better than hers. I have to—yes, but at the very moment of judging, I am disgusted by having done so. Why indulge this destructive habit of measuring? The problem is, I can't seem to help it. I see what I see.

I try to focus on the contrast between the two murals. Of course, their themes are opposite, reflecting the two aspects of forestry, wilderness and industry. In his, nature is to be tamed, made use of; in hers, it is to be preserved and enjoyed. Perhaps these themes were assigned, and yet they also clearly reflect complementary differences in personality. My father's mural, intensely dramatic in its dominance, seems so male. And my mother's, lyrical and diffuse, is so thoroughly female.

"I'm going to miss seeing them every day," the ranger says wistfully as we leave.

My mother and father collaborated again a few times. Years later, there was a children's book—still unpublished—entitled "Look At Me!" in which a poem of my mother's is illustrated by my father. Several of the inventive drawings he made of her poems hang in my mother's house. Two seashells, a nest, a book, a hand writing and a huge pencil all bask under the benevolent light of the familiar hanging lamp in his illustration (see plate 62) for the following short poem:

> I thought I could never
> write anything down again.
>
> Then I put on my cold wristwatch.

When I think of my parents in the early years of their marriage, before I was born, a certain photograph always comes to mind (see plate 12). Taken by my grandfather, Frederick McKim, in the late thirties, it shows Musa and Philip strolling in the autumn woods, smiling into the camera. My father looks rakish and handsome, sporting a mustache and a fedora, with an autumn leaf—placed there, no doubt, by my mother—in the buttonhole of his double-breasted suit. His arm protectively encircles my mother, who looks happy nestled against him. She is wearing a plaid wool coat and sensible walking shoes, but her beret is perched at a jaunty angle and her smile betrays a touch of coyness.

"Your mother is so sweet," people often said after spending an evening with my parents for the first time. "Is she always this quiet?" they'd ask.

Though it mystified me, my mother seemed quite content taking a back seat to my father. When people were gathered at our house, she usually busied herself with emptying ashtrays, refilling drinks, setting and clearing the table. "Why don't you sit down with us, Musa," my father would finally have to say.

"But, Philip—" She would pause, look longingly at the kitchen, then back at him.

"Come. Sit here." He'd pat the couch beside him. "You can do all that stuff later."

My mother would perch on the very edge of the sofa, as if ready to take flight. She hated to be put on the spot.

My father would put his arm around her and smile fondly at her. "Musa has a wonderful eye. She always knows when I'm kidding myself. Even before I do."

She would redden. "Oh, Philip."

"But you do, you know. I'd be sunk without you." Flushed with drink and sentiment, he'd reach over to kiss her.

"Philip!" My mother would push him away and struggle to stand up. "I can hear everything," she'd reiterate firmly, already retreating to the kitchen with the ashtray containing the latest stubbed-out Camel. "I'm happy just listening. Really I am."

My father liked to be the center of attention, laughing, talking, telling stories and drinking until all hours, long after everyone else was tired. My mother would sit quietly at his side, listening intently, but almost never speaking.

To students and acquaintances who didn't know him very well—and even to so ungenerous a critic as Clement Greenberg—my father seemed to embody the romantic image of an artist. Once at Princeton, after listing the ten best painters of the twentieth century, Greenberg was asked why Philip Guston wasn't on his hit parade, as were Matisse and

Picasso, of course, and seven contemporary Americans. "Well, my feeling about Guston is that out of all these painters," the critic replied, "he is *the* personality, the painter more than anybody else."

If my father was the romantic artist figure, then certainly my mother seemed like the consummate artist's wife—gracious and uncomplaining, amazingly tolerant of her husband's unpredictable working habits, his neglect, his black moods, but at the same time an aesthetic companion who understood in the most intimate way what he was striving for.

Close friends saw this. They speak to me of her pride and dignity and delight in his work. How indispensable she was to him. They say things like, "He couldn't make a move without her," and, "Musa was his conscience and his muse—he always said so."

"Without Musa, Philip wouldn't have gone so high, and he might have been far more self-destructive," Mercedes Matter tells me. "Philip had to be his best self with her. He was a very restless person, you know, who always devoured everything in every direction. He strayed a number of times, but he always went back to Musa in a real way, a total way. He always had to have things alive." She pauses, her voice softening. "Musa made it possible for Philip to realize the most of himself. And however difficult her life with him may have been, she knew that she was his primary audience, that she could share in what mattered most to him. She was like a flower turned toward the sun."

"I don't think there would have been the same life in art for Philip without Musa," my father's longtime friend Morty Feldman said. "Musa was a support system the likes of which most people never have."

But this devotion had its costs, of course—for her, for him, and for me. My mother was hardly unaware of the toll my father's self-absorption took. Though she handled herself with grace and a wry, saving humor, at times she must have felt crowded and overwhelmed by his presence. This short play was written while she was studying poetry at the New School during the late fifties:

THE PLUMBING

Persons
Husband   Child
Wife   Cat
The Plumbing

HUSBAND: You are my wife, aren't you?

WIFE: Why do you ask that? You know I am. Devoted. All these long years.

HUSBAND: So they seem long to you, do they?

THE PLUMBING: Hello?

HUSBAND: What's that?

WIFE: The plumbing.

HUSBAND: About that school. Since you've been going there: look at everything!

THE PLUMBING: Hello?

HUSBAND: I'd like to get my hands on the fellow who puts these things into the heads of you women. No time like the present to teach him a thing or two.

WIFE: You'll not find him today. Today he's a bird.

HUSBAND: What kind? Just tell me what kind!

WIFE: A sea gull. He'll be flying over water. You'll never be able to get near him.

HUSBAND: Are you taking his side now?

WIFE: Not at all. I'm trying to help you. Let's see . . . tomorrow's Friday. I think he said Friday he would be either a window, or the Commissioner of Parks.

HUSBAND: Never mind. I'll wait until Wednesday, when he's back to normal. Then you'll see some fireworks. What is it you look for, Wife? Haven't I given you a child, the child a cat—I suppose you want me to give the cat a mouse!

WIFE: Certainly not. We're quite all right as we are.

CAT: Are we, now?

HUSBAND: Who taught that cat to speak? The best thing about that cat was that it couldn't talk!

WIFE: You're beside yourself, Husband. Please calm down. The cat didn't speak: you imagined it.

CHILD: Mother, where is the crust you baked yesterday?

HUSBAND: Under the bed, keeping the dust company.

During the winter of 1964, when my first son, David, was three months old, and I had just turned twenty-one, I visited my father in Woodstock while my mother was away on a trip. That fall and winter I had felt slighted, knowing my father had been in the city several times and hadn't come to see us, as my mother had, during what had proved to be a particularly difficult time for me. So I invited myself up to Woodstock, determined to introduce my father to his grandson.

David slept all the way up on the bus. It was one of those brilliant winter days, the snow-blanketed sleeping figures of the Catskill Mountains sharp against a sky of palest blue. It felt good to escape from the griminess of our two-room tenement on the Lower East Side, where snow was certainly no blessing, to the beauty of this landscape. I'd begun to see life in the city through newborn and vulnerable eyes.

David had been very weak and ill his first two months, spending much of his time in a ward at Mount Sinai Hospital. Strangely, I had not felt I could ask for my parents' help. It seems terribly wrong to me now, that they didn't offer, that I didn't ask. I had no one else, really. Danny had become painfully remote, leaving me feeling frightened and alone with a sick baby. Outwardly controlled, I felt completely lost, and unaccountably guilty. Why was this happening? What was I doing wrong? I concealed the severity of David's illness from Musa and Philip—and from myself, too, I suspect—just as my parents, later, would conceal their own illnesses from me.

My father was waiting for me at the bus station in Woodstock. I could see him sitting there, his cap pulled down around his ears, smoking, lost in thought. His face brightened when he saw me, and he enveloped both of us in a big hug. David woke up and started to cry.

"Is he always like this?" my father asked, after I had finally gotten the baby fed, diapered, and back to sleep in a hastily emptied dresser drawer in my old bedroom.

That night, my father cooked us a wonderful dinner and we sat up late talking in front of the fire, as we always had, about art and philosophy and ideas. What was I reading these days? he wanted to know. I evaded that question. Those last few months, I'd read and reread *Baby and Child Care* at least half a dozen times, but not much else. I hadn't been able to think of anything beyond fevers and diaper rashes. Instead, I told him about the graduate course in Renaissance architecture I was planning to take at NYU in the spring, and we talked about Alberti and Brunelleschi. Hungry for such talk, for the larger world outside, I almost didn't mind that he never asked me about the baby, or how I was feeling. When David awoke in the night, I was at his side instantly, anxious that he not disturb my father.

"How long were you planning on staying?" Philip asked gruffly the next evening. He was facing away from me, chopping vegetables to make a Chinese dinner for us. Suddenly struggling with tears, I couldn't answer his question. Was he really asking me to leave, so soon? I held the baby in my arms more tightly, for comfort.

My father turned and looked at me, with that anguished, hooded look of his I dreaded. "Oh, God," he said. "I thought you understood by now how I feel about my work." He strode out of the kitchen, onto the back porch, and across to his studio.

When David was asleep again, I slipped out the back door. It was a New England picture postcard of an evening, with the snow weighing down the branches of the hemlocks in the backyard to graze an unbroken, sparkling crust of white that covered the still and peaceful scene. It was so cold my feet squeaked as I walked and my breath formed little clouds. I knocked on the studio door and went in.

He was sitting in his chair, staring at his last painting, a cigarette drooping from his mouth. We argued. I wept. More open about my feelings than I had ever been, I told my father why I'd come, what I wanted from him. All the time I was talking, a part of me hovered nearby, listening, somewhat aghast at the words that were coming out of my mouth. The rawness and immediacy of my own child's needs, the urgency of his cries to be fed and held, the hospital vigils—all those frantic hours of worry had altered my perspective somehow, made me brave where I hadn't been before. I knew what was important now, and it wasn't Art.

But it didn't matter, really. I could see Philip felt terribly guilty, but that didn't change anything. "I was working when you came, for the first time in weeks," he said. "It's been so hard for me, recently, to do anything, to feel that I—" He stopped and looked at me. He rubbed his lip with his thumb.

I stared back at him. Ordinarily, I'd have been solicitous, eager to hear his troubles.

He sighed. "Look, Ingie. I'm sorry. Really, I am. You don't seem to realize what an interruption this visit is." Then, after a pause, relenting. "But I did enjoy last night."

"So did I," I said.

"Yes. Well. Maybe we should go back and finish dinner."

I left the next morning. As the bus pulled away, I felt an enormous sense of relief. And then loss—the terrible loss that accompanies saying at last what you have to say, and not having it matter.

During those difficult years of the 1960s, I felt as if I was always missing things. While I was busy having babies and just barely managing to get by, first in a New York slum, later in married-student housing up in New Haven—where Danny was getting his MFA in painting at Yale's School of Art and Architecture—the world around me had been changing. The spirit of Woodstock—the rock festival, not the town—had crested and passed me by, though the festival had taken place not twenty miles from where we were living that summer of 1969, at the Kadish farm near Vernon, New Jersey. We had talked of going, but the local radio reports made Danny decide against it—too difficult, with two young children, he said. He was right, of course, it would have been hard. But still, I felt deprived, those early years, deprived of the music, the experimenting with sex, the drugs and mysticism, missing my chance— my only chance!—at being young and free and wild.

So I was primed for it, I suppose. The feminism of the late-sixties and early seventies, when it finally did reach Ohio, hit me full force. We were living by then near Dayton, in the town of Yellow Springs, close to the Antioch College campus. A town of five thousand, Yellow Springs was—and still is—an anomaly, a town with a tradition of political activism and educational experiment, a tiny hothouse of late-sixties unrest and Esalen-style therapies, set smack in the middle of a flat, bland Ohio landscape of corn and soybean fields. In 1969, Danny had gotten a teaching job at nearby Wright State University in Fairborn, a modern, midwestern campus known affectionately in the town where we lived as "white, straight."

Almost by osmosis, through the Antioch College Counseling Service, where I worked as a secretary, I began to absorb new ideas. The director, Phil McQueen, was a big, gentle Mormon from Utah, but behind his farm-boy looks lay an astute therapist who served *in loco parentis* for large numbers of students. One day, Phil mentioned that he thought I was underemployed. I thought it was a strange thing for a boss to say. But the word kept bouncing around in my head. Underemployed. Though I had finished college, I'd gone to work after my second son was born in a job that didn't require a degree. It was all I could do, I thought. All I was qualified for. And I was a good secretary, efficient, eager to please. But it was the kind of work, as I began to realize, whose essence lay in the satisfaction of helping others—usually male—get *their* work done. So *that* was why I'd been feeling so frustrated. I thought of my parents, of course; how could I not? It all sounded so depressingly familiar.

Despite an upbringing I had always considered unconventional, I discovered in myself an ordinary child of the fifties. I was a little shocked to realize that my parents had played those archetypal male-female roles to the hilt. And that I'd followed suit, without even thinking. Like many another young woman who came of age then, I'd married early and had children right away. By 1970, almost eight years into my marriage, I found myself bitter about a lot of things. I was walking around angry all the time, looking for someone to blame.

One of my minor complaints—or perhaps it wasn't so minor, since it was central to the larger malaise that infected our marriage—had always been that Danny helped so little with cooking and housework. We operated on an economy of scarcity: both of us so starved we gave to one another only grudgingly. Especially Danny, I thought at the time, bent on seeing myself as blameless. It wasn't even an equitable division of labor—male the provider, female the homemaker—anymore, because I, too, was working full time. "But that's your choice," Danny would say when I confronted him.

"Choice," I'd mutter. "Like hell it is. How could we possibly live on what you make?"

"We'd manage."

"Right. Like we did in New York."

The first four years of our marriage we had lived in a tenement walk-up on the Lower East Side, barely subsisting on the small salary he made teaching shop at a private school on Long Island, and occasional handouts from his parents. When we'd moved to married-student housing in New Haven, David was almost three and Jonathan was only six months old. After years without a job, I'd been happy to go back to work as a secretary at Yale, eager to escape the confinement of home and babies into the larger world outside. Now that Danny had gotten his degree and was teaching, I wasn't about to give up working.

I decided to try a different approach. "For God's sake," I said, "look at your father. He's always doing stuff around the house. Cooking. Dishes." It was true. Before we moved, we had always spent weekends and summers at the Kadish farm in New Jersey. Reuben and Barbara shared the chores. Everyone pitched in. I had never heard an angry word between them—about that at least.

I could see Danny's face darken. Being compared with his father always infuriated him. "Well, I'm not my dad," he growled. "And you are not my mother. You have it easy. You don't know the first thing about what it's like, running a farm. They both worked like dogs."

So had he, I knew. This man who appeared to be the son of an artist had really grown up the son of a dairy farmer. Those fifteen years that Reuben had dropped out of the art world had coincided exactly with Danny's childhood and adolescence. Danny was right—I didn't know what it was like. I couldn't imagine being obliged to work five or six hours every day, 365 days a year, for one's father. Danny had told me stories of having to get up every morning at four o'clock to help with the milking, of working after school until it got dark, of being too tired and sleepy for homework, of failing at Rutgers his first year there because of his inadequate rural education.

"You'd never see Barb complaining," he said about his mother. "She'd never bitch all the time the way you do!"

"That's because she has no reason to," I shot back.

Actually his parents did argue over who did the dishes, I was thinking. They'd have these mock disagreements, tinged ever so slightly with martyrdom, where each of them seemed eager to spare the other the chore. "I'll do the dishes," Barbara would say, grabbing a dirty pot from

Rube's hand. "No, you sit down. *I'll* do them," he'd respond, taking the pan back. The opposite of us. Still, despite her assertiveness in some things—her choice to seek a college degree in archaeology and a profession late in life—I could see that Barbara Kadish was in many ways like my mother. Submissive. Devoted to helping her husband do what he wanted to do. The way I had thought I should be, too.

"Well, what about Philip, then?" I asked, knowing how much Danny, a struggling painter himself, admired my father.

"What about him?"

"My father cooks almost every day!"

Danny wasn't enough like my father. That was the real problem, though I wouldn't have admitted it to him, or to myself. Danny wasn't solicitous, nor was he affectionate. And I felt starved for affection, for the kind of sweet compliments and romantic gestures that seemed to more than make up for my parents' conflicts. Instead, we were always bickering. Danny seemed too busy fighting his own battles to have much energy left for me. Uncertain of who I was or what I wanted to do with my life beyond being an artist's wife and mother to his children, I longed for a marriage like the one my parents had, for the sort of paternalistic, protective love my father showed my mother. And in return, I assumed I'd be able to muster my own brand of slavish devotion.

None of it worked for me.

It was during a trip to Woodstock in 1970, with Danny and our two young sons, that I gained a further insight into my parents' marriage, another piece to that puzzle. Jonathan and David were four and six years old by then. Our marriage was on rocky ground, with divorce only two years away. The women's movement had hit me hard that year; I wasn't an easy person to live with.

One night during that visit, I was standing in the kitchen watching my parents prepare a meal, as I had done before, dozens of times. But this time—who knows why—I found myself actually understanding what it was that I'd seen so often before.

Philip *was* a wonderful cook, and they *did* work well together in the kitchen. It was like watching a dance. He led. She followed. My father assembled the ingredients, cooked and served the meal, and graciously accepted all the compliments. My mother did the KP, the dirty work. It was she who peeled and washed and chopped the vegetables, she who set

out everything he needed neatly on the countertop and put it away when
he was done, she who arranged the plates and utensils. And it was she
who stayed in the kitchen cleaning up, long after my father and Danny
and I were sitting, talking, out in the living room in comfortable leather
chairs, enjoying our coffee and cigarettes.

It would be dishonest to say that I had never noticed this before. I had.
My mother cleaned up after me, too—just as I did after my husband and
sons, but with better grace and less grumbling. But that night, for the first
time, what she was doing began to bother me.

I walked back into the kitchen. "Why don't you come out and be with
us?"

"I will. As soon as I finish these." She was wearing yellow Playtex
gloves and was up to her elbows in soapsuds.

"Let me do the dishes later."

She shook her head. "That's all right, Ingie."

"I'll do them now, then." I tried to elbow my way to the sink, but she
stood her ground and nudged me firmly aside.

"Don't be silly! You didn't come here to do dishes. I like doing this.
Go sit down and have your coffee."

"But what about you? Why should you always be the one to clean up?
Doesn't Philip ever help you?"

"No, and I wouldn't dream of letting him, either."

"But why? That's so unfair."

She paused, a plate in one hand. I could see she was genuinely puzzled.
"Truly, I don't mind, Ingie. It's what I do."

Later that same weekend, I saw my mother duck her head and bite her
lip, hurt when my father barged in on what she was saying, not even
noticing he was interrupting the story Musa was trying to tell us. No
wonder she rarely spoke up, I thought to myself. I sat on her bed that
night, watching her undress. "Why do you let him get away with that?"

"Get away with what?"

"Interrupting you. Why don't you ever stand up to Philip? Tell him
you're angry?"

She smiled. "Oh, he knows when I'm mad at him."

He did indeed. When my mother was angry, she refused to speak. It
was very effective. Nothing could have been more punishing for him
than her silent treatment. He couldn't stand it. From somewhere in

childhood comes a memory of her standing at the ironing board, pressing one of his shirts with grim determination, eyes averted, mouth set in a tight little line, while he circled her, ranting, cajoling, pleading with her to tell him what was wrong. My father was transparent. I always could tell when he was disturbed about something. He acted as if he'd explode if he couldn't say what was on his mind. My mother, on the other hand, was mysterious, elusive. When she retreated within herself for protection, it both fascinated him and drove him nuts.

Sometimes, when things got too hard for her at home—as they periodically did, living with such an intensely self-absorbed person—my mother would take off for a few days to be by herself. They would part amicably—my father knew perfectly well how difficult he was to live with. It was understood that she needed to get away from time to time.

I got my first period, at eleven, when my mother was away on one of her trips. I knew what was happening to me. My mother had managed a brief, blushing speech before fleeing from my room one night. It still makes me shudder with embarrassment, remembering that moment of finding the spot of blood on my panties and realizing I would have to tell my father. The mortification of having him look for the box of Kotex in my mother's drawer for me to use! And his delighted exclamations—"Imagine! My little girl, a woman!"

Other than that, I don't remember being apprehensive about her leaving. Withdrawn and moody when she left, she would invariably come back renewed, full of little stories, with new additions for her collections of shells and stones. But I was always a bit mystified by these disappearances, these little "vacations," as she called them. Now I understand, I think, how the solitude and simple daily choices of these trips must have nourished her, and restored her to herself. From time to time, I had longings of my own for such solitary adventures.

"Where did you go on those trips of yours?" I asked my mother recently.

"Oh . . . places," she said, an enigmatic smile on her lips. "South Carolina, an island off the coast of Georgia . . ."

And she handed me a packet of letters my father had sent her on one such trip, when she had gone to Ossabaw Island, off Savannah, in February of 1974.

"My dearest sweetheart," my father wrote in one of these letters. "It has just now begun snowing and a male cardinal is perched in the apple tree—our squirrel is trying desperately to get goodies out of that new-fangled feeder.... I did some shopping and am cozying in—in case snow continues—getting thicker now and steady. Every minute my thoughts are with you—seeing you picked up at the DeSoto Hotel—by whom? Going to the Island—how? How long was the boat trip? And what did you see when you got there? My mind is filled with questions—unfocused images of where you are—but your sweet face and being is always before my eyes and it is in new surroundings of which I have *no image*. If only I knew—had seen Ossabaw—I would feel a little better—but as it is, I feel so lost, so alone without you—BUT!!! I feel myself that it is *good*—good for you to have a little vacation and I shall be strong and not be so self-centered and let you just *be* a bit—with your own feelings and thoughts and experiences—without thinking of me all the time. YES! YES! You must also be at peace for a while—so I have nothing to write about, you see, except to tell you how much I love you for ever and ever. I hope it is warm—that the house and the surroundings please you, comfort you, and that you can feel things for yourself and love me too. I am fine—OK. Please don't think this is too schmaltzy—write me, if only a word. Your Philip."

Food served as a token of love in our household. The dinner table was the one place during the day when the three of us gathered together; it was there that most often I felt my father's affection for me. There was something very intimate, almost sexual, in the way he would take bites from my plate and give me bites from his. "Try this," he'd say, offering me the tenderest morsel. For years, whenever we had chicken, he ritually presented me with the heart—that is, until my mother, thinking I loved this delicacy, served me a whole dish of chicken hearts à la king one night when they were going out to a dinner party. I sat there looking at my plate. How could I explain to her that what I loved was not some gristly little bit of muscle, but the way my father fed it to me? Not surprisingly, it was my father who gave me my first drink and my first cigarette.

An early proponent of health food, my mother played the opposing role—the voice of moderation and control. I longed for white bread and refined sugar. At the dinner table, a small glass of warm greenish liquid would usually await me—the water in which the vegetable had been cooked. "But it has all the vitamins!" she'd say when I made a face. Sweets were hidden. I learned to cook, making cakes and cookies and candies, overwhelming my mother's objections with my creativity.

Both my father and I were scolded for our excesses. It was half game, half serious. She was always trying to modify his diet, especially in later years, when he'd begun putting on weight. A sensible woman, she'd stopped smoking years ago. His cigarette habit, the three packs of unfiltered Camels he smoked each day, she could do nothing about; he was completely unmovable where his smoking was concerned, so she stuck to his eating and drinking. He'd hang his head guiltily as she lectured him, with the half-pleased, half-guilty look of a naughty boy caught with his hand in the cookie jar. But then, suddenly, unexpectedly, she'd remind him once too often that this was his *fourth* whiskey, that it wasn't good for his ulcer, and he'd snarl, "Leave me alone! You're always after me!" The game would be over.

My mother was right. Eventually, it was his excesses that killed my father. He simply wore his body out with drinking and smoking and overeating. His death at sixty-six of a heart attack could probably have been delayed some years had he just been willing to indulge more moderately. He was not unaware of this, of course. A 1970 painting that shows two "hoods" facing an enormous bottle of booze is actually entitled *Bad Habits* (see plate 60). One of the Klansmen raises a hand to whip himself as he stares obsessively at the bottle. Behind him, a clock face stands at eleven thirty.

One day very soon after he died, my mother went through the house, crying all the while, opening every drawer and cupboard, piling into a big box all the cartons and packs of cigarettes stashed everywhere, the bottles of booze, the vials of tranquilizers and sleeping pills. I watched her, knowing it hurt her terribly to touch anything of his, to move it from its accustomed place. Her hatred for the things that had killed him was stronger than her impulse to preserve everything as it had been when he was alive. Eventually, everything went, even the ashtrays. All she kept were my father's pipes and a lighter, and a few books of matches.

My father could be sentimental and affectionate, too. When he surfaced from days of working, or from one of his black depressions, he was capable of showing gratitude in the tenderest, most touching ways. Perhaps he did this only to assuage his guilt; perhaps he knew these tokens would be irresistible. I don't know. What I prefer to believe is that he felt a genuine remorse for the difficult times he put my mother through.

His work habits were erratic, consuming. No moderation there, either; no regular schedule for her (or me) to count on. Often she'd barely see him for days when he was working late at night. He would paint all night long, sleep in the daytime, and hardly see the two of us. Not wanting to disturb him, my mother would leave him things to eat—a favorite was egg-salad sandwiches on whole wheat, wrapped in wax paper and neatly tied with white string—outside his studio door, always accompanied by a thermos of hot, black coffee.

In the morning, she would awaken to find him sound asleep in the bed next to her. They slept in a king-size bed, which he had insisted on, and which she once wistfully told me wasn't the best thing for a marriage.

"Once, when Philip was showing us around the house," the writer Philip Roth remembers, "he said, 'The bed's so big I can't even find Musa in it.' And she said, in her very quiet way, 'Why don't you look?' "

On mornings after he'd been working all night and had fallen into bed exhausted at dawn, she would get up quietly, tiptoe from the bedroom, often to find love notes from him on the kitchen table, written in the fervor of the night before. Many had charming drawings, like little illuminated manuscripts. My mother has carefully preserved some of these notes in a folder. Here is one, in which each letter is composed of a different, whimsical figure (see plate 76):

> 3 A.M.
> Musa
> You are so
> Wonderful

Or this, on another night, written on several small sheets of a white pad, with a little caricature of him working and her sleeping:

> Sweetheart—
>
> Perhaps I am making love to you this way—by creation—It is so difficult for me to be in *this* world. I think that when you are making another world that is parallel to this one and reflects the strangeness

and mystery of one's life—I guess what happens is that you take from real life only what you need. What? What am I babbling about!!!

I love you—so much—

Your P.

In 1973, Philip used one of her notes to him in a painting. There is the familiar naked light bulb of his late-night painting habits, his arm in a painting shirt frayed at the elbow, her head with its two small frown lines above the eyes, sunk below the horizon. On the kitchen table lies her note about some leftovers, which he used for his title, *The Rest Is for You.*

A t its best, their marriage was filled with tenderness and respect. But at its worst, when they were in crisis, it often seemed to me that my father was unable to see past his own distress, that he showed little concern for my mother. I found this hard to forgive. I wanted him perfect. I wanted him strong. Each time my mother was very ill—first, with spinal meningitis in 1971, and then, in 1977, when she had a serious stroke that damaged her memory and left her with difficulty finding the words to express her thoughts—my father was beside himself. He tried to be compassionate. I'm sure he tried. But his own feelings seemed to overwhelm him. "I couldn't call anyone for fear that I would burst into tears," he wrote to a friend in 1971. "I guess I am not as strong as I thought I was."

I remember sitting with him in a Hungarian restaurant on the East Side eating wiener schnitzel (like my father, I possess a highly developed memory for food), when my mother was in New York Hospital, listening to his fears about what the stroke had done. "She's not the same person, Ingie," he grieved. "I've lost her."

"You haven't lost her, Philip. She has difficulty speaking and remembering. Inside, she's the same." But I, too, was scared about what had happened to my mother, the strange, garbled non sequiturs that emerged from her mouth, the foolish, inappropriate smile she wore sometimes. He was right; she didn't seem herself—but I didn't want him to say that. It made it all the more real.

His face was contorted, his eyes filled with tears. "No, you don't understand. I've lost my sweet Musa. And I don't think I could live without her. I couldn't!" There was an edge of hysteria in his voice.

"Philip, please don't," I said. "It's only been a few days. Let's just wait and see what the doctors say."

The waitress set our plates on the table and we began to eat in silence.

Halfway through his meal, my father began talking—ranting really, for his speech had a pressured, urgent quality—about his plans to leave the McKee Gallery, his mistrust and despair about the art world in general. None of the late work had sold, he told me; it was still being reviled and misunderstood by the critics. Have patience, David McKee kept telling him, the work was difficult, but they would come around. But how long would that take? What was the use of going on showing in New York, subjecting himself year after year to that insanity? It was hopeless. Hearing him go on about this made me angry. All I could think about was my mother and what the stroke had done to her. Why did he have to keep drawing attention to himself? I kept my eyes on my plate and listened.

"What else can I do?" he said. "I've really tried this time. David's not like the other dealers. He really has an eye. He cares. But it doesn't matter. Each time you hope things will be different, but they never are. It's really intolerable, all of it. You don't know. You have no idea how it is. I can't sleep. I can't work." He shook his head, sighed, lit a cigarette, then picked a shred of tobacco from his tongue. "But what should I tell David? God, I don't want a fight with him. That's the last thing I need now. I just want to be free of the whole thing. What should I do, Ingie?"

I looked at him. His eyes were shrouded, deep pockets of pain. It was like falling into a bottomless hole. "You really want to know what I think?" I asked.

"Of course I do," he said.

I took a deep breath. "I think you should wait until Musa is out of the hospital and back in Woodstock before you decide about leaving the gallery. Wait until things calm down. You're too distraught right now."

"But that's *why*, I'm telling you. If I could just get *that* settled—"

"But isn't it Musa who's important now?"

"Of course! Don't you think I know that? What kind of an ogre do you take me for?"

Oh, God, now I've done it, I thought. I should've kept my mouth shut. Now he was angry at me, on top of everything else.

"I'm sorry," I said.

"Don't you see?" he continued, ignoring my apology. "That's why I want to get this whole mess with the gallery straightened out," he said. "It's for her. So I don't have to think about that any more."

"Aren't you going to finish your schnitzel?" I said, pointing at his plate. "It's getting cold."

The next day, we sat in the neurologist's office. Dr. Schaefer, the results of my mother's CAT scan in his hand, had been talking about speech and memory. "But what about her—her spirit?" my father interrupted. "What about her poetry? Will she ever be able to write poetry again?"

"Ah, now that is quite a different story, I'm afraid." An Australian with smiling blue eyes, John Schaefer spoke with a broad accent. "Mr. Guston," he said, standing and putting a steadying hand on my father's arm. "Let's just take one thing at a time, shall we?"

My father had been right to be concerned. New poems, as it turned out, were impossible for my mother after that, but her capacity to revise and edit previous work, something she'd always done with great care, was unimpaired. It had something to do with the way in which words were recognized and retrieved.

It was very hard for Philip to accept what had happened to my mother. He was often impatient with her, finishing her sentences, supplying names she had forgotten, interrupting her laborious attempts to complete a thought. Sometimes—and this made me furious—he seemed to be treating her like a nonentity, ignoring her as if she weren't even there. She was having a hard enough time, I thought. Finding herself stuck after a sentence or two of an anecdote, unable to remember what she wanted to say, or the name of that crucial person or place, she became even more reluctant to talk when others were present.

He may have brushed her aside then, and been impatient with her, but my mother was always present in his mind and spirit. She appears often as a subject in his paintings, particularly during the last five years of his life. In 1975, her name appears on a scroll, beside the brushes and tubes of paint in *The Palette*, as if she is actually a part of his materials.

In the emblematic *Source*, done in 1976 (see plate 72), her head, haloed like a saint's, eyes looking up at heaven, rises—or is she setting?—like an inspiration, a muse, a sun over a bright blue, slightly tilted sea. At Whitechapel Galleries in London, where a major exhibition of my father's late work was mounted in 1982, a large, removable slit in the floor is used to move oversized paintings from the first to the second floor. Wandering upstairs as they were hanging the show, I stopped in my tracks, transfixed by the sight of those two incredible eyes looking up at me from the floor below.

During those last years, my father seemed capable of revealing—and redeeming—himself with unrelenting, unflattering honesty. His drinking, his smoking, his bloodshot eyes, his anxiety, his narcissism—it's all there in those paintings. The mask is off. And the sadness is leavened with comedy—a wild sort of vegetable humor animates some of these late self-portraits. How can one not laugh at the kidney bean profiles, the Mr. Potato Heads with their cauliflower ears?

But it's harder to know what to make of his images of Musa, at least for me. I know what I would like to believe, some version no doubt of every child's ambivalent wish to see her parents' love quite simply and romantically. Fascinated and repelled, I stand outside the locked bedroom door. But the truth, of course, is more complicated and more impenetrable.

The Musa in my father's mind and heart—"his muse, his conscience," as their friends said—was in some way, I suspect, as iconic as her image in his painting. She was, for him, an object of contemplation. There were the small details he loved in her, the corkscrew tendril of wispy hair at one temple, the two tiny vertical frown lines that appeared between her brows. He never seemed to exhaust the mystery of her sweetness, her silence. She was his lovely source. But whether this icon was meant to live and struggle with her own life, as an independent person, is much less clear.

"A very queer, composite being thus emerges," writes Virginia Woolf about the portrayal of women in fiction by male writers. "Imaginatively, she is of the highest importance; practically she is completely insignificant. She pervades poetry from cover to cover; she is all but absent from history."

Recently, we have acquired a portrait of my mother from the early forties, a picture my father had lost track of years and years ago. A dealer contacts me about it—am I interested? Interested! I'm thrilled by the idea of owning this painting.

The portrait, when we go to pick it up, is unframed, covered loosely in plastic bubble wrap. The dealer handles it too carelessly, it seems to me. Outside on the street, the wind buffets the canvas; rain threatens. We are absurdly careful of the painting in the taxicab. It is probably quite sturdy, but the canvas looks so old and delicate. The portrait is as small and light, I realize, as deceptively strong, as my mother herself has become in her old age.

Arriving home, we hang the painting in the living room. My husband and I are standing there admiring it, when Tom asks, "How old was your mother when this was painted?"

I calculate the numbers in my head. "Thirty-four," I answer. "Why?"

"She looks so young."

And it's true. But for an ineffable sadness and distance, the face could be that of a very young girl. The composition is simple; it is a half-length portrait, no more. But the ethereal quality is pronounced, that grave stillness and sense of remove my father so loved in Piero della Francesca and Corot is very clear. Is this really how he saw her? Was she actually like this, then—so remote and childlike, and in essence so mysterious?

When I show it to my mother, who hasn't seen the painting in forty-five years, she smiles and says, "He really caught me, didn't he?" She means the seashells strewn on her lap in the painting. "He knew all about my bad habits, even then."

Instantly, I conjure a memory of my parents on a beach in Florida. I can see them both, so clearly. My father sitting on a bleached wood bench, smoking, staring off at the water and waiting for his wife none too patiently. His posture suggests that martyred, long-suffering state of being that men seem to affect when their wives are doing something that bores them, like trying on clothes or gathering flowers by the roadside. He is humoring her, taking the daily constitutional she insists is good for them. My mother is far down the beach, somewhere in the middle distance, bent over, beachcombing, picking up a shell, rinsing it, then tossing it away, or perhaps, more rarely, slipping it into her pocket. Her slight form is like a sandpiper's at the water's edge.

My mother is still looking at her portrait. It is the details that capture her attention. She is trying to remember precisely where it was that she lost the Mexican silver bracelet she'd been wearing in the painting, the one that he gave her before they were married. "That was a pajama top," she says, pointing out the blue striped shirt she wears in the painting.

Glad as I am to have the painting, I can see that it's far less complex and interesting an image than the portraits he made of her during the last five years of his life. By 1977, after her stroke, my father was picturing Musa both more tenderly and more savagely. No longer a singular emblematic image of inspiration or beauty, my mother becomes, in these painful, deeply felt last works, a real person at last. In *Tears* her two huge eyes—like a close-up of those same upturned eyes of *Source*—are brimming with sadness. In *Head*, a rectangular incision has been made into the back of a featureless head, bald as if shaved for surgery, exposing a robotic tangle of wires. In *Red Blanket*—companion piece to his own *Sleeping*—she is in bed, the cover pulled up to her eyelashes (see plate 74).

Often the two of them appear together, caught in a spider's web or swimming in a black or red tide that threatens to drown them, her head half sunk below the sea horizon, his with its single staring eye morosely contemplating the deluge. *Couple in Bed* shows them huddled together under the covers, his hand clutching his paintbrushes (see plate 53). In *Melancholy Studio* the head of Musa—ghostly and faceless, invoked here as a gentle but persistent voice of conscience—takes its place between Philip and his drink.

Writing of the "spare but luminous" *Night*, 1977, in which my parents appear immersed in a black sea, Robert Storr comments, "One must look to Rembrandt to find a comparably moving or candid portrait of a marriage lived in the shadow of age and loss."

There had been an even darker time before this, a dozen years earlier, during the mid-sixties, a time of actual separation, when it had seemed to them both that their marriage was over. My father was in crisis with his painting, just as he had been in the late forties when he went to Italy. He had no gallery; the art world sickened him. His retrospective at the Guggenheim in 1962 had left him nowhere to go. His paintings, becoming darker and more dense during the early sixties, were by then heavy with black forms that seemed to be collapsing in on themselves with an implosive force that was, a few years later in 1968, to explode outward again in a cascade of images that the art world would find even more shocking and unacceptable. But he couldn't have known that, then, of course. By the end of 1965, he had stopped painting altogether.

Everything—his work, his marriage, his stature in the art world—seemed uncertain, in flux. For some years, acting out the familiar story of male mid-life crisis, my father had been restless, looking at other women, women who were younger, more outspoken, more certain of what they wanted, more—something—than my mother. There had been brief affairs, but never one that had really threatened their marriage.

I wasn't privy to any of this. It was not the kind of thing, after all, that parents usually confide to their children. Even now, I confess I'm not eager to know the specifics.

I was still living in New York then, struggling with a sick baby and my own faltering marriage. For once, I didn't care about my father's reasons, his needs. All I knew was that at fifty-three (old enough to know better, I thought), he had left my mother for some young photographer from the Museum of Modern Art barely older than I was. I couldn't forgive him that. Since my mother seemed so resigned to the whole thing, I'd be angry for her. The only good thing I could see to come out of it was that my mother was out on her own, living in the small apartment they'd taken the year before across from the firehouse where my father had his studio, and working at the Studio School—and spending more time with me than she had since I'd left home. That year, without my father's dominating presence, I felt as if I got to know my mother.

I was pregnant with Jonathan then; she would come over and baby-sit sometimes with David, who was two years old. He was a shy, fearful child, and often ill. By then he'd been hospitalized seven or eight times with asthma. My mother was good with David; her gentle ways, her own shyness, made him trust her.

There's a vivid memory I have of a blizzard that year, of walking by myself in the newly fallen snow all the way from the Lower East Side up to her Chelsea apartment. The walk became an adventure, I remember. The snow, glistening at twilight, reflected the dusky orange of the sky. The whole city felt snug and cozy, with its edges softened and its grime concealed.

I didn't see my father that year, or hear from him, except once, when he called to ask how Musa was. It was years before I found out anything more about his affair. Apparently the woman had come up to Woodstock to take pictures for an exhibition at the Jewish Museum, photographs that were never used. "I love your work and I want to photograph every single thing you've ever done," she told my father when they met, according to a friend. "She's a serious photographer," Philip said at the time. "She can set my house in order."

After my parents had separated, my father insisted that my mother come to the opening of the Jewish Museum show. She remembers that Robert Phelps took her to the opening, and that Dore Ashton pointed out my father's new friend to her, saying, "You haven't met her? There she is."

My father's drinking was out of control. Robert Phelps remembers visiting my father in the hospital during this time, where he was drying out. "They had the most hectic, frenetic relationship," he says of my father and the photographer. "He talked incessantly about her, how madly in love with her he was—but then half an hour later it all came out in the wash."

"I'll never forget when Philip left me," my mother told me many years later. "It was in the morning. He actually had me call his 'friend' to tell her that I approved. 'You have to speak to her,' he said. 'Tell her you're giving me up.' We said good-bye and he drove off to New York. I went back to the stone studio feeling stunned, but sort of normal. Then it hit me. I came back into the house and all day long sat on the sofa without daring to move, just rocking my head back and forth. I couldn't have gotten up—" She paused, her eyes filling. "Like an animal, like a tiger pacing back and forth in its cage. I couldn't stop. Finally I must have fallen asleep. The next day, I knew I wouldn't do anything to myself. I knew I would survive."

My mother told me this the summer after my father died. We were sitting together at the kitchen table making a card file of my father's paintings and drawings. We had a system going—I would letter a card, printing the title and date of each painting, its medium and measurements, then she would paste the photograph on it. I was trying hard not to be impatient with her slow, methodical way of doing things; she was trying to be tolerant of my slapdash methods. It was hot, I remember. The fan was blowing and the shades were drawn.

"But he was alive, then," my mother said, almost as an afterthought. "And that makes all the difference."

It was hard to listen to her story. Though I knew she needed to tell it, it hurt to hear it. Think of the good things, I wanted to say. The good times you had together. Why torture yourself—and me—with memories like that? But I'm glad now that I listened, that I didn't cut her off or change the subject.

I'd been so worried about her that summer, concerned that she'd dissolve in her grief, that I'd lose them both. Several times, she'd made references to the traditional Indian custom of suttee, where the wife lies down beside her husband on his funeral pyre. "I would like to have done that," she muttered.

But what she was saying now was different, very different. My mother had always seemed so delicate and tenderhearted; like everyone else, I often underestimated her strength and endurance. It took me a while to catch on.

This wasn't the first time. That was what she was telling me in her own way. Philip had left her once before. Somehow, she had managed to live with that. Perhaps she'd survive this time, too.

In the early part of the summer of 1966, before she left for the MacDowell Colony in Peterborough, New Hampshire, my mother wrote this poem and took it to read to her sister.

SOME MUSIC

Maybe this time you have gone so far,
been away so long, that you take lacunae
for the moccasins
of your new princess.
Or maybe, by now, the princess is real.
Maybe what is real
is that you have a new princess.

I have looked for you everywhere.
In watering places, in dry places.

Where were you during the sirocco?
Should I have looked for you in the speedboat?
Did the flags get my message twisted?
Were you there, but was I asleep
and therefore invisible in the crowd?

I look for you in Woodstock,
East Hampton, the Cape, and New York.
Should I have looked in Europe,
or the Orient?

I look for you in fancy restaurants.
And at Wah Kee's—even at Sing Wu's.
And in the old stamping grounds.
There, all is as quiet
as earth from the air.

I look for you in the air,
stopping and questioning every jet.
The air hostesses smile and say,
"Thanks for stopping PAN AM." Or Eastern,
or American.

I look for you in sky-writing
thinking, sooner or later,
you will send a message that way.

When last we met you said,
"Should I ever want to be looked for
by anyone, it would be by you."

Soon the birds will be perching on my eyes.
Although it is not only with my eyes
that I look.

The neighbors, one of whom is a sculptor,
have built a fence around me
they are so disgusted.

I ease the pain by trying to evolve
into something else.

What could that be, though,
since I am fitted only
for looking for you?

Why, instead of distress
signals, don't I broadcast
the news, the weather report,
some music?

In the winter of 1966, when all of my father's dark paintings had played themselves out, he gave up his affair with the photographer. There had been an abortive trip abroad, to visit her family. Apparently, she had delivered an ultimatum. No more having it both ways; he must end his marriage. And my father could not bring himself to do that.

Philip was in Florida, then, in the house he had built on Siesta Key, across from Conrad and Anita Marca-Relli. My mother says that he called her repeatedly, begging her to come and be with him. Finally, she agreed. "The moment he hung up, Philip confessed," she wrote later, "he regretted asking me to come down. As for myself, I wept, in my roomette on the Silver Meteor, off and on from New York to Washington."

The image she retains of that terrible time is of my father sitting there in front of the fan, in his shorts, for days, not talking, not moving, clearly in agony over the breakup with the photographer, yet not wanting my mother to leave. Time passed. My mother walked on the beach, wrote poems like this one, which he later illustrated.

UNHAPPY DRUGSTORE

The temperature is frigid. The counter
comes up to the middle of the waitress'
thigh. The seats are cruelly close together.
The man on my left has a small magazine
open to an article entitled
"Your Dentures." Two women speak of someone
they knew who dropped dead in a pew in church.

Very gradually and with great difficulty, they resumed their marriage. "And so it had gone," my mother wrote, "our attempts to get together again, Philip contending that so it was bound to be at first."

My father put the house in Florida up for sale. He began drawing again, those single lines and simple forms he later called the "pure drawings." They traveled to the Yucatán in Mexico, to see the Mayan ruins. They came home, to Woodstock.

And my mother disappeared from my life again. That was the way I knew my parents were back together.

SEVEN

Painter's Forms

Untitled, 1968.

No revolution, no heresy is comfortable and easy. Because it is a leap, it is a rupture of the smooth evolutionary curve, and a rupture is a wound, a pain. But it is a necessary wound.

—EVGENY ZAMYATIN

"There is something ridiculous and miserly in the myth we inherit from abstract art," my father had written as early as 1960. "That painting is autonomous, pure and for itself, and therefore we habitually defined its ingredients and define its limits. But painting is 'impure.' It is the adjustment of impurities which forces painting's continuity. We are image-makers and image-ridden."

By 1966, when my parents abandoned the New York studio and apartment for a permanent move to Woodstock, my father stopped painting altogether. He did scores of charcoal and brush drawings that difficult winter in Florida. Some of them were abstract and gestural; others were clearly figurative, but deceptively simple.

"I remember days of doing 'pure' drawings," he told Dore Ashton later, "immediately followed by days of doing the other—drawings of objects. It wasn't a transition in the way it was in 1948, when one feeling was fading away and a new one had not yet been born. *It was two equally powerful impulses at loggerheads.* I would one day tack up in the house a bunch of pure drawings, feel good about them, think that I could live with them. And that night go out to the studio to the drawings of objects—books, shoes, buildings, hands, feeling *relief* and a strong need to cope with tangible things. I would denounce the pure drawings as too thin and exposed, too much 'art,' not enough nourishment, and as an impossible direction with no future. The next day, or day after, back to doing the pure constructions and to attacking the other. And so it went, this tug-of-war, for about two years."

In the end, it was no contest—the objects won. In 1968, the forms which had been gathering, coming into focus, burst into being. And they were, at first, the simple things of daily life. Books, windows, cups, shoes. There was something inevitable about this. Obvious, even. It was as if the forms my father sought had been under his nose, at home, all the time (see plates 64 and 65).

"There are times in one's life," he wrote poet Bill Berkson, "when you begin all over again, from the beginning, a true turning over—a heave—in my case. As if I have metamorphosed again, perhaps from something in flight into some kind of grub . . . They are so simple, these drawings—I don't know truly if they are any good or not. A line or two, a vertical, an arc, a banal shape. Yet, to learn all over again is the only joy left to me."

As always, Woodstock provided the necessary solitude and quiet, as well as a fundamental vocabulary of images that began to appear in the paintings and drawings. My parents' house had always been filled with compelling objects. Furnished piecemeal, it was a dwelling of things, a gallery of *objets trouvés,* each stone and lamp and shell and nest evoking some point in time, some transition in their lives. Most of this was my mother's doing. Everywhere you looked there were odd talismans: surreal hairballs in a glass box (actually, a growth of some sort of seaweed, my mother tells me, from a beach in Tarquinia); a big weathered gray wooden key that had been a locksmith's sign; a cast-iron stag beetle—whose horns were made for pulling off one's boots; a carved wood owl with glass eyes and a hinged head, whose belly contained old keys.

Philip shared my mother's taste for the odd and interesting artifact, the object that would remain resonant, or evoke a particular memory. She would bring him pieces of driftwood, which he would carve or paint, or otherwise alter in some slight way to free the forms he saw there. A bit of driftwood with two painted eyes became a sphinx; a snail's shell in a knot of wood turned into the eye of a bird, the broken branch its beak. On their mantel sits a slim hand with tapered fingers that he carved, and a wax Toscanini-style mustache shaped from a block of paraffin.

For my mother, who'd grown up in the Canal Zone in Panama, the natural world was always fascinating. Her childhood seemed exotic and tropical to me. I always thought of her mother, who loved animals, as I had seen her in early photographs with lush palms in the background and an ocelot kitten or a puma cub draped across her shoulders like a fur wrap. Or I thought of the picture my grandfather had taken of my mother, at ten, posed like a snake charmer, wrapped in a sarong with her flat chest painted like a dancing girl's, a six-foot-long boa constrictor twined round her shoulders and arms (see plate 4).

My grandfather, Frederick McKim, was a gentle, soft-spoken man who wrote poetry and long, affectionate letters to his daughters. Some are still in a box in the bottom of my mother's file. Her father worked for the Property and Requisition Bureau in the Canal Zone and was an amateur anthropologist whenever he could get away. He became known as an expert on Indian affairs and was often consulted by the Panamanian Indians in their dealings with the authorities. When he died, my grandfather asked that his ashes be sent to the Cuna Indians of the Bayano River, to a remote area he had called the Forbidden Land in a monograph published posthumously in a Swedish journal of anthropology, *Etnologiska Studier*.

Once, when my mother came home from art school in Brooklyn, her father had taken her for two weeks to live among the Cuna Indians on the islands of the San Blas, atolls off the coast of Colón and down into Colombia. It was an experience that stayed with her all her life—and the photographs of this trip, the carved wood figurines, the sweet-smelling satiwawa wood, and all the other precious items of Cuna jewelry and clothing, folded and packed away carefully in tissue paper, made it real for me, too.

When I was little, I loved the Cuna beadwork. I would get all dressed up, dance around the room wearing a *mola* (a shirt with intricately sewn designs in reverse appliqué on the front and back), festooned with long necklaces of fish vertebrae and monkeys' teeth, latticework beaded bibs, from which a row of cowrie shells hung, and—I particularly loved this one—a clattering, wreathlike syrinx of animal-bone flutes, which I would tootle in accompaniment to my father's old seventy-eights of Fats Waller and Meade Lux Lewis.

Nothing of my grandmother is on display, beyond a photograph of her as a girl studying the violin in Dresden, which hangs above my mother's dresser. Though she lived until I was twelve, and for a number of years I played her violin, I barely knew her. Once, when I was ten or eleven, my

mother and I visited her in Oil City, Pennsylvania. I presented my
grandmother with a birthday cake I had baked and put on a puppet show
for her on another occasion when she visited Woodstock. Her gauntness
and her age frightened me a little, as I remember; she was not at all the
hefty, jolly-looking woman I knew from pictures.

My grandfather, who died when I was three, interested me far more.
Though my mother rarely mentioned him, I understood, without being
told, that father and daughter had been very close. And that it made her
sad to talk about him.

In addition to various *molas* and carved figurines, my mother kept a
box of photographs of Panama. I looked through them periodically, as I
did through the boxes of shells and buttons, and the scrapbooks my
mother made of photographs from *Life*. More taken, it seems to me now,
with the exotic locales, I felt little sense of my own connection with what
I saw. The Cuna Indian women with their beads and nose rings were far
more intriguing to me than the pictures of my grandparents.

But one photograph in particular both terrified and fascinated me. In
it, a white man and a group of natives from the island of Taboga, off the
Panamanian coast, are holding up a man's severed foot they have cut from
the belly of the huge dead shark at their feet. The photograph must have
been given to my grandfather, who in turn gave it to my mother. But in
my early memories of this photo, it was my grandfather who had hunted
down and shot the shark. I was surprised, looking through this box of
pictures recently, to discover that he hadn't, after all. The man holding
the foot doesn't even look like Fred McKim. Yet I had seen pictures of
my grandfather; I knew what he looked like. I must have combined my
remote, romantic image of the man—the idea of his leaving civilization
to live among the Indians—with some girlish fantasy of the great white
hunter.

As I write this, I'm sitting at my mother's old desk in the stone studio
behind the house in Woodstock. With its square window facing a
grove of ash and maple saplings and its unused wood stove, this room has
been a storage place these past few years; I've had to dust and sweep away
the spiders' webs and dead flies. There is a special musty feeling here, a
fecund, friendly odor of mildew and rot that signals the ultimate return of
things to their former state.

Across the room, a set of shelves holds a row of birds' nests, some with a lining of mud, others fallen out of a tree that was being cut down. There is the nest a blue jay had built too close to one of the hammock hooks one summer; because the jays had screamed at us so, we had finally taken the hammock down and stayed away until the babies left. On another shelf, a gathering of snail shells, all sizes, mysteriously empty. An assemblage of fossils my mother and I have gathered over the years from the rocky shores of the Ashokan Reservoir nearby sits on the heavy trestle table beneath.

All during my childhood, while my father was at work in his studio, or away teaching down in the city, my mother and I went on expeditions to the Ashokan Reservoir, a lake twelve miles long and part of the water supply for New York City. I loved these treasure hunts; they were forays into my mother's imagination. I learned to see the world around me from these trips.

From the land around the reservoir, we collected blue and white glass bottles discovered in the old foundations of deserted houses lost in the woods. On its shores, we picked up bits of smoky flint that gave off a burning smell when struck together, blocks of shale that crumbled in my hands like a Chinese puzzle, fat conglomerates we called pudding stones. Some rocks were so thick with fossils that they were layered like the uncut printed pages of a book—they could be split at any point to reveal a new stratum of shell shadows, like small, trailing wings. Others revealed a single leaf or fern or fat trilobite, or were chosen for their shape and size, their heft and smoothness in the hand, or the way they split like sliced bread. We always went home lugging stones, our pockets stuffed.

These walks were intense experiences for me; all my senses were wide open. Sometimes, overwhelmed with the richness of it all, I would have to sit on the beach and close my eyes. Waiting for my mother, I'd assemble a palette of colored pebbles, and draw on the warm, flat glacial stones we called whalebacks, or skip flat stones and watch the ripples disturb the perfect reflection of the distant blue mountains. Though my mother was far down the beach, bent over, still looking, I felt we were together. Soon, she would amble in my direction, show me her booty and admire my pebble drawing, or the necklace of splashes I'd make for her in the still water.

Another magical place of my childhood that we visited together was an old hotel on the top of Overlook Mountain. Originally constructed in

1870, but abandoned after the crash of 1929, Overlook House had been one of many palatial mountain resorts in the Catskills. Now, only the concrete outer shell remains, but when I was young, the complete structure still stood in all its disarray. People were still climbing the steep three-mile dirt road and pillaging the hotel for its plumbing fixtures and stone cornices. Scaling the steep slope to its summit became an annual adventure.

We'd poke around the ruined grounds, finding fascinating things— old bottles and tiles, the long-toothed skull of a porcupine, and even, once, the pale twin lobes of a rattlesnake's rattles, which made a delicious noise. I took this find home, I remember, and hid it in my jewel box. The grand ballroom of the old hotel was littered with bits of decaying red velvet and fragments of mirrors, which cast prisms of sunlight every-where through a great, gaping hole in the floor above. The dozens of rooms on the upper floors lacked partitions; we walked through walls from one end of the building to the other. Anchored with rusting guy wires to the roof, a wooden spire, churchlike, rose four more stories.

My mother always became worried when we got this high. She'd stand on the flat roof of the hotel, which was solid enough, pointing out the view. "This is far enough," she always said. "We don't need to go up there, do we?" Then, when I insisted, "Oh dear," and, "Please be *very* careful."

Trembling a little, avoiding the places where the wood had rotted away, I carefully climbed the spiral stair to the topmost aerie with its diamond-shaped windows. And there, with ridges of blue spreading to the horizon in every direction and the Hudson River laid out like a wide silver ribbon, I was on top of the world.

Every walk with my mother became an opportunity to collect some-thing. Dried flowers thickened the pages of books, shelves were covered with dusty nests and shells, shoeboxes in dressers and in the attic held the overflow. Sometimes my mother and I still go foraging together. Two years ago, when we compared our day's haul after beachcombing in Boca Grande on the Gulf Coast of Florida, I realized how different our tastes had become. I had kept only perfect specimens—tulips, scallops, turkey wings, cowries—while she had chosen oddities—fragments of clam shells riddled with holes, a twisty worm shell, bits of sea glass, the gothic inner chambers of a whelk. These bits she glued to shirt cardboards;

44. *Mother and Child*, 1930.

45. *If This Be Not I*, 1945.

46. *The Tormentors*, 1947–48.

47. *The Room I*, 1954–55.

48. *Painter*, 1959.

49. *Riding Around*, 1969.

50. *Painting, Smoking, Eating*, 1973.

51. *The Painter*, 1976.

52. *Painter's Forms II*, 1978.

53. *Couple in Bed,* 1977.

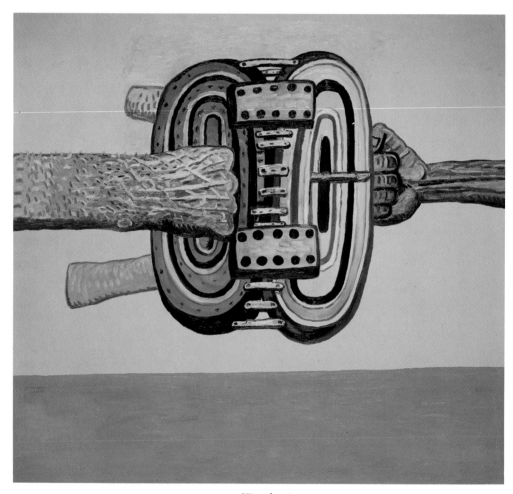

54. *Hinged*, 1978.

arranged in rows like her polished phrases, they seemed to me like lines of poetry.

ALONE WITH THE MOON

What about the small game
and the dew falling?

The dry leaves of autumn
magnify the hop
of the lightest bird.

Why don't you lie down
to pass the time?
Why not sleep—and never meet?

Let the witnesses
be distant mountains.

Should I get back to the city?
to be with the guilty?
Or stay with the tree,
unconscious of me?

My father's new cinder-block studio, grim and gray as a factory on the outside, but huge and light on the inside, was completed by Christmas of 1967. He brought back all his work from New York, and my parents settled in for the winter.

"At last I can spread out!" my father exclaimed when Danny and I visited with the kids the next summer. "I can breathe!" Months of construction problems, leakage, being unable to paint with the workmen there, were forgotten now as he proudly showed off the new studio. "But I do feel bad for them," he said, pointing in the direction of his neighbors to the east. Their house was invisible now behind the monolithic bulk of the new studio. To them, the new building was a high, windowless wall of gray cinder block rising almost in their dooryard. But they never complained.

In this studio, as in the house, were found objects—railroad spikes, antique flatirons, a pair of dumbbells. And it was in the new studio that my father finally gave in to the image, beginning a succession of small panels, oils on masonite, of objects—shoes, light bulbs, books, paintings on walls, bricks, cups, stretchers, easels, boxes, balls, clocks (see plate 59). His rough notes at the time reflect an explorer's excitement.

> September 1970. In a drawer I find scraps of paper with these notes. *Thickness of things. Shoes. Rusted iron. Mended rags. Seams. Dried blood stains. Pink paint. Bricks. Bent nails and pieces of wood. Brick walls. Cigarette butts. Smoking. Empty booze bottles.*
>
> *How would bricks look flying in the air—fixed in their gravity—falling? A brick fight.*
>
> *Pictures hanging on nails in walls. The hands of clocks. Green window shades. Two or three story brick buildings. Endless black windows. Empty streets.*

He had rediscovered the "pleasures of narrative," as he told Bill Berkson in an interview for *Art News:* "You're painting a shoe; you start painting the sole, and it turns into a moon; you start painting the moon, and it turns into a piece of bread."

"Pictures should tell stories," my father had decided. "It is what makes me want to paint. To see, in a painting, what one has always wanted to see, but hasn't, until now. For the first time."

As he worked, he began to feel he was discovering a new place, a topography peopled with new beings—the characters who would populate the larger works of the next several years, the hooded figures of Ku Klux Klansmen (see plate 49).

"They are self-portraits," he told students at the University of Minnesota during a slide talk there in 1978. "I perceive myself as being behind the hood. In the new series of 'hoods' my attempt was really not to illustrate, to do pictures of the Ku Klux Klan, as I had done earlier." In these pictures, Philip seemed to be claiming a fuller, more complex sense of himself, as a painter and as a man. "What would it be like to be evil? To plan, to plot," he mused.

"Isaac Babel gave a lovely ironic speech to the Soviet Writers' Union," Philip told his audience. "He ended his talk with the following remark. 'The party and the government have given us everything, but have deprived us of one privilege. A very important privilege, comrades, has been taken away from you. That of writing badly.' "

After the two most intense and prolific years of his whole career, my father was ready to show what he'd been up to. Thirty-three paintings— many of them very large—and eight drawings of the new work were shown in October 1970 at the Marlborough Gallery, which he had joined in 1966, some years after leaving Sidney Janis. It was at Marlborough that Philip met David McKee, who was to become his dealer in 1974 and his friend for the remaining years of his life. Frank Lloyd, director of Marlborough and as yet unsullied by the Rothko scandal, came up to Woodstock for a look and decided to take a chance on what he saw (see Notes). The show was the first Philip Guston exhibition in New York in four years, the first since the Jewish Museum show in 1966.

In 1969 and 1970, my father had begun working big, some of the canvases as large as six by ten feet, grander in scale than anything he'd done since the old mural days of the 1930s. There were Klansmen everywhere, their blank slotlike eyes and patched hoods innocent and evil and funny all at once; every time you turned around, there they were in chalky, up-tilted landscapes across which bricks were flying—reminiscent of George Herriman's inspired comic strip, much loved by my father for its quirky metaphysics and endearing desert vistas of mesas and buttes and cacti. Despite the best efforts of Offissa Pup, the brick tossed by Ignatz the Mouse at Krazy Kat never fails to carry its ambivalent load of love and cruelty straight to its mark.

Sometimes Philip's dramas took place in furnished rooms, under the harsh light of unshaded bulbs, or outdoors, in cityscapes with plump layered buildings rising behind them; or the hoods would be riding in cars, plotting like petty gangsters, participating in sinister interrogations and flagellations, cringing at accusative fingers, gloved like Mickey Mouse.

"About these hooded men," my father explained in the lecture notes he made for a talk in 1977. "The KKK has haunted me since I was a boy in L.A. In those years they were there mostly to break strikes, and I drew and painted pictures of conspiracies and floggings, cruelty and evil. . . . In this new dream of violence, I feel like Isaac Babel with his Cossacks; as if I were living with the Klan. What do they do afterwards? Or before? Smoke, drink, sit around their rooms (light bulbs, furniture, wooden floors), patrol empty streets; dumb, melancholy, guilty, fearful, remorseful, reassuring one another? Why couldn't some be artists and paint one another?"

In *The Studio*, 1969, a hood, cigarette in hand, is busy painting a self-portrait, surrounded by his brushes, paint cans, and palette (see plate 57). "Caught red-handed," as Ross Feld observes. "If we think the Klansmen are happy monsters, riding around in the clunky cars with their sticks and cigars, gaze here upon the Painter—and see the truest, happiest Monster of all. This cheerful allegory, in attention-tweaking reds and pinks, establishes what is most essential to the gaiety, spirit, and meaning behind Guston's heresy."

Ross Feld published this analysis in 1980. But between the public's first glimpse of the work at the Marlborough Gallery in 1970, and the grudging acceptance that began to emerge ten years later when the Guston retrospective opened at the San Francisco Museum of Modern Art, a great deal of critical writing was devoted to what was considered to be my father's "heresy," most of it resoundingly negative. From all quarters, his new work was attacked for being clumsy, crude, artless, cartoony, affected, klutzy.

From the perspective of sixteen years later, the reaction provoked by the new Guston paintings shown at Marlborough in 1970 still seems extreme. But it has to be seen within the context and prevailing critical wisdom of its time. The sixties had been a decade of intense ferment in American painting, a clear reaction against abstract expressionism.

"On Halloween in 1962," Harold Rosenberg wrote in *The Anxious Object,* one of the better analyses of this period, "Sidney Janis, whose gallery represented de Kooning, Rothko, Guston, and other top Abstract Expressionists, opened a two-locations exhibition of 'factual' (i.e., illusionistic) painting and sculpture. Under these auspices and after fifteen years of the austerity of abstract art, the new New Realism hit the New York art world with the force of an earthquake."

This exhibition led the abstract expressionists to leave the Sidney Janis Gallery in protest. Nineteen sixty-two was also the year of the Guston retrospective at the Guggenheim Museum. For my father, perhaps more than for any of the other painters of his generation, it was the end of an era.

Pop art had arrived. There, across 57th Street in Janis' new showroom, were Oldenburg's soft sculptures and plaster cream puffs, Lichtenstein's comic strips, Warhol's soup cans and silk-screened multiples of pop culture icons. Public attention began to turn away from the New York School. "Philip and I and Barney Newman were in a taxi once, talking about Andy Warhol," Elaine de Kooning told me, "and Philip said, 'Oh, Warhol, he's like giving a Jewish kid a hot pork sandwich on the day of his bar mitzvah!' Barney and I didn't exactly know what he meant, but we said, 'That's it!' "

Photorealism, with its billboards and monumental portraits, and op art, with its optical effects and vibrating colors, were two other forms of illusionism that came into vogue during those years. Minimalism traced a direct lineage from the simple and monumental stripes of Barnett Newman, the somber chromatic floating grids of Mark Rothko, and the black-on-black paintings of Ad Reinhardt. "A joke went the rounds," Harold Rosenberg once said, "to the effect that Newman had closed the door, Rothko had pulled down the shades, and Reinhardt had turned out the light."

It was an era of pushing the limits, of "happenings," of earthworks and transitory mixed-media pieces, and the general transformation of abstract expressionism or action painting into what became known as color-field and hard-edge painting, with the work of artists like Morris Louis, Frank Stella, and Ellsworth Kelly.

But in a time of seeming diversity, one direction in particular seemed forbidden to American painters—that of a subjective and personal expression. Never mind that by 1980 a "new" wave of neo-expressionism would take the fore again and enshrine Philip Guston as one of its principal ancestors. The critics of the sixties and seventies, apparently, were rooted in the art of the moment; a longer view didn't matter. Rosenberg presented this dilemma of the sixties: "The proposition that man-made images *are* the American reality underlies the naturalism of the painters of comic-strip blowups, store-window items, and billboard parodies, who often incorporate the objects themselves into their works. Like the nineteenth-century genre painters, the new art of daily life accepts the prevailing esthetic forms as the forms of fact. Reacting against the radical effort of Action Painting to break through the scene to the subjective reality, the art of the facade declares any other American reality to be either nonexistent or inaccessible."

"Woodstock, September 20, 1970," my mother wrote in her diary. "Drove to N.Y. to Hahn Brothers Warehouse at 134th Street, where, on one of the floors Marlborough rents, were 65 of P.'s paintings, to meet the *Time* correspondent. An English-Australian Captain America he turned out to be, in striped jeans, embroidered denim jacket, and helmet, his Honda safe inside the locked iron gates down below.

"In Rome, a couple of weeks later, Varujan Boghosian and P., having tracked down a copy of *Time International,* stood at the foot of the Spanish Steps, by the Barcaccia [Bernini's barge fountain] and read Captain A.'s review, 'Ku Klux Komix.' Which koncluded, 'In three minutes of film . . . the movie camera can disclose more about the kind of reality that appalls Guston than his whole exhibition has done. . . . As political statement, they are all as simple-minded as the bigotry they denounce.' !! P. was disgusted. Said he should never have taken Captain A. to lunch."

Captain America was, of course, the critic Robert Hughes. Like so many others, he completely misunderstood the relationship of my father's paintings to cartoons. "If the truth is to be had, it must be found," Ross Feld wrote ten years later. "The act of finding is resonantly and invariably private. Since it is private, no amount of clear outlining, impoliteness, gross ballooning, or self-mockery will ever do anything but honor its inviolable mystery."

Yes, of course he had loved the comics as a boy, Philip acknowledged. "I used to dream of having my own strip one day." But the resemblance of these paintings to cartoons was superficial. These pictures weren't crude at all; they were painterly works indeed, and highly artful. "In the old painting I love," my father explained, "early Renaissance painting, the 'information' is fast, no? But the 'painting' is slow, dwelt upon."

"Before they were shown at Marlborough," my father told the audience during a slide talk in 1978, "Tom Hess, who was then editor of *Art News,* heard something was up, so we went over to the warehouse to see them. He looked at this painting here, one with a piece of lumber with nails sticking out, and he said, 'What's that, a typewriter?' I said, 'For Christ's sake, Tom, if this were eleven feet of one color, and one band running down on the end, you wouldn't ask me what it was.' I said, 'Don't you know a two-by-four with red nails?' "

But the real problem seemed to be that my father's work was changing, not with the temper of his times nor the vagaries of the art world, but in response to forces within himself that demanded the invention of unique imagery, a return to sources, and a putting together of all that he'd learned as a painter in an entirely new way. It was Philip's position outside the successive stylistic upheavals of the art scene that seemed to antagonize the critics most.

"It says almost everything about our art world," wrote English critic Norbert Lynton in 1982, "that we should place so high a premium on authenticity and originality, yet either punish outright or seek endless excuses for leaps like the one Guston demonstrated in his amazing Marlborough (New York) show of 1970. . . . The later turning point was announced in words that were widely quoted, often against him: 'I got sick and tired of all that purity! I wanted to tell stories.' Can a painter be allowed to get sick of what the critics have praised in him?"

Here Lynton manages to put his finger on the real problem that critics had with the new work. "I have no personal knowledge of Guston to adduce," he continues, "but the impression his work gives is that of a man refusing to choose, or refusing not to be free to choose, to stay with one choice, refusing altogether to associate significant art with papal bulls and sacred cows. All around him he saw colleagues locked in the idioms they had chosen in the name of freedom. . . . I see Guston's last paintings as monuments against Rothko, Still and Newman, or at any rate against the easy piety and ready greed they engender—sublime ripostes to their much vaunted sublimity."

In the wake of abstract expressionism, all subject matter, especially all personal narrative, was looked upon with suspicion. What was deemed valid as art, it seemed, was formal in nature—that is, when it was not capricious or faddish. And the new Philip Guston just didn't fit in.

In 1970, virtually all the reactions the new paintings got were confused and negative. And no wonder. They must have seemed threatening indeed to the art establishment. How could these images not call into question most of what was passing for art in the galleries? And how else, in the light of eventual acclaim, can one explain the degree of vituperation my father's new work engendered at the time?

I wasn't sure what to think of these pictures myself. I was charmed by the small panels, overwhelmed by the larger works. Their directness seemed abrupt, shocking. But my father's elation and enthusiasm were contagious; he was, as he said, "onto something." During this time, he was working freely, prolifically, with an almost joyful abandon. His pleasure in what he was doing was greater than I had ever known it to be before, and so I was happy for him. I let myself be caught up in his excitement, without really understanding the pictures themselves.

The year before, in 1969—a month after half a million of my contemporaries at the Woodstock festival had trampled Max Yasgur's farmland in Bethel, New York, to muddy pulp—Danny and I and our two young sons had moved to the Midwest.

Life in Ohio seemed very remote—in more than distance—from the life I'd known in New York, far more of an exile, especially in terms of culture, than the two previous years we'd spent in the hallowed groves of New Haven. I gave up all thought of continuing to write art criticism, which I'd begun to do on a small scale as a free-lancer for the New Haven *Register*. There was simply nothing to write about. This wasn't urban conceit or New York chauvinism: apart from watercolors of the local waterfall and bouquets of flowers in the town bank, and an annual crafts fair (plus what little Wright State University and Antioch College could manage to show of their faculty and students, of course), art was scarcely to be seen in southwestern Ohio. To console myself that first year or so, I kept up my subscription to the *Village Voice* and read the Sunday *Times* and the art magazines.

I came to New York for the Marlborough opening, which I remember as a crowded, confusing affair. People, as always, stood with their backs to the paintings, which seemed shockingly immediate and alive in the big, dark gallery. I was somewhat prepared for the new work, having seen it in Woodstock the summer before. But it stunned me a bit, seeing it there. I still didn't know what to think. My father, as usual, was in the center of a cluster of people, talking and laughing a little too loudly, barely concealing his anxiety. I had come with friends; there wasn't enough room for us at the restaurant afterwards. I barely saw my parents.

The most memorable review of the Marlborough show appeared in the *New York Times*. In his article "A Mandarin Pretending to Be a Stumblebum," the art critic Hilton Kramer first set my father up as a "sacred figure" of the New York School, according him the faint praise of "authentic minor lyricist," then knocked him down:

"As the prestige of painterliness began to wane in the 1960s, owing to the combined assault that Pop Art and Color-field painting inflicted on the painterly mannerisms of the New York School, Mr. Guston was second only to Willem de Kooning in commanding the allegiance of those who found in both the ethos and the esthetics of Abstract Expressionism the last embodiment of the 'New' they were prepared to make without reservation."

In fact, Kramer insisted, Guston had really always been a sort of Johnny-come-lately to the New York scene, a latecomer working away years earlier in what Kramer termed the "heyday of Monet-mania," while actually readying himself to make this exit from abstraction. "In only one respect can some of us claim to have anticipated him: we tired of 'all that Purity' long before he did. . . . For in offering us his new style of cartoon anecdotage, Mr. Guston is appealing to a taste for something funky, clumsy and demotic. We are asked to take seriously his new persona as an urban primitive, and this is asking too much. . . . Throughout the history of modern painting, the primitive has repeatedly been called upon to rescue and rejuvenate the vitality of 'high' art, and Mr. Guston is clearly seeking such a rejuvenation in turning to the popular visual slang of the old cartoonists as the basis of a new pictorial style. But it doesn't work. For one thing, there is no vitality here to rejuvenate."

Reading Kramer's attack served to crystallize my own feelings. I was outraged. Knowing what my father's reaction would be to a hostile reception, I wanted to champion him, defend him, cushion him somehow against it. For the last several years, since they had gotten back together, I'd been feeling closer to both my parents, and more protective. From our infrequent talks in his studio when I visited, I was beginning to have a sense of my father's despair over the state of the art world and his place—or lack of place—within it. I wanted to protest, to do something. But who was I, the artist's daughter, to question the opinions of a famous critic, to undertake what would certainly be an embarrassingly emotional defense of my father? I sat down and wrote my angry letter anyway. To my utter amazement, the *Times* published my letter that December in its entirety under the heading "A Personal Vendetta Against Guston?"

"As Philip Guston's daughter," I wrote, "I will not pretend to possess a great deal of objectivity toward my father's recent painting. I feel compelled, however, to say that as a critic Hilton Kramer exhibits even less objectivity than I do. . . . The process and content of self-disclosure in art is an esthetic which has been all but forgotten in the influx of depersonalized conceptual art of the last decade. I will not contend that art concerned with the baring of the artist's soul is by any means the only valid direction that art can take, but it was a direction taken by Abstract

Expressionist painters. To me it is more than exciting to see where these sensibilities have carried a painter like my father. I find myself disturbed, fascinated, moved and repelled by this work, by the honesty and humanity of its vision in which the terrifying and ominous rub shoulders with the pathetic and comic."

But it was the position Kramer took as a critic that disturbed me most: "If Mr. Kramer looks at the work of an artist and cannot see beyond political intrigue, one-upsmanship and self-service, then one has to question his right to be in a position where his opinions carry the weight that they do. . . . Perhaps Kramer would do better to write about all the artists who have sold themselves to critics and dealers in an all-out effort to merchandise art that is little more than the inflated, impersonal relics of a sick, schizoid society."

Someone sent my letter to my father, who was in Italy with my mother. He wrote that he was touched and pleased by my defense of his work. A dozen or so others, loyal collectors and old friends of the family, thanked me for my letter.

"He did a real hatchet job," my father said years later of the Kramer review. "I had asked the gallery not to send me any clippings. I just wanted to have a vacation. We were in Venice in November and in a weak moment I went to American Express for mail. The 'Xerox underground' had caught up with me and in it was the article from the *Times*. I was angry for about half an hour and then I threw it into one of the canals. Why should I be depressed in Venice? So, when I returned about eight or ten months later, I was at Yale and a student asked, 'How did you feel when you read the review in the *Times*?' I explained to him that I was in Venice and that I started thinking, 'That's a hell of a review. Jesus, what if he had *liked* it, then I would have really been in trouble!' So that solved the problem."

Of course, it didn't. But nearly a decade later, with the increasing recognition his new work was at last receiving, my father was able to talk about this dark time with a certain tongue-in-cheek bravado: "When what people have been calling the 'New Paintings' were first shown at Marlborough in 1970, they seemed to shock the New York art world a little bit—or so I heard. We fled to Europe just after the opening. But there were some who understood. When Bill de Kooning saw the show, he said he liked it very much. You know, everybody thought those paintings were about the hooded figures, and the bad conditions in America, and so on, and that was part of it—every artist hopes to give his own interpretation of the world—but they were about something else, too. When de Kooning saw the show, after embracing me, and congratulating me, he said: 'You know, Philip, what your real subject is? It's freedom!' "

Not all his friends understood. Morty Feldman's failure to react favorably to the new work hurt my father deeply. Their friendship never really recovered, although Morty was always on Philip's mind and in his heart; in 1977, my father painted *Friend—To M.F.* It is a poignant image, as Robert Storr observes, of "their mutually regretted estrangement"; Morty's head is half turned away from the viewer.

"Why did you have to go and ruin everything?" one painter said angrily at the Marlborough opening. My mother wrote in her diary, "P. said Lee Krasner hadn't spoken to him at the gallery; had told someone that the work was 'embarrassing.' "

There were a few dissenting voices. Harold Rosenberg wrote favorably in *The New Yorker* about the new work, titling his review "Liberation from Detachment," and emphasizing its political content. To address concerns over crudity and clumsiness, he cited something Picasso was reported to have said that might equally have been said by my father: "When I was a kid, I drew like Michelangelo. It took me years to learn to draw like a kid."

For Rosenberg, "Guston's new crudeness has, however, an important expressive function: it enables him to give a simple account of the simple-mindedness of violence.

"The separation of art from social realities threatens the survival of painting as a serious activity," he maintained. "Guston has demonstrated that the apparent opposition between quality in painting and political statement is primarily a matter of doctrinaire aesthetics. . . . Other contemporaries have done political pieces for special occasions. . . . Guston is the first to have risked a fully developed career on the possibility of engaging his art in the political reality."

All my father wanted to do at the time was to get as far away as possible from all the controversy. Two days after the opening, my parents set sail for Genoa on the *Michelangelo.*

"Can't believe we are in such motion," my mother wrote the day after the opening. "To the extent of getting on a boat and sailing away to Europe! For which plans of all kinds, well ahead of time, have had to be made. What put the fire under P. was of course the need to get away while the show is on, and to be distracted for a while against the blank reactions, the slow takes (usually about ten years), the stupid, if not spiteful, write-ups. Tomorrow's the day! Early!"

Safe in Italy after a rough crossing, living again at the American Academy in Rome, where we had stayed the summer of 1960, my father painted dozens of oils on paper—using only red, white, and black—the Roma paintings, he called them—of fountains and statues and trees and ruined walls; the formal gardens of Rome. Most of these small paintings are elegant, pacific images (see plate 66). A few, though, are anything but peaceful. In these disturbing works, the eyes of the hooded figures have expanded into black, empty windows, clearly a quote from the tortured mannequin in de Chirico's *The Jewish Angel* of 1915. James Thrall Soby—in *The Early Chirico*, a book always at hand on my father's shelf—wrote that these disturbing figures were like "men whom pain has brought to despair, but not yet to death." Their vacant eyes, Soby writes, are "imponderable wounds, deep beyond cure."

For nine months, my parents traveled in Italy, revisiting favorite places and paintings, then on to Sicily and Greece. When they returned to Woodstock in 1971, my father had recovered from the Marlborough show and was eager to plunge back into his work.

"You didn't hear from me in Europe," he wrote a friend the following summer, "because I didn't have anything to say. I mean I became so depressed—deflated and low over the reception, rejection, misunderstandings of the show that the only thing I could do to mitigate my bitterness was a resolve to clam up and travel extensively—which we did. . . . I was in a state of rather extreme paranoia and it was just as well that I was not here. . . . I guess I was shocked the 'official' art world (of *Modern Art!*) could be as bigoted as it was . . . And by now I feel that things really *never* change and that it is pure illusion to ever think that it can. I am back to 1950 again except that it is worse—because of the extreme codification of beliefs and the institutionalism of everything. . . . I just have to—*must*—try to forget the neglect. I am truly on my own now."

In 1972, he painted the first *Painter's Forms*, a strange, self-referential work, a lexicon of coughed-up objects—shoes, bottle, stretcher, bricks —emanating from the open mouth of the painter, whose rather calm self-portrait appears, in profile, in the painting's upper left (see plate 55).

By the time, six years later, my father got around to painting a second version, *Painter's Forms II* (1978), the spigot had been jammed fully on. From a wide and disembodied mouth, the previous spray of "stuff" has become a flood, a parade of forms evolved into a purgative, frightening stampede of marching legs and feet (see plate 52).

By then, he was immersed, totally, in his new language of form—the collection of objects begun ten years earlier with the small panels of shoes and books. In these works, Robert Storr writes, "Guston was not toying with codes of representation. On the contrary, he painted as if speaking directly in the language of 'things.' . . . Chosen from the everyday objects that surrounded him, the things that filled Guston's work were painted on small panels as 'statements of fact' before being incorporated into larger works, where they became the nouns, verbs, and punctuation of his stories."

This "language of things" was a language I learned early. Maybe it was my first language. Long before I understood who my father was, long before art meant anything to me, it was the strangeness and beauty of the evocative objects that were lying around our house that taught me to cherish what I saw. I am convinced that it was the eloquent lexicon of my mother's collections, the places we explored together, and not my later studies in art history, that shaped my aesthetic sensibility. My father often talked about the necessity for innocence in art, saying he wanted to be like "the first painter," to create without convention or tradition. Of course, he could not. Nor can I see his paintings with innocent eyes. Still, I like to think that I respond to my father's late works as I did when I was very young, with a sort of childlike fascination, not as "Art," but as real things in the world, painter's forms to be reviewed again and again.

Referring again to Isaac Babel, a writer he often thought about during this period, my father spoke of the new concreteness, the resonance of simple forms he'd discovered in the last ten years of his work:

"I like Babel," my father said, "because he deals totally with fact. There can be nothing more startling than a simple statement of fact, in a certain form. As Babel says, there's no iron that can enter the heart like a period in the right place."

EIGHT

Drawing Aside the Curtain

Untitled, 1974.

If anyone had suggested that by moving to Ohio with our young children, Danny and I were repeating my parents' sojourn in Iowa and Missouri, I would have denied it. Teaching jobs in the East were hard to come by, after all. It was mere coincidence, I would have argued. Just as it was coincidence that my husband, like my father, was a painter. A painter, moreover, who, as a young man of thirty with a family, found himself far away from the center of the art world, teaching art for a living in a midwestern state university.

By 1972, after two and a half years in Ohio, I was desperately unhappy in my marriage. Danny and I had been married almost ten years; David and Jonathan were nine and seven years old. Surely we could find some way of working things out. A separation seemed unthinkable. But the "things" we had to work out had become huge and amorphous and bitter, encrusted with years of accumulated grudges and misunderstandings.

At the same time that life at home was falling apart, my work had begun to interest me again. Antioch College was offering a paraprofessional counselor training program that was "experiential"—which meant learning by doing—using an eclectic mix of Gestalt and Rogerian and other "humanistic" therapies. And the program was open to staff as well as students. The training, which relied heavily on co-therapy and groups, was intense and exciting. At last I felt I had some sense of what I wanted to do with my life. I was good at it, too. A childhood of staying attuned to my father's emotional states had equipped me with an ability to listen empathically and well. Three years after I had started work as a secretary-receptionist at the college, I was a counselor there with a full-time case load, busy training other counselors—but on a secretary's salary.

A new world was opening to me. I began examining my own life, and my connections with others. How isolated I'd been, and how starved for attention and affection. It was the heyday of Esalen and "touchy-feely" encounter groups, and I was a zealous convert to their powerful techniques. I learned to ask for hugs and take blindfolded "trust" walks. I confessed my secrets and dreams. I wept and screamed and pounded pillows in anger. The lonely child belonged at last: I was rocked by the group, held and reassured as I had never been before—or since. And all of it seemed very real at the time.

I'd come home at night from a training group, brimming with excitement, high on this remarkable "new" process of self-disclosure, thoughts and feelings flying around my head, only to be greeted by a stony silence. I didn't understand it.

"Talk to me," I begged. "What's wrong? Why are you acting like this?"

No response.

Well, my new words could be weapons, too, I was learning. "Why is what I'm doing so threatening to you?" I asked.

Danny shot me a dark look. "You know perfectly well why."

And I suppose I did. It was obvious to both of us that my involvement with this training group was some sort of repudiation of him, of our life together. Naively, I still hoped I could take him along with me, teach him as I was being taught. "Maybe we could see a therapist together?" I said. Silence. "Once, that's all I'm asking. Just one time?" No reaction.

I went over and touched his arm, but Danny stood there woodenly. "This damn therapy stuff is turning you into—" He pushed past me. "I don't want to talk about this," he said.

I stood in the center of the kitchen, my arms crossed. Now I was angry, too. There I was, more my own woman than I ever had been, yet all he could see was that these people over at the college were corrupting me. "Into what, Danny? What is it turning me into?"

"Someone I don't recognize, that's who."

"And what does *that* mean?"

"You figure it out." And he was out the door, slamming it behind him, on his way to the studio, or to a bar.

I opened the door, ran out onto the porch. "Danny, wait!" I called after him. "Stay and talk with me. Please."

He stopped and glared at me over the roof of his car. "Talk? What the hell for? You've made up your mind." He slid into the driver's seat and started the engine. The car pulled out of the driveway, spitting gravel. I watched his taillights round the corner of Whiteman Street and disappear.

Later, when he came home, we would pick up where we had left off, I knew. It was a familiar scene by then. My pressuring, his silence; his accusations, my tears. I would cajole and harangue. He would turn his back, refuse to speak, finally lash out at me. Sometimes I convinced myself that reason—and enlightenment—were on my side. It appalls me now to remember how self-righteous I was. At other times, I felt swamped with guilt. He was right—why was I ruining our lives? How could I do this to him, to the kids? Our fighting began to seem inevitable and pointless. Silence replaced the arguments.

Only much later did I realize we'd been part of an epidemic. I have an image now of that time, of hundreds of such confrontations—perhaps thousands—occurring simultaneously in kitchens and bedrooms all over the United States. Hundreds of wives—compliant fifties girls galvanized by the new feminism—jolted awake by therapy, or some consciousness-raising group or other, or by being back in school, trying to "convert" their angry, bewildered husbands. And hundreds of scared children cringing at the loud voices of their parents' arguments. A few marriages evolved into something better. Some women capitulated, went back to old ways, biding their time until their children were older, or simply gave up. Many of them left, as I did.

During the spring of 1972, I found a job with Encounter Programs, an "alternative" mental health agency that specialized in group therapy with drug abusers. I had enough money—just barely—to support myself and my sons. Danny wasn't going to change, and I wasn't willing to settle for our life as it had been. It was time. Danny had agreed to a trial separation that summer; he would take the kids back east to his parents' farm in New Jersey while I decided what I wanted to do. But the day they left, I knew.

It was with some misgivings that I wrote my parents to let them know about the separation. I didn't want to tell them. But this was obviously something I couldn't keep secret, as I had our marital conflicts, and my growing unhappiness. When we visited once or twice a year, I had always trotted out a prettied-up version of our lives for them to see. I was absurdly grateful that Danny refrained from his usual criticism of me in my parents' presence. It wouldn't be right to burden them with my troubles, I told myself. More to the point, I wanted to conceal my sense of shame from them. I felt I had failed.

For my parents the news of my plans to divorce Danny came as a shock. It must have seemed like an impulsive, unfounded move on my part. Still, I didn't anticipate any real trouble. My mother would be worried, of course. As for Philip, I thought he'd express regret, concern, perhaps a little mild, cautionary disapproval. Though he'd never said so directly, I sensed that my father hadn't been particularly thrilled by my marriage in the first place—but I thought that was because of the awkwardness of having to continue his long-defunct friendship with my father-in-law, Reuben Kadish.

"I don't think you realize what you're doing. There is more at stake here than your personal happiness," his special delivery letter said. "This divorce is a *terrible* mistake. And you will one day regret it." The letter went on to talk at length about my failure to act in a mature fashion and to assume responsibility—by which he meant stay in the marriage, no matter what.

I wish, now, that I still had this letter—it was so full of raw emotion. Though I was stung by it, I also felt strangely gratified that my father could get so upset about my life. But I was in therapy at the time, and tearing up his letter seemed like a marvelously cathartic, symbolically liberating thing to do. I do remember that where the word "terrible" was underlined three times, his pen had ripped right through the thin blue paper. I wrote an angry letter back.

A year and a half passed without our speaking. My mother acted as mediator, lending me money from her own account—I was gratified to find that she had one—to buy my first car, which I saw as a symbol of my newfound independence. I began graduate school, determined to get credentials as a counselor. The divorce became final.

Briefly, I toyed with the idea of changing my last name, but what would I change it to? My father's name? I remembered how relieved I'd been when I got married that people no longer came up to me and asked me if I was related to Philip Guston. I didn't want that again. And I didn't want some made-up feminist concoction.

Though I didn't know of this until years later, my mother and father invited my sons to Woodstock for a weekend that first summer Danny and I were separated. It was the first and last time such a visit occurred; at other times, my parents weren't particularly demonstrative or eager grandparents. David and Jonathan were unusually subdued and well-behaved that weekend, my mother remembers. There were drawing lessons, and trips for ice cream and to the town pool. On the way back to the Kadish farm in New Jersey where Danny had the boys for the summer, Musa and Philip got lost at one point on the country roads. An argument ensued over the right directions, during which my mother remembers looking in the back seat where David, then nine years old, sat with his knees drawn up, hands over his ears and eyes screwed tight shut, shutting out their angry voices. For her, and then for me when she told me about it, that single image of a frightened little boy doubled up in the back seat expressed the entire ruin of my marriage, and its irreversible consequences.

But for me, the end of my marriage came as a relief. At thirty years of age, I was finally free, I told my friends, of the men who had overshadowed me—both of them. As if by divorcing Danny I had resolved my feelings about my father. Yes, I did feel free, but it was a rebellious sort of freedom, a freedom founded on rejection and the necessary indulgences of a late-blooming, long-delayed adolescence. It was not a true liberation.

In March of 1974, I came east for the opening of a Philip Guston exhibition at Boston University, where my father had begun teaching the year before. I hadn't seen my parents since my divorce, almost two years before.

A few weeks earlier, my father had grabbed the receiver from my mother's hand while she and I were talking on the telephone, as we did every month or so. "I have a terrific idea, Ingie," he said. "Come to Boston. For the opening. I'd love it if you would." He would pay for my airfare, he said, and put me up at their hotel. How could I refuse? My need for autonomy crumbled instantly. As always, I was thrilled that he wanted me there.

Philip didn't look well. That was the first thing I noticed when I arrived at their room in the hotel on Commonwealth Avenue. He'd put on weight; his color was florid and his cheeks were drooping into jowls. For the first time, he looked old.

"It's so *good* to see you!" he cried, enfolding me in a big hug. "You look wonderful!" He held me at arm's length, gazing at me fondly. I blushed. He was acting as if nothing had happened between us. I wasn't really angry with him anymore. After all, he had made the first conciliatory move. I wanted to forget what had happened, let it recede into the past, like all the other regrettable parts of my divorce. My mother sat on the bed and smiled at us.

I told them my news. I was in graduate school by then. And I was in love. I'd met Tom Mayer when he was an Antioch undergraduate and I was still working in the Counseling Service. Tom was eight years younger than I was, but I wasn't worried about that. My mother was five years older than my father, and her mother, the first Musa, had been some nine years older than my grandfather. I was a third-generation older woman. I told them about Tom, about how capable and affectionate and attentive he was. How happy we were together. How David and Jonathan, despite their loyalty to their father, seemed to accept him. My father listened without comment.

"Well," my mother said finally, "I hope you're not going to rush into anything." No, I assured her, we were going to live together for a while, then see how we felt. "Good," she said.

Though my father and I never spoke of it directly, it became quite clear to me that his reaction to my divorce had been fueled—at least in part—by his own difficult recommitment to my mother six years before. My father had come back to his marriage and stuck it out, and so should I—that was his message.

At the dinner before the opening that night, I sat at a table in the wood-paneled faculty dining room at Boston University with my parents and my father's friend of the last several years, Philip Roth, the novelist. Witty, urbane, as skinny as my father was portly in those years—was it my mother who first referred to the two Philips as Mutt and Jeff?— Philip Roth entertained us during that meal with his stories. My father laughed gratefully and drank too much to calm his "opening" jitters.

It was that night, too, that I first had a chance to speak with David McKee. I'd been curious to meet this Englishman my father spoke so highly of. David had known my father at the Marlborough Gallery. Disillusioned once again after his 1970 show had failed to produce any major sales, my father had left Marlborough in 1972, moved all of his unsold work to Woodstock, and shortly thereafter begun teaching at Boston University. "The gallery is good for dead artists—or rather their widows," he wrote to a friend at the time. "All the rest is manufacturing, the same old dreary crap."

In the wake of the Rothko Foundation scandal, which had directly involved Frank Lloyd, the head of Marlborough, David McKee had left Marlborough himself and opened a gallery of his own on Lexington and

63rd Street on the second floor of the Barbizon Hotel. And he'd managed to convince my father to join his new gallery—quite a coup for a young dealer. Knowing my father's problematic history with dealers, this new loyalty intrigued me.

That night, as David walked me back to the hotel, he spoke of his admiration for my father and his paintings. The new work, he said, would turn the art world around. I spoke very little. Tall, prematurely gray, articulate, and self-possessed, David McKee seemed much older than I was—though I knew he was close to my age, and also recently divorced. There was little in him of the usual British reticence and formality. Quite the opposite, in fact; I could well imagine David and my father sitting up all night, drinking and talking. A little shy myself at first meetings, I found his volubility and enthusiasm a bit intimidating.

"What did you think of the show? Doesn't the work look marvelous?" he asked me. I said something noncommittal. I didn't know what I thought. I felt remote from the paintings. Looking through that catalogue now, I am surprised to discover that I must have seen, for the first time, some of the pictures that have stirred me the most since then. But they didn't register. Not even *Painting, Smoking, Eating*—a portrait of the artist tucked up in bed, with frightening lima bean head and one giant eye surveying the light bulb and shoes and paint pots massed behind him, a butt in his mouth, and a plate of french fries on the blanket. Disturbing and blunt and touching as this painting is to me now, I don't remember even seeing it that night. In the two years since I'd seen him, I had strayed very far from my father's vision. It would take more than a cursory look at a crowded opening to put me back in touch.

"You know," David McKee said, stopping and peering out at the damp Boston night, "the critics, the art world—they don't even realize what they're looking at yet. Philip doesn't fit into their categories. I keep telling him that it will take time. The new work is difficult. Very demanding. But they will eventually come around. In the end, your father will be recognized as one of the great painters of this century."

I looked up at him. "Do you think so?"

"Oh, absolutely. There's no doubt in my mind," he said. "No doubt at all."

How fortunate, I remember thinking, that my father had finally found a dealer who believed in his work so passionately, who actually seemed to celebrate his changes rather than worrying about how they would affect the market. Four years after my father's initial exhibition at Marlborough, and six years after the first small figurative panels had differentiated themselves from the "pure" drawings, the new work still met with confusion. Critics didn't understand it, found it puzzling and crude. Only a handful of drawings and small paintings had sold. But at least the work was being seen. "I torment about all this exposure," my father wrote to a friend. "The biggest part of me wants to hide, but I want to see it up on walls too."

"Now, it is all over—opening and all," he wrote when he was back in Woodstock from the Boston show. "I wish I could take it down, bring them back here—feel lower than a snake's ass—studio empty—start again? I never have gotten used to this damn exhibition business—gets harder all the time."

While I had purposely kept away from the art world and anything connected with it, I was still at least marginally aware of what was being shown and promoted in New York, and of my father's growing disgust with it. Going through his desk recently, I found several sheets of his angry scrawl, torn from a yellow pad, that I believe date from the early seventies.

"American Abstract art is a lie, a sham, a cover-up for a poverty of spirit. A mask to mask the fear of revealing oneself. A lie to cover up how bad one can be. Unwilling to show this badness, this rawness. It is laughable, this lie. Anything but this! What a sham! Abstract art hides it, hides the lie, a *fake!* Don't! Let it show! It is an escape from the true feelings we have, from the 'raw,' primitive feelings about the world—and us in it. In America.

"Where are the wooden floors—the light bulbs—the cigarette smoke? Where are the brick walls? Where is what we feel—without notions—ideas—good intentions? No, just conform to the banks—the plazas—monuments to the people who own this country—give everyone the soothing lullaby of 'art.'

"We all know what this is—don't we?"

Pop art, color-field painting, and minimalism had held sway in the New York marketplace for the fifteen years since the "fall" of abstract expressionism. Certain of my father's contemporaries—Motherwell, de Kooning, Rothko, Kline, Pollock—were granted their places, enshrined as masters of a past generation. But the newer work I saw in the galleries and art magazines was puzzling to me. It was so tidy, somehow. It seemed increasingly media-oriented and self-referential.

"In a recent article which contrasts the work of a color-field painter with mine," my father told an audience at the University of Minnesota, "the painter is quoted as saying, 'A painting is made with colored paint on a surface and what you see is what you see.' This popular and melancholy cliché is so remote from my own concerns. . . . I think that the idea of the pleasure of the eye is not merely limited, it isn't even possible. Everything means something. Anything in life or in art, any mark you make has meaning and the only question is, 'What kind of meaning?' . . . Regarding the general situation in art today . . . something must be wrong somewhere, because there is this overwhelming success and at the same time such an overwhelming apathy."

It wasn't only the impoverished aesthetic of the art world that disturbed my father, but the contrast between it and the social and political upheaval he saw around him—the assassinations and police violence, the televised horror of the Vietnam war, and the unreal antics of the Nixon administration. For him, as an artist, there was a terrible irony in this, as he recounted some years later: ". . . when the 1960s came along I was feeling split, schizophrenic. The war, what was happening in America, the brutality of the world. What kind of man am I, sitting at home, reading magazines, going into a frustrated fury about everything—and then going into my studio *to adjust a red to a blue*. I thought there must be some way I could do something about it. I knew ahead of me a road was laying. A very crude, inchoate road. I wanted to be complete again, as I was when I was a kid. . . . Wanted to be whole between what I thought and what I felt."

Despite his distress at the world outside his studio, it seemed that my father managed to arrive at a new self-sufficiency of being and working in isolation. As if he'd been able, finally, to do what he had always claimed was necessary—to step outside of the art world and to leave it behind him. At times, he seemed able to transcend his bitterness and actually welcome the solitude and time his lack of recognition gave him—or at least to put it to good use.

Something John Cage had said to him during the 1950s often came to his mind. "When you start working, everybody is in your studio—the past, your friends, enemies, the art world, and above all, your own ideas—all are there. But as you continue painting, they start leaving, one by one, and you are left completely alone. Then, if you're lucky, even you leave."

He treasured Willem de Kooning's use of the word "freedom" to describe his "heresy" at the Marlborough opening in 1970. It meant something that a painter of his own generation could see what he was doing as an act of liberation. "The other important thing that de Kooning said to me," my father told an interviewer in 1980, "which I think is wonderful, was this: he said, 'Well, now you are on your own! You've paid off all your debts!' . . . I think I am. . . . I don't look at my pantheon of the masters of the last 500 years of European painting as I used to. Or when I do I see them differently."

But it was a profound, emptying sort of liberation that was involved, one that cost him a great deal. Letters to his friends during these years show him moving from despair to elation and back again. "I think I've got some 19th century poet's nervous disorder that machinery can't solve," Philip wrote a friend from Johns Hopkins Hospital in Baltimore, where he was being given a battery of tests. Deep, crippling depressions —"I'm more like Oblomov than ever"—and a painful ulcer that wouldn't heal had put him there.

"The head internist thinks I'll be around for at least twenty years," he wrote jubilantly when he was released from the hospital late in October 1974. "Think of all the painting I can do in all this time!"

"I am in a big painting streak," he wrote in March of 1975. "Keeps on going, stranger and more mystifying than ever . . . So this is what I've been after so many years—a good, heavy foot in the door of this room, finally. What a difference—to *live* out a painting, instead of just painting it."

By August of that same year, he was in despair again. "From where— where—do these doomed feelings come—and why, why are we so vulnerable?" he wanted to know. The letter went on to talk of Rilke's poetry, of the strange allegories he'd been painting: ". . . the counterpart of melancholy can become unbearable excitement, nervousness about the recent images. Either way, it's touch and go. You'd think I'd be familiar by now with all these goings on—but that's not the way it works, is it?"

He was reading Russian writers again. His letters to friends are larded with quotes. "When a Russian refuses consolation, it means that things are bad, it means that there really is no consolation. Without consolation, one can live only on love, memory and culture." This was from Joseph Brodsky's review of Mandelstam's *Hope Abandoned*. "I feel such identity with this," my father said. "This is what my recent painting is about, in a way."

With the work of Zoshchenko, Biely, and especially Isaac Babel, he found real connection. "There is a *doubleness* of looking so sharply at life," he wrote. "Apart, yet at the same moment the writer's heart is *so deeply* involved—and in a subtle, formal way."

Isaac Babel was a Jew from Odessa, the birthplace of my father's parents. Babel's gifts, as Lionel Trilling points out in his introduction to *The Collected Stories*, are "rooted in the memory of boyhood." In one of his stories, the Odessa pogrom of 1905, from which my grandparents Leib and Rachel Goldstein fled, is powerfully compressed in the vision of the young boy thrown to the street, the entrails of his beloved pigeons streaming down his cheek. "I close my solitary unstopped-up eye so as not to see the world that spread out before me. This world was tiny, and it was awful. . . . The earth smelled of raw depths, of the tomb, of flowers. I smelled its smell and started crying, unafraid."

Beneath the "brilliant" surface, the "lyric and ironic elegance" of Babel's story, Trilling says, it is the "elemental simplicity" that surprises the reader. "We are surprised, too, by its passionate subjectivity, the intensity of the author's personal involvement, his defenseless commitment of himself to the issue." It is precisely these qualities in my father's paintings of the 1970s, it seems to me, that lend these pictures their intimate and universal power.

"For beyond the difficulty of communicating oneself," as Virginia Woolf once wrote in an essay on Montaigne, "there is the supreme difficulty of being oneself." It was to this difficult process of "being oneself" that my father, with great relief—and utmost trepidation—had finally surrendered.

"There is nothing to do now but paint my life," Philip said in a note to himself in September 1972. "My dreams, surroundings, predicament, desperation, Musa—love, need. Keep destroying any attempt to paint pictures, or think about art. If someone bursts out laughing in front of my painting, that is exactly what I want and expect."

During the early 1970s in Woodstock, my father found comfort and humor in the friendship of Philip Roth (see plate 61). The novelist had beaten a retreat to the Catskills after the hullabaloo that followed the publication of *Portnoy's Complaint*. They met at the home of a mutual friend. "It was through lightheartedness that we connected," Philip Roth tells me. "We discovered we both liked American junk. We'd drive over to Kingston, have a walk around, take in whatever was hideous, have lunch in my favorite diner, the Aim to Please."

After my father returned from Italy in 1971, the two friends found that they shared a growing sense of dismay over recent political events. At the time, Roth was working on *Our Gang*, a satire of the Nixon administration; a few months later, my father began his own parody on Nixon's life, a series of caricatures he collected together in a volume he called *Poor Richard*. The drawings, which begin with Nixon's boyhood, are rendered with a savage—and frequently obscene—humor. Only a few have been reproduced. Apparently, Grove Press was approached and expressed an interest in doing a book, but by then the Watergate scandal had blown up and Richard Nixon had resigned from office. Philip Roth has a number of these drawings, he tells me. "When Irving Howe, the critic, attacked me in *Commentary*," he recalls, "Philip did a drawing of an artist stabbing a critic to death. I've got it framed over my desk."

Clark Coolidge, a poet friend of my father's during those last years, remembers Philip consoling him over a bad review in *Poetry* magazine on one of his visits to Woodstock. "Philip kept patting me, saying, 'Don't worry. Don't worry about it,'" Clark says. "Actually I wasn't that worried about the review. But Philip seemed so concerned."

To my knowledge the following story about his friendship with Philip Roth is the only piece of its kind my father ever wrote.

THE APPOINTMENT (A TRUE STORY)

Once there were two Philips who were friends. One was a very famous writer, a celebrity, the other, a painter who had some degree of fame. Philip the Painter, who lived in the mountains and whose solitude was always being interrupted by the telephone, decided to put a stop to this thievery of time. He installed a switch that turned off the ringing telephone. This was a luxurious feeling for him, since he could telephone out to the outside world, but the outside world could not reach him at all.

Philip the Writer, who lived in the city (by preference, he once said, where he could roam the streets at will, eat in foreign restaurants, and taste all sorts of imported delicacies), had been trying to telephone Philip the Painter for six months. Then, after a trip to European cities, Philip the Writer tried again to telephone Philip the Painter. Again without success. Finally, Philip the Writer wrote this letter: "For Christ's sake let your phone ring. The world isn't just shit heads and monsters wanting to disturb you at your sacred foolishness—there's also me, your old pen and brush pal. Call me."

Philip the Painter waited a week before he telephoned Philip the Writer, whose answering service said he was busy and that he would telephone Philip the Painter. But remember, Philip the Painter's telephone couldn't ring, and since he again went back to his "sacred foolishness" in his studio, weeks went by. He received a second letter from Philip the Writer. This time in capital letters. "HOW CAN I CALL YOU BACK IF YOU WON'T ANSWER THE TELEPHONE? HUMANLY IMPOSSIBLE. TECHNOLOGICALLY IMPOSSIBLE. HOPELESS SITUATION, NO?" Then, as if they were secret agents, a designated time was chosen (through a third party, a neighbor) for Philip the Painter to telephone Philip the Writer. Philip the Writer couldn't believe his ears when Philip the Painter called. Philip the Writer pretended he wasn't home when he answered the phone call.

The dilemma was overcome when Philip the Writer agreed to visit Philip the Painter a week later for dinner and some talk. With the stern admonition, however, that since Philip the Writer couldn't telephone Philip the Painter, the appointment had to be firm and definite. This appointment made Philip the Painter more nervous than usual. He never knew from minute to minute how he felt. He couldn't control his moods, which changed like the shapes of clouds. The commitment to a definite time of meeting might mean that he would have to telephone Philip the Writer again in order to change the time of the meeting to a future time. Naturally, this made him even more nervous.

This story ends happily, however.

Through a new source of willpower, Philip the Painter overcame his nervousness and was calm as he prepared to entertain his friend, Philip the Writer. His determination was accomplished by the feeling of security that they would spend their evening, during and after dinner, leisurely discussing their mutual nervousness about the time stolen from their work by the world outside. He knew they would exchange their fears of the ringing telephone. Philip the Painter knew that he and Philip the Writer would speak of their miseries and would plan strategies to prevent the frightening theft of time.

It was a warm early spring day when I went to interview Philip Roth; midtown traffic could be heard through the open window of his hotel room. The immediacy and warmth of our conversation surprised me, as it had before from time to time in talking with my father's friends. Despite what he was telling me about the lightheartedness of their friendship, Philip the Writer seemed very sad as he talked about Philip the Painter. He was only in his late thirties then and twenty years my father's junior, he said; the passage of time had not been as poignant for him then, nor the sense of isolation.

"I sensed this terrible, terrible loneliness," Roth said. "It was crushing. He was alone in his work. He was alone in Woodstock. He was alone with Musa . . . I think I saw him at his best, protected by his house. But you pay a terrific price in loneliness for that protection, and it's torture for your mate . . . If you're working with excitement, you're a lovely fellow. But if it's not working out—or if you've been hammered in public, or slighted—but, particularly, if the work is not going well, that secluded life is a nightmare."

My mother had always suspected that the first of the Zuckerman novels was about them. A bit hesitantly, I asked about this, knowing that most writers of fiction hate such literal attempts to pin them down.

Philip Roth smiled. "Sure," he said. "In the world, they all thought Malamud, Singer . . . *The Ghost Writer* has a lot to do with Philip. And certainly I thought of Musa. . . . What I thought of was their situation. I did know something about being alone with a mate and this art obsession. It's like being a religious zealot."

The evenings they spent together in Woodstock were always great fun. "You'd get a sense of his gregariousness," Philip Roth said, "when they had six people over for pasta. But he couldn't leave the cave in which he hibernated because his nerves were too subtle for the travail outside. He was too wounded."

I sensed it too. After those two years of our not speaking, my connection with my father became gentler, more tender. Our hiatus had had some sort of cleansing effect. Gradually, we developed a different way of being together, based on my new profession. I was appointed his therapist ex officio. I was flattered by this role; it gave me a chance to test my hopeful theory that creativity and suffering did not have to be intertwined. My father played along with this. He would take me into his studio and confide his fears and doubts, and I would counsel him. He always acted as if I was amazingly helpful, which could scarcely have been the case.

Once, though, I surprised myself during one of these annual or semiannual visits. We were sitting at the drawing table in the studio, my father in his big red office chair, I on the swiveling oak stool. It was late on a winter afternoon, and getting dark. I'd been listening, mostly in silence, as he spoke about his frustrations and anxieties for several hours. As he reached over to switch on the light, I commented rather mildly, and without anger, that he almost never asked me how *I* was feeling, or what *my* struggles were.

He stopped in mid-sentence, opening his eyes wide, as if the thought had never occurred to him before. "You know, you're right," he said. "You're absolutely right. God, what a selfish creature I am. I get so wrapped up in my own stuff." He smiled tenderly and put his hand over mine. "Can you forgive me, darling?"

I nodded dumbly.

"*You* talk now," he said. "*I'll* listen."

As he sat there, waiting for me to speak, I was overcome with embarrassment. There was nothing I wanted to say. I didn't really want to confide in him. It was an old wish, the wish of a little girl wanting to climb into her father's lap to be comforted. And the time for that was long past.

Tom and I were married in May of 1976. My mother and father came out to Ohio for the wedding, which pleased me enormously (see plate 71). It was the first time they had visited me in the seven years I had lived in Yellow Springs. After the wedding party was over and we were all back at the house, Philip sat down at the kitchen table. David and Jonathan brought him their tempera paints and brushes and a pad of newsprint paper. While we looked on, my father gave my sons a drawing lesson, and painted one of his funny little cars with the two of them riding in it. "Now I can go home and *know* what it's like where you are!" my mother said, and her tone made me think rather wistfully of her visits to me in New York years before, when my father had left her.

At times, I knew, my mother felt isolated up in Woodstock. While my father painted, Musa kept herself busy, running errands, reading, working and reworking her poems. Philip needed her there, and she knew it. But she missed New York, missed going out and seeing people—not their friends, necessarily, but just people. She longed for the street life of the city. In desperation, she'd drive out to the Pinehill Bakery in Shokan, order a ham and egg on a seeded roll, and chat with the Swedish family who owned the place, or she'd sit at the counter at Duey's, in Woodstock, and have a vealette sandwich.

In 1976, she wrote "Honorarium," a short story told from the point of view of a painter living with his wife off in the woods.

It was autumn. The squirrels, invisible all summer, had been tearing around cutting down and burying their poems, which were in the shape of acorns. The oaks, several kinds of them, were turning deep shades of purple. My wife was going crazy with admiration for all the different leaf-shapes, and practically every book in the house was filled with leaves being pressed. To relieve a nagging suspicion that we were being buried alive, we often went out in the morning for coffee. To be with others. Garage mechanics, State Troopers, truck drivers, hunters, and, on weekends, churchgoers, and stunned city dwellers most likely from Queens bound for we always wondered where in the Catskills. Every one of them, automatically, without thinking about it, took a little of our burden onto them-

55. *Painter's Forms*, 1972.

56. My mother in the kitchen, Woodstock, 1975.

57. Philip with *The Studio*, 1969.

58. Philip with *Smoking I*, 1973.

59. The small panels (1968–70) hanging on the wall of my old studio were the beginning of a new figuration in my father's painting.

60. *Bad Habits*, 1970.

61. Philip Guston and Philip Roth, 1972.

62. My father often illustrated my mother's poetry.

63. Musa and Philip on the night of the Marlborough opening, 1970.

64. *Clock*, 1969.

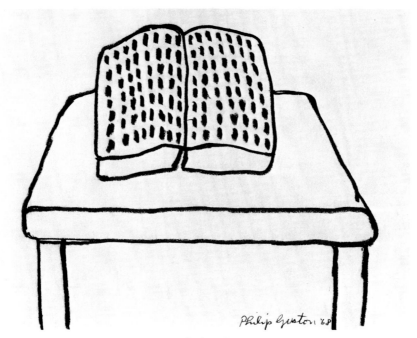

65. *Book*, 1968.

66. *Box Tree—Rome*, 1971.

67. *Sanctuary*, 1944.

68. *Alone*, 1971.

69. *Allegory*, 1975.

70. A wall of my father's studio.

71. My parents came out to Ohio when I married Tom Mayer in 1976.

72. *Source*, 1976.

73. *The Door*, 1976.

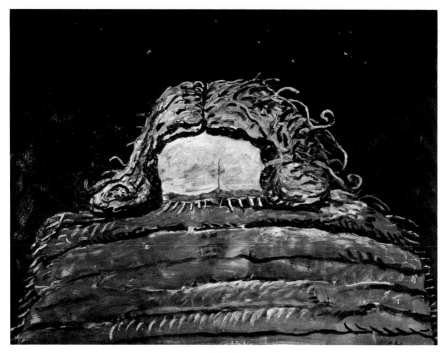

74. *Red Blanket*, 1977.

75. My sons, David and Jonathan, and I in Philip's studio, with *Monument*, 1976.

76. A late-night note from Philip to Musa.

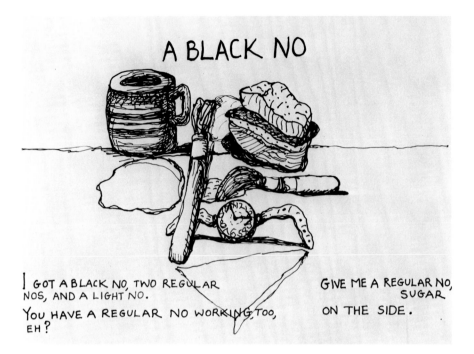

A BLACK NO

I GOT A BLACK NO, TWO REGULAR NOS, AND A LIGHT NO.

YOU HAVE A REGULAR NO WORKING TOO, EH?

GIVE ME A REGULAR NO, SUGAR ON THE SIDE.

77. This poem of Musa's was one of my father's favorites.

78. The family at Muir Woods, a few weeks before my father's death in 1980.

79. Untitled (Head), 1980.

80. Untitled (Ladder), 1980.

81. Philip in his studio, 1980.

selves. I presumed we did the same for them. At least I was out of the woods.

"I've been painting around the clock, 24 hours or more—sleep a bit and go back—it is totally uncontrollable now," my father wrote during the summer of 1976. "Phone has been off for months and I look at mail only when a painting is done. They are large, ten feet or so, and take complete possession of me. . . . It is a new "real" world now that I am making—and I can't stop. One to another and the sensation that there is always one picture—the last one. But then the need to staple up another canvas. Time—time! Is it my age or does it really take forty years or more to become an artist?"

Perhaps it had. "In these last years Guston was a man mad with painting," wrote Joseph Ablow, a colleague of my father's at Boston University, in a recent essay, "exploding with the energy of an artist who has discovered his full powers. He had also entered into his old age. Kenneth Clark has written about a group of artists—Rembrandt, Donatello, Michelangelo, Turner and Cézanne among them—who worked at the end of their lives in what Clark termed baldly 'an old age style.' This is a way of working not defined essentially by chronological age but by certain attitudes: a newly discovered freedom, a belief in instinct, a sense of isolation, a feeling of holy rage developing into what Clark calls a 'transcendental pessimism.' "

But age was taking its toll. My father's health was poor. His smoker's cough had gotten progressively worse; conversations with him were punctuated by a painful, strangled hacking that went on and on, until you wondered where the next breath could come from. Once, in New York, when we had gone to dinner and a movie, he'd had to leave in the middle of the film, his face pinched and white with pain. "This damned ulcer!" he said, and went back to the hotel to dose himself with vodka and milk.

"I hope I have the stamina and guts to enter old age as other artists have," he wrote. "I'm not sure at all that I do." His great sprints of work were interrupted constantly by health crises, his own and my mother's. In May of 1977, my mother had a series of small strokes. She was in the hospital a month; convalescence was expected to take a year. "Our way of life will have to change," he wrote despairingly. "Continued painting as I've been doing is for now, out."

But he kept on working anyway. Every day more of the geography of his inner world was being revealed to him. "If I speak of having a subject to paint," he scribbled one day during the late seventies, "I mean there is a forgotten place of beings and things, which I need to remember. I want to see this place. I paint what I want to see."

The stretch of years from 1974 until the time of my father's first heart attack, in March of 1979, was by far the most productive of the entire fifty-year span of his career. Dozens of huge canvases took shape on his wall—so many, finally, that he had to have another cinder block addition to his studio built to contain them. "They don't seem to be pictures anymore, but sort of confessions—exposures," he wrote. There were five one-man Guston shows at McKee Gallery during this six-year period—one of them in two installments to accommodate the many big paintings—and eight elsewhere in the U.S. and Europe. But still, no one was buying. Students and younger painters came in droves, but the critics still didn't know what to make of the strange, discomfiting images they were seeing.

"Officialdom still says thumbs down," he wrote. "You know, museums, big collectors, etc., but now, so say people, letters I get and so on, that my underground support is real and solid. Well, it pleases me mightily—sort of a real reward. The only one, no?"

In hindsight, it seems bitterly ironic that the art world finally "discovered" the late work in 1980, the year of my father's death. "This return to prominence seemed almost a resurrection," Robert Storr writes in his book on Philip Guston, "and it is perhaps tempting to romanticize Guston's comeback as another example of the myth of the genius belatedly, if not posthumously, discovered. But Guston was neither unknown nor forgotten; rather, he had been placed under a kind of critical 'house arrest.'"

This house arrest, however disheartening it may have been for him during the 1970s, did give Philip the time and space to develop his new work unencumbered. And his loneliness was eased by visits from friends like Clark Coolidge.

"We would always begin by complaining," Clark recalls. The first two hours of every visit, he says, were spent in mutual complaints about the worlds of poetry and art. "Nobody discriminates," Philip would lament. Then my father would cook something for dinner, and the two men would sit, talking and drinking, for another two or three hours. "Then, at last, and almost reluctantly, as if we weren't really there to do that at all, we'd go into the studio to see the new work." Clark would move from one painting to another, excited, telling stories. Finally, late at night, back they'd go to the kitchen, to have a melted cheese toasted under the broiler.

It was quite an experience, visiting Woodstock during this time. You never knew what you were going to see. A disembodied overcoat, shoes packed under its arms, a rising red tide that threatened to drown, a wide eye staring resolutely at a bottle of booze, an open pit above which a painting-within-a-painting depicted fire raining down on a red sea. Just when you'd had enough horror, there'd be something funny or touching or lovely—a sandwich with a bite out of it; my mother's face, haloed, saintlike; a pair of apples huddled together; or a row of cherries, their stems like grenade pins (in 1981, Patterson Sims, of the Whitney Museum, eager for an iconographic point of reference, asked me if this painting, *Cherries* [1976] wasn't really the Last Supper—together, we counted the twelve cherries, one of them black). Certainly, the images seemed emblematic, unmovable—a white ladder scaled by a pair of stringy legs against a background of pacific blue, the beaded pull of a light cord. And everywhere there were legs—feet and shoes and legs.

The strangeness of these works is invoked by their sheer inviolability. Whatever else they may be, they are undeniably real. They exist. It is as if the paintings are windows on another world, some crazy parallel universe with a logic all its own. Finally, my father had managed to capture the otherworldly quality he so admired in artists like Piero, de Chirico, and Picasso.

"De Chirico's thought was not willed," my father scribbled on an undated sheet of notepaper. "It was so perfectly balanced that his forms never seem to have been painted. His walls and shadows, his trains and cookies, his mannequins, clocks, blackboards and smoke. They could all disappear. Yet they appeared. They have known each other for centuries. De Chirico drew aside his curtain, revealing what was always there. It had been forgotten.

"Picasso, the builder, re-peopled the earth—inventing new beings. We believe his will.

"Marvelous artists are made of elements which cannot be identified.

The alchemy is complete. Their work is strange, and will never become familiar."

During this period, Ross Feld often came up to Woodstock to see my father's new work. A slight man, possessed of a quick wit and powerful tenderness, he understood this strangeness. "It's what Kafka knew also," he wrote. "That beyond imagination, all is calm—and triply terrible, since the mind there, bespelled, surrenders its freedom. Past a certain point, nothing is more 'normal' or 'regular' than the odd; and whatever it was that brought this image of dismembered limbs to Guston—nightmare, intriguing structural complexity, remembrance—whatever it was, he goes about illustrating it innocently and generously, as parents are innocent and generous who add to the world they know not what."

Increasingly plagued by ill health, my father continued to plunge into this world, day after day. It wasn't easy for him. "One time, in Woodstock," Ross Feld said, "I stood next to Guston in front of some of these canvases. I hadn't seen them before; I didn't really know what to say. For a time, then, there was silence. After a while, Guston took his thumbnail away from his teeth and said, 'People, you know, complain that it's horrifying. As if it's a picnic for me, who has to come in here every day and see them first thing. But what's the alternative? I'm trying to see how much I can stand.' "

NINE

Coronary Care

Dawn, 1971.

"I called to see how your father was doing." Mark Clark, a friend who lived in Virginia, was on the phone. It was March 1979, and I was standing in the kitchen of our house in Ohio.

"My father?" I repeated woodenly. "What about my father?"

The Chrysler Museum in Norfolk, Virginia, where Mark was a curator, had been about to mount a Philip Guston exhibition, he told me. David McKee had just called to cancel the show, saying that my father had suffered a massive heart attack.

"God, I'm sorry," Mark said. "I can't believe you didn't know."

I called my mother, letting the phone ring and ring. No answer at the house in Woodstock. Maybe they were out for dinner. Maybe . . . But no. Two more phone calls and I knew what Mark had told me was true. My father was a patient in the Coronary Care Unit at Benedictine Hospital in Kingston, New York. I asked to speak to the nursing station there, and was told that my father had that morning suffered a second serious heart attack after his first three days before, and was now in critical condition. There was more, the nurse said; her voice sounded irritated. My father was agitated, delusional, and disturbing the other patients in the Coronary Care Unit.

I hung up and walked into the bedroom. I sat there on the bed, shaking. Three days ago! It was intolerable that I couldn't be there, immediately, with him. Surely I could do something, anything. I dialed Woodstock again, listened to the phone ring and ring, then slammed the receiver back in its cradle.

Looking back on it now, I can see that it was just as well I couldn't reach my mother at that moment. I was beside myself. Why hadn't I been called? Didn't they care how I felt? Didn't she realize how important this was to me? But I knew perfectly well why my mother hadn't called. We were trying not to worry you, she would say, if I pressed her. We didn't want to burden you with our problems. Oh yes, I knew all about my parents' exaggerated sense of privacy, the way they guarded their lives against intrusions. And that I was not supposed to feel slighted by this; it had only to do with my father's need to work. The same old story. But I did feel slighted. I had never resigned myself to the fact that I could be seen as an unwelcome intrusion.

There had been other serious illnesses these past years; often I found out about them only months later, by prying information from my mother. I suppose I seemed very remote to them, living seven hundred miles away, in Ohio. And yes, some part of me was always relieved to find out after the fact, relieved to have escaped the usual filial tasks, the demands and obligations most of my friends labored under with their aging parents. But I hated being in this state of vigilance, this perpetual worry that something terrible would occur without my knowledge. And now it had.

One thing seemed clear that night—they didn't need me. There were always devoted people in the wings—students, friends—people ready to lend assistance. No, it was just as well my mother wasn't home at that moment. I would have railed at her. And she didn't need that. Not then.

There were no more flights to New York from Dayton or Columbus that evening. I would have to wait until the morning. It would be late afternoon by the time I got to Kingston.

I stood there over the half-empty suitcase, trying to pack, unable to think of what I might need to take with me. Finally, after repeated calls, my mother was at home. Her voice trembling, she told me how the heart attack had happened. My father had been on the phone talking with Mercedes Matter, an old friend, when it began. Abruptly ending the conversation, he had staggered into the kitchen, vomited into the sink, and collapsed, unconscious, on the floor. The emergency squad had taken him to the hospital.

From the way she spoke of my father's condition in the most indefinite of terms, it was clear that she didn't understand what a heart attack was, exactly. Or how bad his had been. How did he seem now? I asked. What did the doctors say? She wasn't able to tell me that either, at least not in any detail. I wondered what they had told her. Sensing her fragility, had they withheld information? Or had she simply forgotten? Hearing the only slightly submerged panic in her voice, I tried to be as comforting as possible.

Since her stroke two years before, my mother's short-term memory had become very poor. She had difficulty with words, particularly with names, and with grasping the meaning of events and their consequences.

It was worse when she was tired or upset. This wasn't only the stroke, though. My mother had always been a tenderhearted and innocent woman who wept easily, who would shrink away from anything to do with pain or illness. In a way, the stroke had only exaggerated her natural and rather sweet vagueness of temperament, while her poetic response to life, her love of the unusual gesture, the odd detail, had been retained.

"I don't see why they have to keep him in that dreadful place," my mother said tearfully. I mumbled something about how they probably had to monitor his heart, but I knew what she meant. My father was a chronic insomniac; he easily became stir-crazy. Once, visiting me in New Haven, unable to sleep, he had insisted they leave to drive back to Woodstock in the middle of the night. If a single night in a guest room made him claustrophobic, I could imagine how imprisoned he must feel in a Coronary Care Unit. I remembered hearing something about an abortive visit to Johns Hopkins Hospital in Baltimore for a checkup a year or two earlier when my father had signed himself out after the first few days of tests and fled back to Woodstock, undiagnosed.

I wanted to be there with him, yet I dreaded seeing him robbed of his vitality and privacy. Out of context, out of his studio and away from his work, my father might lose that patina of greatness he wore so well, that sense of being larger than life, and become just another sick and frightened old man. I need not have been afraid of that. If anything, the opposite was true. Even now, after all that has happened, that same ideal, heroic statue of a father still manages to stand, somewhere in the center of me. But more pressing than my fear of seeing him weak and helpless was another, stronger impulse, something more elemental. I just wanted to be with him. I wanted to touch him, and be touched by him, before he died.

My father's bed lay at the end of a long line, painfully circuitous and slow to unfold, a line that began in the cold, wet March dawn in Yellow Springs, Ohio, and extended all that next day across the flat grays and browns of Ohio, Pennsylvania, New Jersey, then up through the drab winter-bearded foothills of the Catskills along the New York Thruway, finally into the city of Kingston, the hospital corridors, to my mother's pale face, latticed with worry, as she walked behind me, in through the twin doors that said QUIET, PLEASE!

The beds in the Coronary Care Unit of Benedictine Hospital were arranged like spokes in a wheel around a central nursing station. Harsh fluorescent lights spread their white glare on the banks of monitors, the white beds, the chrome equipment. Human sounds were overtaken by the clicking, beeping machines. A frightening place, calculated for efficiency.

Other patients looked up at us as we passed. My mother hung back, as if she didn't want to approach him. It was my turn. At this last moment, I became afraid again; after coming all this way, I wanted to leave. My father's bed was cranked up as high as it would go. With the side rails up, the bed looked like a big crib. I looked at the form in the bed, the bulk of it seeming both large and insubstantial at the same time. Maybe it wouldn't be my father, I thought. But then I recognized the unmistakable shape of his big feet and I knew that it was. I approached the bed. His wrists were tied with strips of cloth to the two side rails. Angry tears sprang into my eyes. They had put my father in restraints! As I approached him, he began thrashing weakly, moaning something unintelligible. I stood over him a few moments, unable to speak.

"Philip," I said, finally. "It's me, Ingie. I'm here." I took his hand, which was hot and dry, and he quieted, his eyes seeking, then focusing, on my face. He said my name, thickly, and tried to smile. I could hardly bear it, seeing him like this. Convinced that I had to be strong for him, for my mother, I stood there fighting my tears, looking down at him. His color was a ghastly gray-green under the cold white light. Wires emerged from nipplelike circles glued to his hairy barrel chest leading to a cardiac monitor that made uneven green zigzags over his head. My father had for years combed a long growth of hair over the bald place on the crown of his head; this mostly white plume of hair was wild now and stood out from his head on the pillow in a sad, long tuft. His deeply set eyes were dark, and glittering with fear.

He began mumbling something about Nazis and interrogations. As he tried to speak, his tongue lolled in his mouth as if it didn't belong there—this from the Thorazine they'd given him when he'd begun to hallucinate the day before.

Leaning on the side rail of his bed, holding his hand, I tried to understand what he was telling me. I forgot to be afraid as I tried to piece together what he was saying. From what I could tell, he wasn't delusional any longer. He knew where he was. He knew why. He seemed, in fact, to have a much firmer grasp on his condition than my mother did. He reported, with more fascination than alarm, it seemed to me, his remarkable experience of the night before. SS officers had come for him, he said. He remembered their polished black boots, the click of their heels. When I told him this had been a hallucination, he said, "Really?" He thought about this for a minute, then looked at me sheepishly. "Do you really think so?"

I nodded. "Why did they tie you up?" I asked, touching the cloth that bound his wrists.

"I think I tried to fight. I remember kicking one of them," he said, with a small bad-boy's smile that was incredibly heartening. "I was trying to get out of here," he said.

I looked around at the chrome and glass and tile, at the stupid half-length shower curtains that were supposed to provide privacy. "I don't blame you," I said.

There was a weak pressure from the hand that still held mine. "I'm so glad you're here," he said, and closed his eyes.

After a few hours had passed with no further incident, the nurses, seeing that he had calmed down considerably, agreed to untie the restraints and to call me that night if my father became agitated again. When I left him, he was sleeping quietly.

By the next morning the more obvious effects of the Thorazine had worn off. His speech was no longer thick and he seemed less drowsy. I waited outside the CCU while the cardiologist examined him, then waylaid the doctor in the hall and asked for my father's condition. Did his dour face usually carry such a gloomy expression?

"It's too early to tell, after this last episode," the doctor said. He lifted his eyes from the floor. "You must realize, your father is very weak."

Very weak. I knew that doctors often spoke in code, that the meaning was there if I cared to recognize it. What was he saying? My father still seemed so full of life. Even in that dreadful place, I could feel the force of his intelligence.

Like my father—and unlike my mother—I have always hungered to know where things stand. Some people prefer not to know how serious an illness is; leaving a grim prognosis hazy and indefinite allows for hope. They'll actually say they don't want to know. I've never understood that. I always find myself imagining the worst, anyway. The truth is usually a relief. I wanted to know exactly what the doctor meant.

I glanced at my mother, who was sitting nearby. Since I had arrived, she'd allowed me to handle things, giving me her trust in the same childlike way she permitted my father to make most of the decisions and plans in their lives. Now she was sitting there on a bench in the hospital hallway, letting me talk to the doctors, too.

I lowered my voice. "Yes, but how bad is it?"

The doctor shook his head. "It doesn't look good. His heart has suffered a tremendous insult. . . ."

I looked at him levelly, waiting for him to finish the sentence he'd let trail off so delicately. He didn't.

"Shouldn't he know?" I finally asked.

"No. I don't think that would be wise," he said, frowning. "He's had quite enough stress as it is."

"I'd want to know, if it was me."

"Look, let's just hope for the best, shall we?" the doctor said, putting his hand on my arm. "I've asked for a psychiatric consult. I trust that's OK with you and your mother?"

I nodded. "What made him hallucinate like that?"

He shrugged. "Hard to tell. People sometimes lose their sense of reality in the CCU. Tell me, how much was your father drinking, Mrs. Mayer?"

"I—I don't really know. Not that much, I think. Why?"

"There's a good chance he may be suffering from delirium tremens."

I knew he drank to calm his nerves and relieve pain; his preferred treatment, when his ulcer bothered him, was a glass of vodka and milk. Come to think of it, while we sat and talked, my father was usually drinking something from a jelly glass. And there were refills, too, repeated trips to the pantry, where the liquor was kept.

I tried to think back, to remember. I had never even seen him drunk. Or had I? The truth was, I had never seen him *acting* drunk—out of control, tearful or belligerent, slurring his words, falling down or passing out. None of the conventional signs. But I had worked with drug abusers; I knew enough about addictive behavior and alcoholism to know that all drunks didn't behave that way. Could it be? Maybe alcohol was actually *causing* some of his awful swings of anxiety and depression, rather than providing relief. One thing was certain: I didn't like thinking of my father as a sick man. Not this kind of sick.

In his studio that evening, I looked at his paintings. It wasn't as if he had hidden anything; the signs were clearly there. I simply hadn't wanted to see. In *The Desire,* painted only the year before, a fist lies on a high red wall, clenched, as if to avoid clasping the highball glass beside it. And *Head and Bottle,* from 1975, has his lima bean–shaped head with its enormous, all-seeing eye glaring down fixedly at an empty green bottle. When I opened the kitchen cabinet my parents used for their medications, there were bottles and bottles of pills meant to help with anxiety and insomnia—Librium, Valium, Seconal, Dalmane.

Now, years after my father's death, when I tell Norman Burg, the internist who treated both my parents for years, that I am writing about my father, he stops examining my mother and gets a distant look in his eyes. "Yeah, he was quite a guy." He sighs and shakes his head. "Remember when he had the d.t.'s? That took me completely by surprise. I knew he took a drink now and then, but I had no idea. No idea. Did you?" I shake my head. "I guess he had us all fooled," Dr. Burg says.

Hearing this now, I feel vindicated, a little. But at the time I remember feeling shocked and guilty, as if I could have done something, had I known. I glanced at my mother. I could hardly blame her. But *someone* should have seen what was happening. Someone should have been able to do *something* before it came to this. I looked at the cardiologist, then stared at the floor of the hospital corridor. "I guess I could try to find out from my mother how much he was drinking," I ventured doubtfully.

"Why don't you do that," the doctor said.

After he left, I sat down in the hallway on the bench beside my mother. "The doctor says Philip is very weak," I said. A crowd of chatty candy-stripers passed by in the hallway, silencing us with their cheerful banter. We sat there without speaking until the elevator doors had closed on them.

I didn't tell my mother anything more. She didn't need to know my father was close to death, I reasoned; why face it unless she had to? And why should I upset her with questions about his drinking? She wouldn't be able to tell me anything. For all my training, it never occurred to me that I was retaliating against her for having withheld the news of my father's heart attack.

Ten minutes of every hour, they let visitors into the CCU. When the next visiting period came around, I told my father there was a chance he might not recover from this second, more serious heart attack, that the next day or so would tell the story. He listened with his eyes closed, then looked up at me and began to weep, silently, tears welling up and sliding down his cheeks into his ears.

"I want Kaddish said for me," he whispered. "It's very important. Tell Musa. There are three men I want to say Kaddish for me. Do you understand?" I nodded. The three men were Morton Feldman, Philip Roth, and Ross Feld—the three dearest and deepest friends of his life. "But my poor dear Musa," he murmured. "What will happen to her?" Thinking of my mother brought fresh tears. I tried to reassure him that I would take care of her as best I could.

In the few minutes that followed, there were other instructions, too, about what he wanted done with his work. "After what happened to Mark," he said, "I didn't want anything like a foundation. I never knew what to do about it."

Vaguely I knew what he was referring to, at least that the Rothko Foundation scandal had been a nightmare for everyone involved. Of all my father's contemporaries, Mark Rothko had been the most obsessively concerned over the way his work was exhibited and sold—and that obsession had led to the forming of this foundation. It was painfully ironic.

Knowing how little I understood of Philip's life in the art world, and sensing, perhaps, the role that I might be called upon to play when he died, my father educated me that day in the Coronary Care Unit, making me privy for the first and only time to his intentions. This conversation was something I have been grateful for many times since, in moments of doubt. In a weak voice, pausing frequently for breath, he made sure I knew about the people he trusted, about their loyalty to him.

When I left him that day, I was sure I had done the right thing. But as it turned out, my father's stamina and tenacity had not abandoned him, after all. To the doctor's surprise, he made it through that day and the next. By then, it appeared that the immediate danger was past.

Strangely, he seemed better able to deal with the imminence of his death—perhaps all those years of reading Kafka and Kierkegaard and thinking about death had prepared him for it—those next days and weeks than he was with the continuation of his life, with his body's ongoing and progressive betrayals, with all the petty indignities and humiliations a hospital stay was bound to exact from him.

Illness and death had been much on my father's mind since my mother's stroke in 1977. His painting had taken a decidedly more somber and personal turn since then. Image after image of mortality filled his work. Rising black or red tides threatened to drown. The heads that managed to keep barely afloat were unmistakably those of my parents. Sometimes they were entrapped in elaborate spiders' webs; still other paintings showed them huddled in bed together.

As he began to recover, it became increasingly difficult for my father to tolerate the atmosphere of the Coronary Care Unit, especially the loss of dignity and privacy. Once I came in to find him sitting on a bedside potty, glowering. The constant harsh lighting and noisy machines, the chatter of nurses and the groans of the other patients, and the occasional episodes of cardiac arrest were deeply upsetting to him. He continually complained of being unable to sleep. As he became stronger, he became a fractious and difficult patient—demanding, complaining, arguing. Though he could barely stand up unaided, he begged to be released. He refused their food. At first, the nurses treated him with an amused tolerance, but then, as he became harder to deal with, they began to show a condescension toward him, as if he were a child. Finally, there were moments of outright hostility.

One day a new nurse sailed in with a flurry of efficiency. "And how are we today?" she asked breezily.

" 'We' are terrible. 'We' are dreadful. 'We' would like to get the hell out of here," my father muttered, fixing her with his baleful glance.

I watched the nurse's brittle smile harden. "Is there anything I can get for you, Mr. Guston?" she asked.

"A nice stiff whiskey and a cigarette would be fine."

Her face became serious. "Oh now, you know I couldn't do that."

My father let his head sink back on the pillow. "Then just leave me alone," he whispered bitterly.

When my mother and I were there he was calm enough, but when we weren't the nurses had no time to make my father the center of their attention. They had other, sicker patients there now, patients my father was disturbing.

I was used to making allowances for my father. I had learned to excuse his dark moods, his self-involvement, his unpredictability as the necessary foibles of his genius. In my mind at least—and in my mother's—my father was exempt from ordinary standards of conduct. And there was usually a greater or lesser degree of worshipful adulation going on when I had occasion to see my father with other people. By turns loquacious, witty, and philosophical, he was accustomed to attention. Students clustered around him, awaiting words of wisdom, collectors were fascinated with his stories.

That's what I was used to. Seeing how people in the hospital reacted to my father came as a shock to me. Here he was, at his worst, ranting and raving at the poor hospital staff, who were no better, no worse than any other such staff—at times inattentive and frustrating, at other times surprisingly considerate—and they were treating him exactly as they might anyone else who gave them problems.

I tried to intervene. Couldn't he be moved to a private room? Well, yes, they said, his heart could be watched through telemetry that broadcast an EKG signal down the hall to their monitors. But he had to have someone with him at all times. My mother and I assured the nurses we would be there. We began spelling each other at the hospital, taking turns spending the nights as well as the days there, on a small, sprung bed that folded up into a hassock by day. My father slept, but I didn't. I don't know if my mother did. What I remember is lying awake in that hot, airless hospital room, listening to his groans and snores. At least once a night, a nurse would come running in, concerned; in his sleep, my father had dislodged one of the several EKG leads attached to his chest. It made for an exhausting routine.

One afternoon, my father asked for pencil and paper to do some drawings. When he was asleep, I took them from his hands and looked at them in the dim light. One was a humorous portrait of himself in the hospital bed, a sort of reverse get-well card to the McKees, with a heart pierced by an arrow. There was a special message for Gavin McKee, David's ten-year-old son, and a picture of Alfie, their dog. They reminded me of the drawings he'd done for my sons after my wedding to Tom three years before, caricatures of people he'd seen that day, with captions like "hungry person at the wedding" and "angry person at the wedding."

A psychiatrist began coming around for visits. He was a short, rotund man with a halo of curly hair and round glasses, and his air of false conviviality put me off immediately. The first time I had met him outside the CCU as he was about to interview my father, he asked me what kind of work I did. On learning that I was a counselor, he handed me the thick book he was carrying. "You'll find this interesting, then," he said, smiling, his little round eyes beaming at me. I sat in the hallway and leafed through the book while he spoke with my father. It was on anorexia nervosa, a collection of theoretical essays on object relations and eating disorders, written in the most impenetrable analytic jargon.

On the psychiatrist's second visit to my father, I asked if I could stay in the room. I was curious about the man's techniques. Listening to him, I had to suppress a smile. He was attempting to do with my father exactly what he had tried to do with me: Establish a Relationship. It was a patently obvious, transparent maneuver. "I understand you're an artist," the psychiatrist said. My father nodded. "Well, what kind of painting do you do?" he asked.

"What kind of painting?" Of course my father had been asked this question hundreds of times. I could tell he was playing with the doctor, making it difficult for him.

"Yes. I mean do you paint abstracts or landscapes or portraits? Are they realistic or what?"

"At times they seem very real to me."

"Or maybe surrealism, like what's his name—Salvador Dali. I like his work very much."

"Do you?" my father said.

"Yes, well, Dali is very expressive, isn't he? Symbolic. But what kind of painting do *you* do?"

"I wouldn't know how to describe it to you," my father said wearily. "You would have to see it."

"I'd like to. Is your work in any museums?"

My father closed his eyes and didn't answer. I jumped in, unable to resist. This man simply inspired smugness. "Have you ever heard of the Museum of Modern Art in New York?" I asked sweetly. He nodded. "Well, how about the Guggenheim or the Metropolitan Museum of Art?"

"Very impressive," the psychiatrist said. I could visualize him rubbing his chubby hands together, beaming with satisfaction at the prospect of taking on a famous patient. What he couldn't have known was that my father didn't like to talk about painting, especially his own painting, except with other artists and writers. When he was with other people, he wanted to know what they did. And actually, he was quite interested in therapy and psychology, although somewhat suspicious of it, too. He had read all of Freud and Jung. We had often discussed the different personality theories related to my work as a counselor.

The psychiatrist began to question him about the past. "Tell me a little about your childhood, Mr. Guston. Where did you grow up? What did your parents do? Did you have brothers and sisters?"

My father groaned. "Oh, God. What good does it do, at my age, to resurrect all the old ghosts?"

"Age is hardly a factor in these matters." The psychiatrist drew himself up. "And, as you so rightly imply, the past can return to haunt you."

"Yes, well . . ." Philip was silent for a moment. "Surely you know what Rilke said on the subject."

"Who?"

"Rainer Maria Rilke. The great German poet. He said, on refusing to enter psychoanalysis, 'I am afraid, if my devils leave me, my angels will take flight as well.' "

I've forgotten the psychiatrist's facetious response, but I remember that my father and I exchanged a look. It was clear to both of us, I think, that this man couldn't be much help beyond prescribing medication and acting as intermediary with the nursing staff.

"But *you* understand me, Ingie, don't you?" my father said when the psychiatrist had left. "Talking with you always helps me. If that doctor were half as smart as you, then . . ." He smiled as I blushed, pleased. My father was capable of the most shameless flattery.

But such moments were few. For the most part, Philip was cantankerous and difficult. By the time I left, a week or so later, to go back to my job and family in Ohio, I had very nearly exhausted my fund of patience. I was relieved to go.

For days, he'd been begging me to smuggle in cigarettes for him. At first, I'd resisted, but eventually I gave in after he spoke passionately, and with anger, about not wanting to make any compromises in his life. Even if it killed him. Which it was evidently going to do, if things went on as they had been. His dour-faced cardiologist had made that quite clear. Even if my father would stop smoking and drinking, the doctor wasn't optimistic. After two weeks of caring for my father, of putting up with his moods and petulance, I was furious at this cavalier attitude about smoking. Here we were, trying to keep him alive; it was as if he was determined to do himself in. No compromises, indeed! *He* might be ready to die, but what about what I was ready for? What about my mother? How could he be so damn selfish?

Cigarettes were part of him; they appear everywhere in his work. Almost every photograph of my father I've ever seen shows him smoking. In a painting that hangs in my study now, entitled *Language II*, among the familiar symbols of the shoe, the wheel, the manhole cover, the green glass shade, is the image of a cup of coffee with a butt in a little cloud above it, that represents, as my father told me, "a cup of coffee dreaming of a cigarette."

It was he who had given me my first cigarette, at fifteen. Only three years before my father's heart attack, Tom and I had finally managed to give up smoking. I'd been able to relinquish my two-pack-a-day habit only with great difficulty. Now I was something of a crank on the subject. I tried to persuade him to stop. Even though I tried to convince him that it could be done, that he could quit, I knew that a fifty-year habit of three to four packs a day wouldn't be given up unless he really wanted to, which he clearly did not. No compromises, he said. Sick with myself for doing it, I finally gave in and brought him his cigarettes. But I felt like a traitor, putting that pack of Camels in his hand.

I walked off the plane into my husband's arms and wept openly for the first time since I had left Ohio. Every muscle in my body ached from the tension of the last two weeks. I was exhausted.

My father was discharged from the hospital a couple of weeks later. I waited a few days before calling my mother to see how things were going. My last act, before leaving, had been to hire a practical nurse to help my mother take care of my father after he went home. This was my idea. She was a stand-in for myself, I suppose, to lessen my guilt about leaving my parents in such a bad way. An officious, opinionated woman with her own way of doing things, this nurse had turned out to be exactly the sort of woman my father couldn't stand. I smiled at my mother's description, imagining some hefty Brünnhilde in a white uniform bathing my father, him glaring at her. There was an awkward silence on the line before my mother told me, rather apologetically, that they had fired her on the second day.

After months of slow recovery, my father was able to begin painting again. The works of that year are small; he hadn't the stamina to stand and paint large canvases. "The truth is I am an old man," he wrote his friend Bill Berkson in August of 1979. "I always knew it was a *pact* and the *price* to pay. So the hell with it. I can't drive and the docs say it will be a year anyway to get back to 'normal' if I 'live right'—i.e., change my way of life—and who the hell is going to do that?"

My visit had left an impression. My father painted a picture of me sometime that summer or fall, the only image of me as an adult that exists in his work. Not one of his best efforts, the painting remains, blessedly, untitled; it may be an affectionate portrait, but it is far from flattering. But why should he flatter me? Why should I be exempt from his honesty? No one else was. His late self-portraits are merciless, and in his last images of my mother the ravages of her illness are dissected and laid bare. Perhaps I should be grateful I didn't draw more of his fire. There in the painting is my curly hair, yes, and a pair of roly-poly shoulders that suggest the extra twenty pounds I carry around. A string of pearls is around my neck; my eyes are inexplicably crossed.

What is so disturbing to me about this picture? Why am I always so embarrassed when Tom pulls it out to show to visiting friends? I'm not so thin-skinned and humorless that I can't see that it's funny. It's not a likeness, after all; it's clearly more caricature than portrait.

For a long time, my reaction continued to mystify me. Only recently have I understood that what disturbs me about this painting is its precise, ruthless statement of the relationship between the painter and his subject. It is a companion piece to one of the same size he called *Nurse*, a portrait of Sue, one of the RNs at the hospital—the only one, as I remember, who had a sense of humor, who could kid my father out of his black moods. With her, I was cast in the role of caretaker. That was who I was, to him. No more, no less. And I knew it then; wasn't that why I had come to Woodstock, after all—to take care of him? But still, it hurts to know that *he* saw it too, so clearly. It cruelly punctures my fantasy. Deflated, I can no longer entertain the hope that somehow, through taking care of my father, I had come to mean more to him, not as his nurse, but as his daughter.

At home in Ohio, I became immersed in my life again, seeing my patients, taking care of my own family, and turning over the soil in the garden for spring planting, preparing to sow the early seeds. Woodstock, the hospital in Kingston, all of what had happened began gradually to recede, as such things do.

But some part of me was vigilant, all that year, always just waiting for that phone call from Woodstock, that inevitable phone call I knew one day would come.

TEN

Openings

Untitled, 1975.

In 1980, the San Francisco Museum of Modern Art had a second major Philip Guston retrospective—the first such comprehensive exhibition of his work since the show at the Guggenheim Museum in 1962. It contained more than one hundred paintings and drawings, and traveled to Chicago, Denver, Washington, and New York.

That April, as if in rehearsal for the opening of the retrospective, I promised my father I'd go to another exhibition of his paintings, in Akron, Ohio, since he wasn't well enough to attend the opening himself and it was only a few hours' drive from where we lived. It was the first opening I'd been to since the one in Boston six years earlier, and the first—but by no means the last, though of course I didn't realize that then—I'd attended in his place.

Tom and I stood around awkwardly, drinking white wine out of plastic glasses, admiring the installation of the eight large paintings, the renovation of the museum, not knowing quite what to say to the museum staff. I was grateful for the Dixieland band that played in the entryway, making talk difficult. I tried to be as gracious as I could, but inside I felt as stiff as one of the George Segal sculptures that peopled the other half of the museum. I phoned my father that night. "The show looks terrific," I told him, because it had.

"Wait until next month," he said. I was pleased and a bit surprised to hear the excitement in his voice. It wasn't what I expected.

I told him I was looking forward to seeing the show in San Francisco. But I had never enjoyed my father's openings; in fact I dreaded them when I was a child. Each one was different, of course: different galleries, dealers, paintings, guests. But Egan or Janis, Marlborough or Peridot, museum or gallery, uptown or down, the things that bothered me remained constant: the crush of people, the loud voices and smoke, the incomprehensible talk.

My father hated openings, too, particularly his own. Those of his friends he found merely tedious, I think, but sometimes trying, too. I remember him groaning aloud at the prospect of going to another painter's opening, a man whom he liked but whose work he felt was mediocre. Philip had it in him to be a loyal friend, a friend who was exquisitely sensitive to the impact of criticism or indifference, and so the business of finding something to say to the artist whose work he didn't care for—or worse, thought was canny, commercial—the problem of striking a balance between insult and falsehood weighed heavily on him.

"After the show at the Jewish Museum in 1966," he told an audience at the University of Minnesota in 1978, "I must have done hundreds of paintings of shoes, books, hands, buildings and cars, just everyday objects. . . . I couldn't produce enough. I couldn't go to New York, to openings of friends of mine like Rothko, de Kooning, Newman. I would telephone Western Union with all kinds of lies such as that my teeth were falling out, or that I was sick. It was such a relief not to have anything to do with modern art. It felt as if a big boulder had been taken off my shoulders."

Even during the heyday of abstract expressionism, there was very little painting being done that my father cared to go and see. He sometimes told this anecdote: "At the first exhibition of Barnett Newman's painting, de Kooning was in the gallery. We left together in total silence, down the elevator and through to the street. More silence. Then after a coffee he said, 'Well, now we don't have to think about *that* anymore.' "

During the fifties, when my father's work was often copied, de Kooning once remarked, "Well, Phil, they're imitating you now instead of me, putting all the paint in the middle. They always imitate the part you most hate about your own work."

Picasso, Léger, Mondrian, de Chirico—and a precious few other twentieth-century painters—notwithstanding, it was the Italian Renaissance masters my father loved the best. In 1973, he made a painting he called *Pantheon*. In it are two of his perennial studio symbols: an easel holding a primed, waiting canvas, and a naked light bulb, the source of illumination for an artist who painted at night, as he had since that boyhood closet in Los Angeles. In this painting, the names of five artists hover in the anxious air of the studio: Masaccio, Piero, Giotto, Tiepolo, and de Chirico. He would sometimes tell a story, his half-joking, half-serious fantasy of meeting the great masters in heaven, when he had gained acceptance into that confraternity, of one of them patting him on the back and saying, "Not bad, sonny. *Pas mal.*"

Because of his own early acclaim, my father struggled for almost fifty years with the problems of recognition and success—and the lack of it—fighting to maintain his privacy and integrity from the onslaughts of public expectations. Certainly, he understood how seductive fame could be; he must, at times, have longed to rest in some comfortable, easy niche rather than take the risks he did. Openings would not have been these grueling public occasions at which the painter, naked and defenseless, offered himself to the world.

But my father's openings were excruciating to him, especially during the fifties—or perhaps this is simply the period, the Sidney Janis openings, that I remember most vividly—preceded as they always were by days and weeks of paralyzing indecision and anxiety on my father's part. Was he doing the right thing, showing the work now? Would the critics, the public understand? Or would this show prove to be another lacerating exercise in futility?

It would have started out well enough, of course. These things always did. At the show's inception, there would have been a first flush of enthusiasm—like the starry-eyed beginnings of some new love affair—for the new dealer, or for the mending of fences with a former dealer. After the months of hard work and self-doubt in the studio, how could it not be an intoxicating thing for an artist to have someone believe in his work so unreservedly? However independent of spirit he considered himself to be, how could he resist the siren's song of commercial success without compromise?

My father was no more immune to this than anyone else, at least not then, in those early years. After months of isolation in his studio, he would feel pleased at the dealer's attentions, basking in the glow of friendly blandishments. There would be a flurry of dinner engagements, visits to Woodstock, long evenings spent in comradely drinking and high-flying aesthetic talk. Hearing only the hinted, tantalizing possibilities of museum purchases and exhibitions, the rumors of collectors who cared about art, who covered museum walls with their gifts, and who were eager to see *his* work, my father would almost forget what had happened all the other times. Was *this*, finally, the dealer whose priorities were in order? Who actually understood what he was seeing? Who knew that his paintings weren't products?

But inevitably, such idealism would fade as the preparations for the show continued. Reality would interfere, the fantasy begin to crumble.

Perhaps the dealer, complaining of high overhead, would make decisions that compromised the work, shortened the show, or gave it less space. Perhaps he would insist on hanging the show himself, without consulting my father, or skimp on the announcements or the catalogue, or reveal too baldly that his motivations were tied to the marketplace. Perhaps he would invade the sanctity of my father's studio, bringing collectors looking for investments, who would demonstrate, by their foolish questions, that they neither knew nor cared about art, but who craved a glimpse of the artist in his natural habitat before they bought his work.

Or worse. Perhaps the exhibition itself seemed like a failure. Perhaps the work appeared thin, inconclusive, weak. Perhaps old work was already being invalidated by new. Perhaps the anticipated harsh criticism from certain quarters would be making itself felt, magnifying his already considerable fears. And, feeling this, perhaps my father despised his own thin skin. As the date of the opening approached, the show would have become an infernal, destructive machine set in motion that could no longer be stopped.

For all these reasons, and for others I can only guess at, there were usually strings of sleepless nights before each opening, nights leading to what were, for me as a child, days of tiptoeing around the apartment, taking care not to awaken my father. Often he was there still at the kitchen table in the mornings when I got up for school, not having slept, sitting and chain-smoking his unfiltered Camels, a cup of black coffee at his elbow, eyes hooded by a deep gloom. His smile of greeting seemed so hollow and ghoulish that I'd be relieved when he'd let his face slip back into that familiar haunted look I knew to be his.

I wasn't at my father's first New York opening, at Midtown Galleries in 1945. I was two years old then; we still lived in Iowa City. But by the time I left home for college in 1960, there had been six more one-man exhibitions in New York. It is those openings, at Peridot and Egan, and particularly the later ones at the Sidney Janis Gallery, that have blended into a single pastiche of memory, a jumble of images and sensations instantly evoked by the word "opening" itself.

We always arrived late at my father's openings, making our entrance into the already crowded gallery as if emerging onto a stage. Conscious of his distress, I worried about him. I took all of my father's fears quite seriously, rather as if he had a painful, but not mortal illness. It never occurred to me then that I might view his torments as pitiable, or unnecessary, or even within his control. His anxieties didn't seem particularly strange; to me, as a child, they were inevitable, natural phenomena, to be endured like bad weather. But scary, nevertheless. Still, he seemed more stable than some of the other painters he knew, from the things I'd seen and stories I'd overheard. It was what being an artist was all about, I thought. Certain events brought emotional upheavals. That was how it worked.

On the way to the opening, I would keep stealing looks at my father in the taxi. He seemed so miserable. My mother kept her eyes on him, too. Pale and distracted on the trip uptown, Philip would unfold himself with difficulty from the taxi, then stop on the sidewalk outside the gallery, rooted as if he couldn't move. My mother fluttered ineffectually around him, patting him, trying to calm him down, urging him to go in, telling him that everything would be fine, but only succeeding, if he paid any attention to her at all, in drawing his anger. Embarrassed, I was aware of passersby looking at us. Who was this raving, wild-eyed man? Ah, an artist. That explained it. His fears would rise in a crescendo. The whole thing was a mistake, a terrible mistake, he'd cry. He should be in Woodstock, working. Dealers were parasites, the critics worse. How had he let himself be talked into this madness?

Finally, he calmed down and entered the building grimly, a criminal resigned to his punishment. We got in the elevator and began the ascent, hearing the noise of people talking coming nearer as we approached the floor.

But then, *mirabile dictu,* the elevator door opened, we made our entrance, and my father was suddenly, ineplicably, all right again.

Our arrival was, I see now, like a light turned on in a child's bedroom, where imagined terrors are deflated abruptly by prosaic actuality. But it wasn't until twenty years later that I understood his transformation, as it echoed in me. As a counselor, I hated doing crisis intervention; on my way to the hospital after a late night call, I always imagined the worst. Slashed wrists, bizarre paranoid delusions. But once there, seeing what was what, the mundane invariably provided a calming antidote to my fearful fantasy, just as it must have for my father when he arrived at his openings.

The next moment, Philip was swallowed by a circle of people, leaving my mother and me standing off to one side. Ah, is that the artist? I could hear the whispers. Yes, that's him. That's him. My mother and I stood there, cloaked in our common shyness, cut adrift by his sudden recovery. Someone usually took pity on us and came to the rescue. I mumbled polite greetings and tried to pay attention, but my thoughts were still with my father. Lost in the crush of people, I couldn't even see him anymore, but now and then I heard his voice, holding forth, easy and booming now, that infectious laugh of his strangling into a smoker's cough. Now that he seemed happy again, I wanted to be near him, to have him hoist me up in his arms, as he had when I was a little girl, and give me one of his sloppy kisses, but there were so many people clustered around him, that I knew—as I knew so many things without being told—that I should stay away. He belonged to them now. This was his night, his party. And I tried to be happy for him.

Bored, I let go of my mother's hand and slipped along the wall, around the periphery of the crowd. It seemed to me that the paintings were lonely too; no one was paying much attention to them, despite the fact that they were the reason we were all here.

Finally, someone noticed me, an extravagantly dressed woman, her bracelets clattering. "Oh!" she gushed in a breathy voice. "You're Philip Guston's daughter, aren't you?"

I nodded. It was embarrassing to have a fuss made over me, but some part of me was grateful nevertheless to be special in someone's eyes, if only for a moment.

"Oh, you must be so proud of your father! He's such a wonderful man, so brilliant! I just *love* his work!"

I smiled, blushing. An answer didn't seem called for.

"And it must be so *interesting* to be the daughter of a famous artist!"

I nodded again. I never knew what to say at times like this. Clearly, being my father's daughter was important, a lineage that conferred some sort of distinction. I was somebody. But it was an uneasy distinction—uneasy, even then, because it was unearned, not attached to who I really was.

The woman with the bracelets turned away from me to speak to her bored companion. "Isn't she just darling?"

The noise of talk and laughter became louder. Cigarette smoke formed a visible layer of haze above my head. Drinks were spilled, and mopped up again. And finally—finally!—the crowd began to thin. People were leaving, exchanging kisses, going off to restaurants and theater. A space cleared around my father. He was still deep in discussion with someone, gesturing, a drink in one hand, a cigarette in the other. He was not, at first, aware of me, standing there near him. But then he noticed me. Holding out his hand to me, smiling, he pulled me to him, giving me a squeeze and wet kiss full of whiskey (from the dealer's stash, back in the office—wine was served at the opening) and the smell of Camels.

"This is Ingie. My daughter," he said with a tremendous pride, overwhelming me with a suddenly loving look, as if the very fact of my existence made him happy.

Most of these evenings ended the same way. We were dispatched, in several taxis, to Chinatown, where my father ordered for everyone, without a menu. There was more laughter and loud talk, and rice wine around the table to help the whiskey someone had brought. My father was again oblivious of me, a little drunk now, holding forth to his friends. I sat there, crammed in beside my mother, picking at the strange food on my plate, sleepy but perfectly content.

Was there ever a time when I wasn't aware that my father was important to other people? When I wasn't competing with the world for my claim to his attention? Even when I was four or five, I can remember feeling that uneasy mix of pleasure and embarrassment and jealousy. It was impossible not to feel intimidated by his fame; those effusive compliments I always heard at openings exacted their toll. What right did I have to question him? Who was I to call attention to myself?

We were on a seesaw, my father and I—the more of a somebody he became, the more of a nobody I saw myself to be. And the less right I had to my share of his love. It always seemed that so many other people wanted something from him, that their claims, too, were real, and undeniable. And I saw how put upon he was by their demands. It was impossible not to. He seemed to have such a terrible time saying no, to anyone. Well, then, I told myself, I would be the perfect daughter. I wouldn't be like those students of his, always asking for recommendations, or all the others, the dealers and collectors and academics and hangers-on who wanted interviews, visits, lectures, explanations. Asking, always asking. I would make no demands. Maybe then . . .

By the time I was a teenager, I had learned to make use of his fame.

Pretending sophistication, I was prepared to let myself be dazzled by art world celebrities, to drop the famous names in "casual" references to impress my friends with their "ordinary" fathers. I was trading on this heavily for a while, using my father's name as ballast.

Openings. What emblematic events these are for me. For most of my life, I have felt precisely as I did at my father's openings: invisible until recognized as his daughter, cloaked—no, masked—in that comfortable, curiously eclipsing sense of self which is not me at all. Again and again, it seems, I have to remake the same discovery—that reflected glory yields little warmth.

While the earlier openings blur and become confused with one another, the last of his openings I attended with him is certainly clear— that of the retrospective at the San Francisco Museum of Modern Art in May of 1980.

It was after the San Francisco exhibition had already been scheduled, the catalogue and other arrangements for it well under way, that my father had suffered his heart attack. Even after a long recuperation, he was very weak. A marathon painter only the year before, possessing the kind of stamina that could keep him on his feet for thirty-six hours at a stretch before his huge canvases, he could stand only with effort. He shuffled when he walked. He had to work flat, sitting down, at his drawing table. It was terribly frustrating for him. Feverish with ideas, he felt imprisoned inside a failing body.

During that year, my parents had again retreated from me. I was to be protected, not burdened. Grateful as they might profess to be, they were embarrassed by my having helped them that previous March. Though they said nothing, it was clear to me that they didn't want to feel obligated. Gratitude made them uneasy; my parents worried over emotional debts as if they were back taxes, accruing penalties and interest they could ill afford.

They came to rely on the few they did allow to help them, and these were often people my parents felt they could repay financially—my father's dealer and his wife, David and Renée McKee; his accountant, Louis Bernstein; a former student from the New York Studio School, Steve Sloman, who was then in the process of photographing all of my father's paintings; and Ed Blatter, an electrician and carpenter who did all the physical work around the studio. As frequently as I dared, I called

Woodstock for the occasional, laundered bulletins my mother would give me over the phone.

It was only with great difficulty that I could pry out the real, painful situation from the proffered fabric of reassuring half-truths. Telephone conversations with my mother became inquisitions on my part. Was he sleeping? What did the doctors say? How much was he drinking? Had he at least tried to cut down a little on the smoking?

Consequently, I knew nothing of the preparations for the San Francisco show, the pitched battles between Henry Hopkins, the museum's director, and my father over the selection of paintings, the arguments over itinerary, timing, the catalogue, and all the other decisions that had to be made. I knew little of the genesis of this exhibition, or of the degree of openness there might be to it in the art world, or even how worried my father was. The Guggenheim retrospective in 1962 had been hard for him, I knew, but that had been a summing up, a cutting off, in mid-career. This show, coming after the work of the late sixties and seventies—and especially after his heart attack—seemed triumphant, somehow, a celebration of a life in art. I hoped he saw it that way. For the climate in the art world had finally begun to change; after ten years, there had been scattered, grudging critical acceptance of my father's late work. Beginning late in 1978, there had been a string of important sales—a number of them to Edward Broida, a Los Angeles collector. Ed Broida's interest had been enormously encouraging to my father.

We were all planning to go to California. It was to be a gala occasion, that opening. A family affair. We would all be in San Francisco together —my parents, my husband Tom and I, my sons, even my aunt Jo and cousin Kim. All of us, together, for a week. It would be a wonderful time. My sons—David was then sixteen, and Jonathan, fourteen—who saw their grandparents so rarely, would finally get to spend some time around Philip, in his element, among his life's work. The thought of this was particularly gratifying to me. For years, I'd been trying to put my children together with their grandparents, to kindle some real spark there. But whenever we took the boys for visits to Woodstock, their energy and interests seemed to tire my father, and shorten the time I felt I could spend with him.

We took the red-eye to California from Columbus, Ohio. Somewhere over the Rockies, with the movie over and everyone asleep, our big wide-body jet dropped like a stone in a down draft—a quick, screaming nightmare ride that left us wide-eyed and jumpy for the rest of the flight. On my parents' flight out from New York, I found out later, my father had been breathless and pale—they had given him oxygen. But once we were safely in San Francisco, the momentum of the week took over. My father was putting us all up in style. I was charmed by the elegant hotel room with its fresh-cut flowers and view of the bay. That first morning, still sleepless, Tom and I went riding with David and Jonathan through Golden Gate Park on rented bicycles, all the way to the Pacific and back. The smell of eucalyptus was in the air.

Later that day, we went together to the museum. My father seemed pleased with the installation of his work. We strolled through the galleries where final touches were being put on the show. Paintings from all fifty years of his career stood on the floor, leaned up against the walls on which they would hang. There was *Martial Memory* and *Dial* and *Beggar's Joy*, all of them cheek by jowl, for the first time, with his late work. The earliest painting there, *Mother and Child*, painted in 1930 when my father was only seventeen, had been cleaned for the first time (see plate 44). None of us had seen it since the cleaning. Having grown accustomed to its orangy-yellow appearance, the product of fifty years of cigarette smoke, we expressed shock at its raw, vivid colors. My father smiled at our reaction. "It's just as I remember it," he said.

He walked slowly from painting to painting, visiting each one affectionately, occasionally patting a picture gently.

"This is one show where I can touch the pictures and no one's going to tell me not to," he said, and laughed. He ran his long, tobacco-stained fingers over their surfaces like a lover caressing the cheek of an old sweetheart. It had the feeling of a reunion.

He stopped before a painting from the early fifties. "You know, I remember what I ate that day, when this picture finally came off," he said. "It was in the old Cedar Bar days. I had a studio on Tenth Street. I went in the bar and Bill de Kooning was there with Franz Kline. I'd been on the picture for two or three weeks and . . . I had this look on my face, I guess, because Bill said to me, 'Good strokes, eh? You made some good strokes.'" We all laughed.

Some of these paintings, sequestered in the midwestern museums or in private collections, Philip hadn't seen since his last retrospective, almost twenty years earlier. Many I had never seen, except in reproductions. Behind my father trailed an entourage of family, museum people, David and Renée McKee, Michael Blackwood and his film crew, who were shooting footage for a documentary film. That day, my father was as happy and relaxed as I have ever seen him, talking and joking with everyone. They brought him a chair and he sat and smoked, holding forth, as he always did, to a circle of his admirers.

Predictably, somebody asked him about the change in his style, how it felt to work now, as opposed to the early sixties. "No different," he said. "There's no difference."

Philip looked slightly pained at the question. "You know, comments about style always seem strange to me—'why do you work in this style, or in that style'—as if you had a choice in the matter." He took a drag of his cigarette, and paused to think.

"What you're doing," he said slowly, "is trying to stay alive and continue and not die."

My father spoke of a time when he was working in his big, cavernous loft in Chelsea, over the firehouse. "I hadn't painted for a month or two," he recalled, "and my painting was beginning to bore me, what I'd been doing. I tacked up a ten-foot canvas, and squeezed out tons of paint, and I thought, I'll paint the room, I'll paint all this junk. I had an eight-hour stint. I painted the cracked and broken mirror, the paint table, the floors, the useless wires hanging down and other easels and stacked-up drawings. I looked and painted. I didn't think. And I painted the whole thing. In fact, I ended up with—I looked at the thing and—" Philip gave an embarrassed little laugh. "Jesus, well, I'm a painter, you know—it looked like a Bonnard. Wonderful, lots of colors. And I'd been doing black pictures, these dark heavy pictures.

"We lived across the street. I went across and woke up Musa. It was about four in the morning, and I said, 'You've got to look at this!' And she came, of course, and said it was wonderful. Then I couldn't sleep, because I thought, what's happening? Am I going to have a new career as a painter? Does this deny all my previous work?

"When I came in the next morning to look at it, my euphoria was gone. Just disappeared. And the painting itself looked as if I could just peel it off. It didn't stick. Naturally, I destroyed it."

I drifted in and out of listening to all of this, drawn also by the luxury of a private viewing of paintings in the empty rooms. I went to find *If This Be Not I*, from 1945, and was surprised to see how small it was (see plate 45). From across the gulf of years, I stared at that little girl's round face, my father's image of me, as if she could tell me something, offer me a clue. As if the picture, simply because I was captured in it, must include some special message for me, some particular wisdom my father could impart to me only in that way.

The title, a line from a Mother Goose rhyme, "The Old Woman and the Peddler," had been suggested by my mother, I knew. An old woman falls asleep by the side of the road on her way to market. While she is sleeping a peddler comes by and cuts her skirts "all up to her knees." Awakening, the old woman's sense of herself is shaken. She begins to shiver and weep. Suddenly, she doesn't know who she is. "Lawk a mercy on me, this can't be I!" she cries. Reassured by the idea that at least her little dog will know her, she hurries home, saying, "If it be not I, he'll loudly bark and wail." But her little dog doesn't know her, after all.

I walked back into the large gallery where my father was standing with the museum director, the McKees, and my mother. They were making ready to go. Philip was tired now, I could tell, his tall form stooped with the effort of standing. Before leaving, he turned to survey the entire gallery, where all of his late paintings leaned against the long walls.

My father looked around, then sighed. "It's not so much a painting show," he said. "It's like a life, you know. It's like a life lived."

The rest of that week went by, too fast, in a blur of good food and hospitality and sightseeing. One day we all drove up to Muir Woods to stroll among the redwoods; stopping to rest every few feet, my father listened attentively as my son David talked about the age of the huge trees around us (see plate 78). Another day we drove down the coast. All that week Philip was always just out of reach. Nothing had changed about openings, in all these years; at a distance, there I was, still longing for him. But there were two moments that were later on to assume an inflated importance in my mind.

At the museum, my father collapsed after a particularly strenuous morning and was brought back to the hotel. I found him stretched out, gray and sweating, in a darkened hotel suite, his restless brown eyes set so deeply in their dark sockets they appeared like a mask of his own invention, the skin of his face puffy and florid. My mother was frantic with worry, but he was ignoring her, too weary for any part of her panic. He asked me to sit with him, and I did, feeling the usual pang of guilty satisfaction I always felt when I, instead of my mother, got to take care of him.

He didn't want a doctor, he said. They'd hospitalize him, he knew, and he'd seen quite enough of coronary care units. No, he only wanted a drink, and to rest, he told me, the museum people were running him ragged. I reminded him, as I had before, that it wasn't necessary to give everyone what they wanted. He smiled weakly, pressed my hand. "You're so right, darling," he said, letting his eyes close. "Why do I do this to myself?" We didn't talk much that afternoon, but I stayed there, close by him, until he was able to sleep. And the next day, of course, he was back on his horse again, riding another punishing round of interviews and lunches and lectures.

The opening was at the end of the week, the day before we left. We weren't seated with my parents at the formal banquet at the museum; instead they had put us with my aunt and cousin at another table. I felt angry and hurt, but there was nothing to be done. Left out, once again. After the Dungeness crab and rack of lamb, there were the usual speeches. When it was time for my father to talk, he spoke of his happiness, his gratitude for the exhibition. In his gracious way, he thanked the museum, the corporate sponsor, his dealer, his wife, and his friends. And finally, unexpectedly, he thanked me. Feeling that intense beam of his love from across a sea of tables, I was overwhelmed with tears. It was as if he had reached down to that little girl again and picked her up in his arms, making it all worthwhile.

Little enough, perhaps. To me, it was everything.

It had to be. Three weeks later, at the home of a friend in Woodstock, just as dessert was being served, my father died.

ELEVEN

If This Be Not I

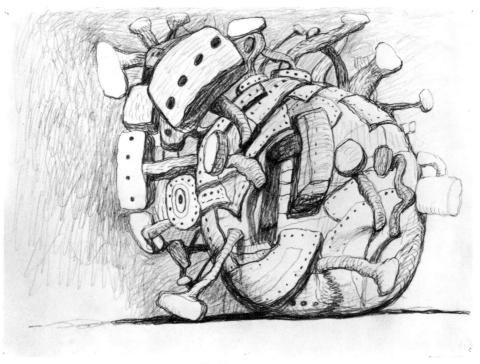

Untitled, 1980.

Shall I say it again? In order to arrive there,
To arrive where you are, to get from where you are not,
You must go by a way wherein there is no ecstasy.

—T.S. ELIOT
"East Coker"

My parents had been having dinner at the home of their friends Fred and Sylvia Elias, a physician and his wife who owned several Guston paintings, when my father had another heart attack.

"He just put his head down and was gone," Fred told me the next day in Woodstock. "I did . . . I mean I tried . . ." He shook his head, as if to clear it of the memory. "What about your mother?" he asked. "She can't stay here alone."

We were standing on the back porch. I stared at the gray cedar shingles, the pattern of the flagstones under our feet. The sunlight poured down like a physical assault. "I don't know," I said. "I haven't had a chance . . ."

"Of course you haven't." Sylvia patted my arm. "If there's anything . . . anything at all . . ."

My mind had halted. I couldn't seem to pull my thoughts together. Karl Fortess, a friend who had met my bus, took me aside. "The funeral home wants someone from the family to . . ." He paused. "I'll take you if you want." I nodded, trying to absorb what he meant.

At the funeral home late that afternoon, I signed the necessary papers for the cremation and stood up to leave. I walked slowly across the room and stopped, my hand on the open door. Beyond the manicured lawns of the elaborate Victorian structure, the shape of Overlook Mountain was flat, a cardboard paste-up against a white sky. "Was there something else?" the man asked. I shook my head. I wanted to see my father's body, but I couldn't bring myself to ask. It was a day filled with things left unsaid.

Waking every morning to the high white ceiling and north window of my girlhood studio, now a guest room, I was twelve or thirteen again. For a moment, it was one of those endless Woodstock summers, and I was lying in bed, savoring the long day ahead of me, riding my bicycle through the blue morning coolness to the life drawing class at the Art Students League, swimming in the heat of the afternoon at the Big Deep, then riding home to my studio, with my poems and drawings tacked up on the walls. My father was back in his stone studio, working; the comforting tap-tapping of my mother's typewriter could faintly be heard from the house. The whole world seemed poised on the verge of something then, limitless in its possibilities.

Coming back to the present with a sickening jolt, I would lie there, sweating, my heart racing. My father was dead. It wasn't possible. I should have made them show me his body. I just couldn't make myself believe it. But then, neither could my mother, and she'd been with him when he died. She kept seeing him through the kitchen window standing beside the studio door. This scared me. I kept on stupidly repeating things to her I thought would be comforting. How good it was that Philip had lived for the opening of his retrospective. How important our time together in San Francisco had been.

I tried to take charge, to make sure the necessary things were done. People brought food and sat around telling stories about my father. The *New York Times* obituary came out. As word spread, the telephone began ringing. What were the plans? When would the funeral be? Would there be some sort of memorial service in the city? And how was Musa? Could they speak to her?

I made apologies for my mother, saying she was resting. As people came and went, she lay in the bedroom, curled up on her side of their big bed, taking up hardly any space. Sealed off somewhere inside herself, she let herself be led through the day's necessities. Occasionally, she would emerge from her room, a polite smile pasted on her face. The conversation would stop. People would get up, offer to get her something. My mother hated being the center of their attention. I could tell how uneasy it made her. Sitting in the oak captain's chair at the kitchen table that had been my father's seat, she would eat mechanically, dutifully, not speaking. But wasn't there anything, people would whisper to me later, anything at all they could do for her? I didn't know. I'd go in and sit on her bed, ask her questions. Did she want to talk to so-and-so? Open the day's mail? No, she didn't want anyone. Only him. Even my presence was barely tolerated.

Finally, the date for the funeral was set. I had some slight idea of what my father had wanted, from our conversation in the hospital the year before. Philip Roth later told me that my father had spoken to him once about being buried. "Better as a Jew than a bohemian," he'd said. And so a rabbi was found, the speakers were chosen. Now, what remained was to find a place for some sort of gathering afterwards.

People in the Hudson Valley recall the spring of 1980 as the worst year of the periodic gypsy moth infestation within memory. The larvae of the insect had completely defoliated thousands of acres in the Catskills. Whole mountainsides were as bare and brown as if it had been mid-winter. In most of Woodstock, it had become impossible to stand under trees without the black, brightly spotted caterpillars sliding down on their silken threads and dropping on one's head and shoulders.

We stayed indoors, with the curtains drawn. One day that week, I remember standing on the back porch, watching with a sort of morbid fascination as one of the caterpillars methodically, in neat, serrated rows like a tiny eating machine, chewed up the last leaf on the hickory tree outside the kitchen window. Awful as it was, it seemed fitting to me, somehow, the devastation outside mirroring the devastation within. Except for the pines and hemlocks, all the trees around my parents' house were bare. The birds were gone. Day and night, the loudest sound outdoors was the rainfall pattering of larvae droppings, and an enormous aggregate of minute chomping noises, a symphony of feeding.

The old Maverick Concert Hall, just down the road from us, the most suitable and natural setting for such a gathering, was out of the question. The woods around it were completely infested. In the end, we were offered the back lawn of the Woodstock Artists' Association, despite the fact that my parents had avoided the local artists' group for many years.

On the day before the funeral, Tom took me to pick up my father's ashes. Inside the white cardboard box was another box, of brown plastic, no larger than a good-sized book, that had been completely sealed. Not what I expected at all, this neat package. I remembered how I'd cupped my hands to receive my share of a friend's ashes in Ohio, the rough gritty feel of the bits of white powder and bone I'd scattered on his land. After the first shock, that had seemed real, and fitting, returning him to earth. But this! This was so sterile and concealed.

I held the box in my lap on the way home, opening the white flap, peering inside at the smooth brown plastic, then closing it. It seemed to weigh nothing at all. My father's remains should have been like collapsed matter, so dense as to be unstoppable, falling through earth. Surely what was left of him wasn't contained in that ugly little box. Shaking, I got out of the car, ran into the studio, and set the box in the center of his large drawing table, under the white hanging light. His presence flowed outward from the table to the corners of the empty room in a big wave.

The studio was cool and bright; every object seemed coated with a porcelain, lucid calm. I tiptoed across the room, then caught myself at it. I still felt like an invader, a trespasser; I had never been alone in my father's studio before this past week. The piny smell of turpentine was comforting, familiar. I walked over to his palette, a glass-topped rolling table that stood beside his painting wall in the center of the studio. Beneath the wall, on the floor, an encrusted line of clotted paint scrapings lay in a thick row. I touched the palette's surface, the swirls and mounds of cadmium red and black and white, and was surprised to find some of the paint still soft under the rubbery crusts that had formed. Had he worked here that recently? But no, the brushes in their can were mired in a thick brown glue; the paint rag was stiff.

On the big, angled wall on the far side of the studio, opposite his painting wall, were pinned his last paintings and drawings, small works in acrylic and ink, done in the last month or two. Secured with pushpins so there was no space at all between them, they formed a quilt of images, alive and complex. They'd been done at this same drawing table where his ashes, in their box, were sitting now.

Some were ink drawings, some painted in acrylics, the forms then shaped and modeled with quill pen and ink. Despite their small size, they had the emblematic power of his largest recent work. I recognized familiar forms, friends: a mound of cherries, a flatiron, a sandwich, a kettle, a ladder with woven, nailed legs, the pull chain of a light, trash can lids.

But there were other, stranger images—crawling forms that attempted to scale a sloping brownish plain, among them a stone tablet, bifurcated like the Ten Commandments, the laws of Moses, but also resembling a gravestone, inscribed "1980 P.G." There was a head—his head, unmistakably—with its huge eye, more nearly round now and gray as stone, the face battered and bandaged, looking up the brown incline as if at some Sisyphean task (see plate 79). In another work, familiar forms—the shoes and legs and lids and stretchers and nails—were snowballed up into a mass of "stuff." A sunset was backdrop—or was it sunrise, perhaps, and the brownish slope some ooze of creation? But no, the ball rolled everywhere, gathering, collecting, clearing the landscape. Emptying the room. In one drawing it made ready to roll out an open door.

> Would it have been worth while,
> To have bitten off the matter with a smile,
> To have squeezed the universe into a ball,
> To roll it toward some overwhelming question,
> To say: 'I am Lazarus, come from the dead,
> Come back to tell you all, I shall tell you all'—

Eliot's lines from "The Love Song of J. Alfred Prufrock" came to me with a shudder.

One of the paintings was very much like a larger work from 1978 called *The Tomb*. "I just did a painting which I shall call *The Tomb* or *The Artist's Tomb*," my father had written when he saw what he had made. "So it is truly a bitter comedy that is being played out. Painting, which duplicates and is a kind of substitute for your life, as lived from hour to hour, day to day. There is no such thing as a picture, it is an impossibility and a mirage to believe so. Nothing is stable, all is shifting, changing."

Just after dawn on the morning of the funeral, my mother and Tom and I went to the artists' cemetery in Woodstock. Our shadows were long and the grass still wet with dew. Birdsong echoed in the woods. Above us, the dome of sky was already a hazy whitish blue. It would be another hot day. Taking the shovel we had brought with us, Tom began to dig; beside me, my mother clutched the brown plastic box.

In the artists' cemetery in Woodstock, the gravestones are all flat, inset into the earth. Nothing can protrude above the level of the grass— no plantings, no monuments, no urns of geraniums. I could almost pretend that we were standing in a mowed field, a simple grassy slope ringed by mountains and woods.

Finally, Tom stepped back and wiped his forehead. My mother knelt and, after a long time, set my father's ashes inside the deep hole. With them we put brushes and paint, tubes of cadmium red medium, mars black, titanium white. His colors. I knelt beside my mother and we refilled the grave together. The earth seemed like a living thing that morning, moist and glistening particles of soil that left no stain or mark on our hands.

The bunches of peonies we'd brought from a neighbor's garden, pink and white and deep crimson red, needed water. I walked up the hill to the monument. From this high vantage point, the graves below lay like necklaces on the grassy breast of the hill. Beyond, the deep green of the woods—untouched yet by the gypsy moths—rolled away to the blue mountains.

How glad I was that we had done his burial ourselves, the family alone, with no help and no intrusion. The rest was for the others. My father belonged to them now; they would make of him what they wanted, give him his niche, his myth, his place in their theories.

At the top of the cemetery hill, an oval bluestone dais, flanked by rhododendron bushes and stone benches, was surmounted by a twelve-foot-tall block of rough quarried bluestone, which bore a plaque, with the inscription, "Encircled by the everlasting hills, they rest here who added to the beauty of the world by art, creative thought and by life itself."

Beside the monument was an old iron hand pump. Setting the glass jars we had brought for the flowers down on the stone, I began to move the handle up and down. There was a delicate fluting sound as water rose in the throat of the well and spilled over into the jar, overflowing onto the flagstones. I cupped my hand beneath the spout to taste the sweetness of the well water mixed with the iron flavor of the old pump.

For a moment, despite the morning's heat, I felt chilled; something—the water's taste, perhaps, or the rusty screech of the pump handle—had hurled me back in time. Inside, somewhere, a door opened, a blast of icy air entered a warm kitchen, and there was my father in his red plaid wool jacket, stamping the snow from his boots, the pail of water in his gloved hand filmed with ice, just the thinnest layer of starry glass on its surface that broke when I touched it.

I walked back down the hill to my father's grave carrying the full jars, passing people I'd known, growing up, my father's friends, names like

Millman, Magafan, Kuniyoshi, Refregier. Wendy Jones, a childhood playmate I'd had a crush on for years, dead at twenty-one on a motorcycle in Putney, Vermont. Carved in the bluestone below his name and dates, a small boat sailed away, heeling far into the wind. A cello was engraved on the stone of Hans Cohn, my doctor when I was a child; I remembered his stern face bent gravely over his instrument, playing in a string quartet at the Maverick Concert Hall. At the bottom of the hill beside the woods, in a sort of shrine with a glazed terra-cotta Madonna and Child in the della Robbia style, was the grave of Ralph Radcliffe Whitehead, the builder of Byrdcliffe, the first artists' colony.

That afternoon, when we returned to the cemetery for the service, without thinking I began to walk toward my father's grave, rather than up the hill to where the rabbi waited beside the monument. My mother followed me, unquestioning, Tom supporting her. Suddenly I stopped, aware all at once that the crowd of people—so many!—had begun to follow us down the hill. They seemed to be closing in, all those sad, aging faces from my childhood. For a panicky moment I wanted to run from everyone, off into the woods, to hide. Before I turned uphill again, to the proper gathering place, I looked across the grass to the spot where the peonies, drooping now in the afternoon's heat, imperfectly concealed the wound in the ground we had made that morning.

I don't remember much of my father's funeral. The heat of the sun overhead. The black yarmulkes on the heads of the men, and the dark, complicated Hebrew words in their mouths—the Kaddish, the Prayer for the Dead my father had wanted his three friends to say for him.

A week later I returned briefly to Ohio to pack more clothes and speak with my supervisor about taking a leave of absence from my job for the rest of the summer. At the time of my father's death, I'd been working with problem adolescents and their families in a day treatment program at a community mental health agency based in a Dayton hospital. My patients were young teenaged boys who were—in mental health lingo—considered "SBD" (Severe Behavior Disordered). In other words, they'd created such a degree of havoc in their classrooms, and were so often truant, that no public school would have them. The Learning Center, where I worked, was a last-ditch attempt to prevent institutionalization. The boys I worked with greeted my leaving with sullen silence and outbursts of misdirected anger. I was letting them down. "Just when things were starting to get a little bit better," one of the mothers said bitterly.

I felt guilty about leaving. I also felt relieved. Nine months of tackling their overwhelming problems had humbled and exhausted me. Let someone else try, I thought.

Besides, I told myself, my mother needed me. She shouldn't be alone, and there was so much to be done in Woodstock. A list of all the paintings and drawings had to be drawn up and each work photographed for an appraisal. We had to find a good estate lawyer. There was too much at stake to leave these things up to dealers and lawyers and accountants, no matter how much my father had trusted these people.

But I wasn't sure where to begin. The art world was a mystery to me; I had never been involved with decisions concerning my father's work. My mother, knowing this, was hesitant to accept my involvement at first, although she was aware she couldn't manage alone. I was an intrusion on her privacy. Her anger when I relabeled some envelopes in my father's desk drawer was crushing to me, in those early days. She'd always been so gentle with me. But she was furious that I'd erased anything in his handwriting. With Philip gone, it was more than she could bear, that first year, for anything of his to be moved, or touched, or changed in any way. His clothes stayed in the closets, his glasses on the table by the telephone. I soon learned to disturb as little as possible.

That summer, through the making of difficult decisions, the doing of all that had to be done, the photographing and listing, the arguing and crying and explaining, my mother and I became close again, as we had not been since the shy days of my childhood, before I had real friends of my own, when we would go out together hunting fossils on the shores of the Ashokan Reservoir.

What took longer, much longer, was for David and Renée McKee and Louis Bernstein, my father's accountant, to discover that I was more than an interloper, an unwelcome—if entitled—family meddler in their well-established and smoothly running business relationship. My father had barely mentioned me, I found out much later from Lou Bernstein, who in time became my close friend. My father had been something of an old-fashioned patriarch—his business was his business. Even my mother had been relegated to the waiting room while Philip and his accountant talked over business matters. I was even more in the dark. A "protected" child, I'd never known anything specific about the family finances. Though nothing was ever said directly, it was quite clear that my participation in the affairs of the Estate of Philip Guston was greeted with a certain begrudging acceptance.

Every week or two, I took the bus into the city from Woodstock. Limp from the assault of New York in summer, I arrived at the gallery for our meetings bedraggled and a bit disoriented. I felt out of place. I listened as they talked, trying to follow the logic of their strategies, the legal reasoning, the plans for shows and sales. At first, I was hesitant to ask for clarification when I didn't understand. I didn't want to reveal my own ignorance; besides, I sensed a certain uneasiness with my scrutiny.

These people had loved my father too, and were grieving his loss. I knew that, and I sympathized. But our needs were at cross-purposes—mine to become a part of my father's life, theirs to keep things as they had been when he was alive, just as my mother was trying to do.

After these meetings I'd call Tom in Ohio tearfully, and tell him how unsure of myself I felt.

"Come on. Don't be so timid," he urged me. "Just say what you think."

But they were the experts, I'd answer. What did I know?

That made him angry. "You're Philip's daughter, aren't you?" he'd say. "Doesn't that count for something?"

Certainly I wanted it to, but I wasn't so sure it did. Not with these people. For a long time, though my sense of ignorance eventually yielded as I did learn more, there continued to be moments of awkwardness, little bubbles of tension, of looks being passed and averted eyes, messages that I—who'd been so good as a group therapist, at coaxing problems out into the open between people—felt helpless to decode or defuse.

In July, David and Renée McKee came up to help us photograph and list the paintings in my father's estate, a process that took several long days. The large cinder block storage area behind the studio, constructed to hold my father's work of the past five years, was like a treasure trove. Paintings I had never seen lined its walls, six and seven deep.

Renée and I set up our cameras on tripods while David masked the glass-block windows and set the bright, hot lights on either side of a clear area of wall. One by one, we moved each painting in front of the cameras, assigned it a number, measured it, determined whether it was oil, acrylic, or gouache, and whether it was painted on canvas, masonite board, or paper. We looked for inscriptions on the front and back. My mother sat there in a director's chair, wide-eyed and talkative for the first time since my father's death. We all enjoyed ourselves, I think. It was exhilarating, this process of inventory, a salute to old friends, a meeting of new ones.

Fully two-thirds of the work I had never seen before. There were bizarre images hidden away in that storage area, paintings too strange or too personal to have been exhibited, works that looked as if my father had been trying to see just how far he could go. Nixon on the beach at San Clemente, dragging a leg swollen with phlebitis, a tear hanging from his stubbled jowl, enormous toes like slabs of bacon. Or a ghoulish, gray fellow with a thatch of hair like a spaniel's ear grinning over a riotous plate of spaghetti, each strand of which was painted with absolute authority and delight. Or two slightly limp hearts, one of them studded like a trash can lid, stacked on a box like tired, trapped intimates—a valentine of sorts. A painting called *Martyr*, clearly a send-up of St. Sebastian—had my father been thinking of the Mantegna in the Ca' d'Oro in Venice?—showed a backless, coffinlike wooden box pierced by arrows in three dozen places.

After the McKees had left, my mother and I continued to work, photographing and listing the drawings. By working methodically, we made our way through the drawers of the drawing cabinets. But finally, there came the day when that, too, was finished, when the last photograph had been taken, the last measurement made. Abruptly, that buoyant sense of daily discovery that had been sustaining me vanished, and I felt as bleak and emptied out as I had in the days right after my father's death. I had seen everything. There would be no more. From then on I would always feel cheated, wondering what my father might have painted next.

"Let's photograph the work that's hanging in the house," I said to my mother, desperate to keep going. We began an inventory of her collection. From the back of a dresser drawer in her bedroom, at the very last, when everything else had been listed, she pulled two rolled-up canvases from the 1930s that I had never seen before. "What's wrong?" I asked, as she handed them to me.

"He never forgave me," she whispered, shamefaced.

"Forgave you? For what?"

"Making him change his name." I unrolled one of the canvases, a highly stylized nude model beside an empty easel. On the left, in small black letters, it said, "Phillip Goldstein, 1935."

Earlier in the summer, we had opened his safety deposit box to find it full of the official papers and petitions about his name change. He had kept every scrap of paper, every lawyer's letter, every form, long after any question of legality was involved. I knew that my father had felt tremendous regret about having changed his name, that in his eyes it had become a shameful, cowardly act. And I knew that after the Second World War and the revelations of the Holocaust, when it became crucial for him to reclaim his Jewish identity, it was too late to change it back. His reputation was already established with the new name.

My mother showed me the place where, on one of his earliest paintings, *Mother and Child* from 1930, he had repainted his earlier signature, carefully matching the pigment to conceal the change. He'd given in to the pressure of her parents' concern over rising anti-Semitism in the years before the war, she told me, weeping. It was she who had forced him to do this terrible thing. But he must have had reasons of his own, I protested. There must be more to it than that. It was hard to imagine my father caving in under family pressure.

Of course, Philip's story—as I learned later, from reports of guilty confessions he'd made to friends—was that he'd decided on his own to change his name, before even meeting her parents, and that my mother had been against it. He'd been certain her parents would accept a Guston more readily than a Goldstein as their son-in-law.

Whatever the reason, there is no question that the anguish and shame my father felt about having changed his name animated, at least in part, one of the lifelong themes in his work—the search for self through the process of masking and unmasking. He loved Venetian painting, Domenico Tiepolo's poignant masked figures of the *carnevale*. His paintings of masked children from the 1940s draw most directly on this tradition, of course, but the later images of hooded figures, the Ku Klux Klansmen of 1968 through 1972, are an even more potent restatement of a theme that had preoccupied him since the early 1930s. By concealing their identities, these masked creatures seem to reveal the truer, deeper selves of their fantasies, hidden wishes, dreams.

Throughout his life, my father waged a war with himself, between, on the one hand, the impulse to be private, secretive—witness his story of hiding in his boyhood closet when the family came—and, on the other, an enormous need he had to unmask, to reveal, to disclose all, and in the most personal, costly way. In the evolution of a lifetime's painting, it's as if there is a progressive struggle and resolution and return to this same conflict again and again. In his late work, when finally all was at risk, he wrestled quite openly, and with a sort of joyous abandon, with the issues of his own culpability.

My mother and I finished the inventory, and I moved on, from the works themselves, to the catalogues and articles, the photographs, his correspondence. I spent my time organizing, filing, grateful that there was still so much to do.

Outdoors, while we had been so absorbed in our listing and photographing, a renewal had begun. The trees, stripped of their foliage by the gypsy moths in May and June, were experiencing a second spring. It was April in August. New leaves burst forth, the bare trees rapidly progressing from a light green haze of buds to the lush deep greens of high summer. A month later, it was as if nothing had happened. I could walk in the woods again.

In September, after the long summer in Woodstock had ended and my mother declared herself able to manage on her own, I went back to Ohio and quit my job. Good Samaritan Hospital offered to extend my leave; although I was flattered, I told them no. I had to be free to spend time in Woodstock with my mother, I explained, and to go to New York for business. But it was more than that.

That summer in Woodstock, I'd begun to rediscover an earlier, neglected self—a young girl left behind some twenty years before, filled with vague longings and wishes for her life. What that meant, exactly, I didn't yet know. Tom was just beginning his doctoral work in psychology and would be immersed in that for the next few years. He certainly didn't need me around all the time. And my two sons were in high school, self-sufficient, involved with their own lives. As for my patients, my work as a counselor, I was, in the common parlance of the day, "burned out." Too much mothering, and too many years of helping others find their way, had left me feeling depleted. What I missed about my job, I discovered, was not the work itself, but the sense of professional identity, that business of being able to define myself in terms of what I did for a living when I met people at a cocktail party or opening. Once again, I let myself slip into that old, eclipsed self I remembered so well. Once again, I was Philip Guston's daughter.

It was a strange, uprooted year, that fall and winter and spring of 1980 and 1981, a year spent traveling back and forth from Ohio to New York to Woodstock every few weeks, never feeling fully at home anywhere. I was floating in a vacuum, not anchored to anything, waiting for some gravitational tug to determine my direction. For the first time in my adult life, I was freed from the necessity of earning a living. All of a sudden, there was money—the result of the acceptance that had finally begun to settle on my father's last paintings. I didn't have to work. I was free to do what I really wanted to do, whatever that was to be. I had no idea. The prospect was terrifying.

That November, we were all gathered one evening on the seventy-fifth floor of the John Hancock building in Chicago, in an apartment belonging to Gerry Elliott, one of the few collectors who'd made an early and risky commitment to my father's late work. As if sharing a well-kept secret, he took my sons into one of the bedrooms for a view of the lakeshore, curving beneath us in a shining web of lights. The living room blinds had been drawn, he explained, because the spectacular view detracted attention away from the art on the walls. "I want people to look at the paintings," he said.

My father's retrospective—now on its third of five legs, after a summer spent at the Corcoran Gallery in Washington, D.C.—looked wonderful in the intimate, gallerylike setting of the Museum of Contemporary Art. At some point during the evening, I found myself talking with David McKee. Flushed with several glasses of wine, I was telling him how much more I understood of my father's painting, now that I had seen it all. The more I got to know the work, I said, the more fascinating I found it to be.

"Hmm." His eyes narrowed in thought. "Have you given any thought to doing a catalogue raisonné?"

"Me?" I was taken aback, but also pleased. "But I'm no art historian. I wouldn't know how."

David waved a hand dismissively. "Oh, don't worry about that. These things are quite straightforward, really. I would help you."

Once he'd said it aloud, it made perfect sense. A catalogue raisonné—it sounded so erudite, so scholarly. So that's what I'd been preparing for, I thought. Until then, all this compulsive organizing seemed like some odd species of grief, a way of keeping my father close to me, yet removed. So it was to have some real use, after all. Naming and structuring the project would give me a purpose, a goal. More important, it would give me a sense of authority in my dealings with my father's estate. In retrospect, though, it seems painfully indicative of my state of mind then that I needed David McKee's suggestion—no, permission, for that's what it was, really—to undertake a project I'd already begun.

Dusting off my slight undergradute art history training, I rolled up my sleeves and went to work. During the next several years, I was able to assemble and then computerize a reasonably complete record of my father's work. For each painting from the fifty years of his career, I compiled a listing of physical details (size, medium, inscriptions, condition), exhibitions, photography, bibliography, and ownership. Though straightforward, as David McKee had said, this quickly became a surprisingly demanding task. In the last seven years I've corresponded with hundreds of museums and galleries and collectors. As an ongoing archival project, the catalogue raisonné has given me a medium through which, it seems, I can continue to distill indefinitely the nature of my connection with my father and his work.

"Don't make it your whole life, Ingie," David McKee warned that night in Chicago.

He was right, certainly. But at the time the work seemed—as it still does—a useful emotional bridge, a way of both having my father and letting him go. Months go by when I am writing and thinking about other things. New works, requests for authentication, trickle in. The provenance—the history of a painting's ownership—is never up to date. But that is the nature of such a project. And strangely—or perhaps it is not so strange—I feel more legitimate, more secure in my role as archivist and caretaker of my father's paintings than I ever did as his daughter.

That first year I followed the San Francisco retrospective as it opened in Washington, Chicago, and New York. I was amazed to see the same paintings look so different in each setting. After paying proper respects to the museum people, our little band of roving devotees would gravitate together—my mother, Tom and I, the McKees, Ross Feld, Ed Broida, and a few others. We would roam around the galleries, go out to eat, and tell Guston stories. "Wouldn't Philip have been thrilled by this show?" we'd say, or, the few times something went wrong, "It's a good thing Philip's not here to see this." And always, we came back to the work, looking and looking at the pictures, hung in varying combinations and different rooms, all of us in some way still investing in the paintings our feelings for the man who made them.

There were many self-portraits among these late paintings, images of the artist, masked and unmasked, that I found difficult to look at, at first. Philip himself seemed inseparable from his pictures, especially those pictures. They were more personal, more telling, than his work clothes, or the contents of his pockets. I often had an eerie feeling standing in the room with them, as if some essence of my father had been mixed in with the pigment and laid down there, on his canvases, some sort of potent trace mineral that continued to radiate his physical presence.

Over time, as the pain of seeing them diminished, these paintings have continued to fascinate me, to deepen in their meanings. Strangely, there is no narcissism in them, as one might expect to find in such an extended series of images of the artist. For the painter of portraits, as Peter Tarnopol points out in Philip Roth's *My Life as a Man*, his own physiognomy becomes "the closest subject at hand demanding scrutiny, a problem for his art to solve—given the enormous obstacles to truthfulness, *the* artistic problem. He is not simply looking into the mirror because he is transfixed by what he sees."

Many of my father's pictures seem to possess mysterious powers of renewal. Even after years of hanging on the same wall and being seen daily, they still surprise and disturb and delight. But I didn't realize that then. If I had, I suppose it wouldn't have been so upsetting to complete the inventory.

"Marvelous artists are made of elements which cannot be identified," my father had written of Picasso and de Chirico. "The alchemy is complete. Their work is strange, and will never become familiar." Perhaps it is this same strangeness that lends his paintings their transformational quality. Perhaps it is their truthfulness. I don't know. What I do know is that I am not alone in seeing it.

The San Francisco retrospective closed at the Whitney Museum of American Art in New York in September 1981, and the paintings were shipped back to their owners. I wandered around the Whitney the last day of the show, I remember, feeling sad and let down. Another ending. But other major shows have followed in the years since, in Europe and Central America, in Australia and in the United States. More exhibitions are planned. And there is always something new to see.

During the fall of 1980, there was a letter from the poet Bill Berkson. The St. Mark's Poetry Project wanted to do a "Homage to Philip Guston" that December. Would we come? And would my mother permit some of her own poems, which Philip had illustrated, to be exhibited? Reluctantly, she agreed, and we made plans to go together.

The St. Mark's Parish House was crowded that night. All the folding chairs had long since been claimed by the time we arrived, late from dinner with the McKees. Embarrassingly, chairs materialized for us from nowhere down in the front of the hall. People were standing several deep in the back and sitting on the floor. I sat there in the audience, feeling both exposed and invisible in that small sea of faces.

Morty Feldman, reading from an essay he'd been writing for the catalogue of my father's last works, which were being organized into a show by the Phillips Collection in Washington, D.C., offered a touching portrait of the friendship between two stubborn, difficult men. "I have resistance," he said, "in talking to anyone who could tell me why Guston assembled these last works the way he did. My attitude is not unlike my father refusing to ask for directions the time we were lost in Hoboken." I remembered that in Woodstock before the funeral, Morty had spent long hours puzzling over the studio wall of these last works my father had left, as if trying to decipher where he and Philip had lost one another. "For me," he continued, "the real research would be in reenacting that special kind of loneliness Guston shared with others throughout the seventies: a concern that something just might last a little longer, that our lifespan would not be a measurement of time documented on early, middle, late horizon. Two rabbis, who were very close friends, survived the Holocaust. One went alone to London, the other, to somewhere in South America. The rabbi in London wrote his friend, 'Too bad you're so far away.'

" 'From where?' was the reply.

"One of the most memorable afternoons I spent with Guston started off with, 'So I'm not Michelangelo,' as I was walking up the stairs to his studio. I looked at the start of a new painting for some clue to his depression. The clue wasn't there. 'O.K. so you're not Michelangelo, you're El Greco.' Guston's face lit up with relief.

"A small Guston painting from 1967 hangs over my desk: on a white ground, just two elongated black shapes about seven inches from each other. Their positioning in the field is characteristic of how Guston *freezes* a painting during the sixties. 'That one on the left,' he said, 'is telling the other one his troubles.' "

"Of all the artists I have been close to through the years," the poet Stanley Kunitz began, "Philip was by all odds the most daemonic. This daemon in him had an enormous appetite—for life and art and food and drink and friendship—and, I mustn't forget, talk—not gossip or frivolous banter, but high talk through the night, on the grand themes that agitate a serious mind, excited talk, with little pockets of moisture that bubbled at the corners of his mouth. Others who drifted in and out of the room eventually collapsed or disappeared; but at dawn Philip was still at top form, replenishing his vehemence with a last or next-to-last nightcap as we raided the refrigerator and brewed a fresh pot of coffee."

The audience laughed gently at this memory, and I laughed with them. I, too, had sat up with my father until dawn, talking. "That is my image of Philip from the fifties and sixties," he continued, "before he turned his back on the New York art world and settled permanently with Musa in Woodstock, a move that somehow signaled for me the end of an era, the breaking-up of an intimately knit world of exhilarating companionships. Things were never quite the same after that."

Kunitz paused, somber, and then his face brightened. "*Volcanic* is another word I think of in connection with Philip. He did not so much occupy his physical frame as seethe within it. His rage was always perilously close to the surface, ready for instantaneous eruption, attended by a darkening of his whole countenance and a creasing of his brow. On such occasions, you could almost watch the horns growing out of his temples. He did not suffer fools gladly, or at all. About his work, he was superlatively touchy. Once a woman, a stranger, gave him a lift after a party. As they were driving along, she made polite conversation by telling him that she preferred his older paintings to his new. 'Stop the car!' Philip shouted, and jumped out on the highway."

The stories continued. Poets spoke of his generosity, of his illustrations for their books, of his inspiration, his humor, the richness of his imagery, his appetite for talk.

Some of what was said was very moving; there were tears here and there. I looked at my mother, but she didn't return my glance. She sat straight in her chair, hands folded, feet tucked beneath her; her face was perfectly still, unreadable. Acutely conscious of all the eyes on her, checking her for responses, she sat there politely, distantly, looking as if she would have liked to disappear. She was enduring this, no more, I thought. Her poems, illustrated by my father, were pinned up around the periphery of the room. What did it mean to her that they were being seen? Was there comfort for her here? Was she less alone in her grief?

I, too, was uneasy as the night wore on. The big room was dense with feeling, airless, as if my father's substance were being sucked up by too many others. Like a gallery opening, this public outpouring of appreciation, far from giving comfort, was threatening to swamp my own tenuous connection with my father.

Surreptitiously, I looked around the room, seeing faces I knew from childhood, and many younger faces I didn't know. Perhaps no one else there that night, not even my mother, had feelings as mixed as my own. Yes, of course I was moved and exalted, filled as I'd been so many times before by an enormous sense of privilege. It was such a gift to have known him, been witness to him, been *exposed* to this man; that was the message repeated over and over that evening.

So what was wrong with me? Why couldn't I pay homage, too? Why couldn't I simply be grateful for the small part of him I had known, my share? And leave it at that. And let him go.

But for me, on that night at St. Mark's, all the eloquence and affection poured out by his friends was at risk of curdling, of becoming another sour episode in a lifetime of not measuring up. The mythic presence of Philip Guston was simply overwhelming; that evening it was palpable. All these young writers and students, for whom my father had become model as well as friend. That he was dead only made it worse, I realized with a shock, for his death fed a new, even more romantic vision in which his flaws, his imperfections, his terrible anxieties—even, now, his anger! —had become the occasion for new mythmaking.

"If you have a hero, look again; you have diminished yourself in some way." So said Sheldon Kopp, the author of *If You Meet the Buddha on the*

Road, Kill Him!, a book on transference in psychotherapy I'd admired back in the days when sweeping changes in personality seemed possible.

For years, I'd believed I had killed my Buddha, had "dealt" with my father, as we used to say at Encounter Programs in my days as a counselor there. In southwestern Ohio, far from the New York art world, none of my friends knew a thing about modern painting, much less who Philip Guston was. Nor would it have mattered to them, had they known. It was another world, completely, from the one I'd grown up in. And I'd been happy there, cut off from my past. No longer wholly obscured by my father, I'd at least managed to reach the penumbra, the area of partial eclipse. With distance and detachment, I concealed my insecure self, containing her tightly curled within me, like a naughty child sent up to her room for making a nuisance of herself. I was grown-up. I was a mature, competent woman with a career and a family of her own. I didn't need my father—or any man for that matter—to tell me who I was.

And then my father died, and I found out how hard, how full of illusions, this business of growing up really is.

E̶ach year, in the fall, my mother takes a different painting from storage to hang in her living room, a new presence to keep her company during the long Woodstock winter. This last year, she has chosen a picture that surprises me. "Are you sure about this one?" I ask before we hang it. She nods.

It is a portrait of T. S. Eliot as an old man, lying in bed, the rictus of death already on the gaunt profile. During his last year, my father had been reading Eliot's *Four Quartets*, the great final work. It was after his first heart attack that my father made this painting and named it *East Coker—T.S.E.* "When I came home from the hospital," he told an interviewer in San Francisco, "I wanted to paint a man dying, because that was what had happened to me." It would have been "too obvious" to paint himself, he said, so he simply began to paint a head, only later noting the resemblance to T. S. Eliot, including the Buddha ear with its long lobe—for Eliot, my father said, had been interested in Buddhism.

It is the last of his bed paintings, the final entry in a series that begins with the dreamy moonlit reverie of a young man lying sleepless in Iowa City—in *Sanctuary*, 1944 (see plate 67), which hangs in my bedroom again now, as it did when I was a child—and continues through the savage and tender self-portraits of the 1970s, where alone or with Musa, my father, heavy with the melancholy of aging and illness and art, takes refuge—like Oblomov—in bed.

An uncompromising work, *East Coker* is as pure and starkly beautiful as it is grim, one of a group of paintings we have come to call "difficult." Some years ago, it was sold to a well-known collector, only to have the collector return it to David McKee almost immediately, claiming his wife couldn't bear to live with it. I remind my mother of this. "Yes," she says. "But *I* always liked it." I nod, saying nothing, realizing how foolish I am to worry about my mother spending the long winter alone with this disturbing image.

After Tom and I have hung the painting, I go to my father's bookshelf, pull out the well-thumbed book of poems, and turn to "East Coker." And it is there that I find—as my father found before me—the elegy I have been looking for:

> Old men ought to be explorers
> Here and there does not matter
> We must be still and still moving
> Into another intensity
> For a further union, a deeper communion
> Through the dark cold and the empty desolation,
> The wave cry, the wind cry, the vast waters
> Of the petrel and the porpoise. In my end is my beginning.

TWELVE

Night Studio

Untitled, 1968.

I shall never get you put together entirely.
Pieced and glued, properly jointed.

—SYLVIA PLATH
"The Colossus"

The studio at night. Everything in place, now. Removed for safekeeping, or put away. The paintings rest in air-conditioned berths in the storage room next door, the drawings in the long drawers of the two gray steel cabinets, the masses of photos filed by year in glassine envelopes. The fifty piles of catalogues and magazines and books have all been sorted through and reside in a tall wooden file of their own.

When my father died, the walls of the storage room beside the studio were lined with big paintings. When I visited him those last years, this big cinder block space with its tiny high windows seemed cavelike to me, like some underground chamber filled with treasure. You walked in, he turned on the lights. And there they were. You were completely surrounded by amazing images, by legs and shoes and ladders, by high red tides and drowning heads. Philip knew where each one was, could bring it to the surface with a minimum of moves. He and Ed Blatter, his helper, would shift the paintings, and their cardboard backings, with a layered, deliberate certainty. It was like a dance, this uncovering, a ponderous ritual dance.

Seven years later, this room has changed beyond recognition. Of necessity, the storage space has become a species of vault, a smoothly humming expanse given over, not to the excitement of planning an exhibition, nor to the sheer surprise of seeing the big pictures for the first time, but to the strict needs of conservation. No images greet the eye on entering. There is only a stark, almost clinical whiteness. The paintings are stored in carpeted racks now, their edges labeled like the spines of books. The air is maintained at the precise correct temperature and humidity.

The studio next door seems empty with its walls bare, but otherwise it looks much the same. There are still the big windows facing north, their lowest panes whitened for privacy. My father's rolltop oak desk is where it was when he was alive, his drawing table, the clunky red vinyl desk chair, the swiveling oak stool. In the middle of the room, the painting wall still stands, but it is a partition no longer needed, a baffle for the silence. A few jars of pencils and brushes remain beside his drawing table, but on the shelves the Higgins black ink has dried in its bottles, and the rolls of masking tape are brittle. Certain evidence remains: a pattern of pushpins in the Homosote wall beside the desk, the placement of tools, a solemn row of flatirons, and the absurd superfluity of an entire cupboard full of Bocour and Grumbacher cadmium red medium, hoarded like pints of blood against some feared and imagined shortage, still in readiness for the next impassioned run of work.

In the center of it all, his claw-foot chair, a stiff leather throne of a seat, with its perennial companion beside it, an ashtray on a brass pedestal. I can still summon up a picture of him sitting there, smoking and looking at his work, but after seven years it is only a memory, and not a haunting presence.

It is in summer that I see him, wearing a worn Brooks Brothers short-sleeved shirt, something blue and striped, with the shirt tails hanging out over floppy khaki-colored shorts. His long, pale legs are crossed, big misshapen feet sockless in unlaced dirty white sneakers. And it is late, sometime after two or three in the morning. Overhead, the fluorescent lights hum. From time to time, my father sighs deeply. Otherwise, he is silent, staring through half-closed lids. One hand cups an elbow, his chin rests on the heel of the other. He only moves to take deep drags from his cigarette, making that familiar two-finger salute of his, then spitting a loose shred of tobacco from his lower lip or squinting against a wisp of smoke. He stares at his painting, the one he is working on, as if it is his adversary. His eyes, set deep and pouched, look almost black, opaque, in the flat, shadowless light.

Pushing himself up with difficulty from the chair, he sighs again, stubs out one cigarette, lights another, and shambles over to the wall where the canvas is stapled. There's something about his long, surprisingly thin legs and bulky torso that brings to mind some anxious, stalking bird, a crane or heron, one of those gawky, elegant creatures that soar so majestically.

He approaches his painting, squints, leans into it, disturbs an area with his thumb, walks away and turns on it again, as if to catch it unaware. He is not finished with this one. No, I can see he is deep in this picture still, worrying it, arguing with it. This looking is only an intermission, a brief cease-fire. The picture has not yet claimed him fully.

And so the battle resumes, the devotional act. For all the excited talk far into the night, for all his wise words on the creative act, for all his wit, his passion and despair, it is this solitary dialogue, most intimate of conversations, that forms my father's essence. The paintings testify; they are the evidence. He is the painter, in his studio, alone.

" 'One has no business to have any children,' St. George placidly declared. 'I mean, of course, if one wants to do anything good.' " So says the Master in Henry James' *The Lesson of the Master*. He has everything, he tells his disciple Paul Overt, but the "great thing." And what is the great thing? the young Overt inquires.

" 'The sense of having done the best,' the Master replied, 'the sense which is the real life of the artist and the absence of which is his death, of having drawn from his intellectual instrument the finest music that nature had hidden in it, of having played it as it should be played. He either does that or he doesn't—and if he doesn't he isn't worth speaking of.' "

A full life, for an artist, is treacherous with compromise; there is always some precarious division of attention and energies to be made. Yet in this story, the Master himself is married; he has apparently renounced the austerity of Art in favor of Life's entanglements. For him, at least, as for my father, the rewards of marriage far outweighed the risk of mediocrity.

But what of his family, the supporting cast? Theirs are the voices we never hear. We never hear what it's like for them, the patient wives of artists. Too modest or too shy, these women are hidden away somewhere, busy feathering a safe nook, fending off invaders, trying to offer their brilliant mates some semblance of what Elizabeth Hardwick calls "the wholeness of the bourgeois, whose health they must have in order to work, but whose happiness they must surrender because of their violent consciousness and vulnerability."

Worthwhile as this enterprise might be, I suspect there would be few applicants today for my mother's position. For that matter, few artists seem to possess my father's passion and single-mindedness. Today's cooler attitudes—not only in art—are more pragmatic, less idealized. And women, rightfully, are eager for their own rewards. Certainly, the next generation, my own, wanted things to be different. Younger artists looked at the lives of the artists they admired, the abstract expressionists who rose to prominence in the fifties, those hard-drinking, work-obsessed painters who died young; they looked at the embittered wives and children of these ancestors, and decided this was not for them. Or so an East Village painter of my generation told me recently. He and his friends wanted to stay closer to their families, he said, to try to be less self-destructive. Whether they were successful, or even representative of their generation, I do not know.

Certainly, I, who tried so hard to emulate my mother, have long ago given up the fantasy of being the artist's wife—or the artist, in the sense that my father was. My own story, I suppose, is one of bending my parents' extremes to my more moderate uses. Strange, then, that in looking at them now, it is still their extremes that move me—not to anger as they once did, but to respect and a bit of sadness, at the cost. But I can only admire the full-tilt intensity of my father's pursuit, the constancy and sweetness of my mother's devotion.

For the stern equation of such sacrifice to prove itself, the gift in question must be very great, the good must be more than merely good. If it is not, all is unbalanced. Whole lives seem wasted and the losses very bitter. Without true greatness to lend an imperative, an artist can turn into a foolish, brutal tyrant, and his wife is in danger of becoming, in Cynthia Ozick's words, a "docile captive, an accomplice, an It," a woman who has chosen the "comforts" of "dependency, the absence of decisions and responsibility, the avoidance of risk, the shutting-out of the gigantic toil of art."

For everything depends on the redemptive power of Art.

How else can I explain that feeling of being caught up, all three of us—my mother, my father, and I—in something larger, something so very necessary? It feels like something I've known all my life, but only now can find the means to say. I feel embarrassed writing these words, as if I were confessing some sort of religious fervor to skeptics. But for me, growing up with my parents, the underlying reality was always this: that we lived with a great and irresistible force that my father claimed and yet didn't claim as his own, a force that moved through him, that tormented and exalted him, and all of us.

What a romantic notion—this mysterious force, this noble suffering! How can I dignify my father's domination, my mother's submissiveness? How can I, who know how very human my father was, add to the pompous mythmaking that follows an artist's death? But what shall I do? This is how I have lived my life, and fashioned meaning from it.

"He was a drastic artist," Philip Roth says about my father. "Every time he wrote the rules to the game, he wanted to break the rules . . . There was such strain, you know? At the end of a BBC film on Malamud, the camera is perched on a ladder, looking down on him writing at his desk. It gave me the chills. I said to Claire, 'So that's what it looks like. It's horrible. There's no point to that.' . . . There was this man, alone, trying to break his own rules, to get further, to get further. And to get to 'it,' to do 'it,' to show what couldn't be seen." He stops, then turns to look at me. "Do you think he would do it again?" he asks.

"Of course," I say, without having to think. "He would have said, 'What's the alternative?' "

"I feel there's none for me, either." The sense of resignation in his voice is sobering. We are silent for a moment.

"It's not a matter of romantic agony," Philip Roth says, "but just a form of professional deformity."

Goethe wrote, "The only way in which we can come to terms with the great superiority of another person is love." This sounds fine, of course, transcendent even, but how do I find such love? How do I live with this man so large on my walls and in my heart? To get on with my own life, shall I diminish his? Shall I build a figure of pity from my father's flaws, create him in my mind as some lesser being, full of anxieties, excesses, and grudges? Is that the remedy?

Sometimes, I admit, I do look for ways to shrink the monument, this larger-than-life creation I and others have made of Philip Guston, to someone more my size—and therefore more manageable. And then he becomes an ordinary man again, imperfect, flawed, someone to rage against and forgive. Someone to grieve for. Then he becomes, simply, my father.

But it never sticks. Philip Guston was more than my father. That was always the problem: that he was more. There is a photograph of him, at ten or eleven years old, that stays with me. The resourceful child of poor Russian immigrants, the young Philip is standing behind the scruffy house plants on someone's front porch. His cap is at a rakish tilt; his pose is confident. Arms crossed, he stares straight out at me, and his eyes are wise, ageless, defiant, as if he realizes already that he is made for something else (see plate 1).

My father was brilliant, and knew it. And I was not, and I knew that too. Each of us was burdened in different ways by this knowledge: he by the responsibilities of his gifts, I by a sense of my own relative unimportance. None of that matters, I now understand. It's only a yardstick best brought over one's knee and broken. "Praise and blame alike mean nothing," as Virginia Woolf once wrote. "Delightful as the pastime of measuring may be, it is the most futile of occupations."

And excellence is only one part given, I finally realize, and two parts (at least) some other quality of mind, some crazy, driven insistence on getting it right, on shunning the glib and easy reach, on letting the line down through the surface glimmer, past the lotus blossoms and baitfish in common view, into that murky place, into obscurity, and, once there, waiting—no, not patiently, but waiting—for the deeper tug of truth.

Surely what Goethe meant by love was more than selfless devotion or simple encouragement, more than the setting aside of one's own ambitions—that gracious and infinitely sad accommodation made by my mother. There is a love that reaches past these things. But there are no words for it that don't sound mawkish or high-handed, or at least none that I, in my embarrassment, can find. It is a love of what is godlike in us, of creation's deep source, a love of Art, if you will—names do not matter. In some very few, it seems this quality is more exposed, more pure. They cannot help who they are. And what they give is given to the whole world, not only to their families. Though we may love them, we can never really claim them. They are not ours to claim.

What I know now, after these seven years since Philip's death, is this: in my life, I have worshiped, hated, and loved my father. I have run from him and I have run toward him. I have tried, desperately, to attract his attention. I have tried to ignore him. In the end, none of this matters. He will always be with me.

For me and for those who knew Philip Guston, two things remain— his art and the memory of his passion for it, a commitment as absolute as he, given his quite human failings, could make it. Now that he is really gone, and not in hiding, pursuing his "sacred foolishness," now that it is no longer his hunger for painting that keeps me from him, but death itself, now that I can at last give up trying to get his attention, I find myself welcoming that passion at last, for what it has left of him for me, for the world.

People ask me what it's like to live with my father's work. As if it must be disturbing or overwhelming, as if it must interfere in some way with my own life. They seem not quite to believe I am being honest—with them or with myself—when I say that it's wonderful. But it is. I get up in the morning, pour myself a cup of coffee, walk into the living room, and look at the paintings. I never tire of them.

Beside the glass double doors to my father's studio is a green curtain, for privacy, so that no one would walk in on Philip when he was working. Though no one is here but me, I find myself instinctively pulling the curtain across the entryway, hearing the brass rings scrape along the metal rod. Still protecting him. I open the curtain again, reach for the lights, and pause for a last look.

The studio walls are bare, with only ladders and light fixtures leaning up against them to disturb their white expanse. Big wooden packing crates for a European exhibition now past, built sturdy as furniture and lined with green felt, are stacked like giant blocks. Stretched, primed canvases stand side by side, waiting. For a year or two, we cleaned in here, but now everything carries a fine coat of pale blond dust.

We call this room "the studio," but it is no one's studio now. No longer steeped in sadness, it is too anonymous for that. It is no longer his. It's just a room, an empty room. It could be anyone's space, with its flat lights, its silences, its dust.

I listen to the high whine of the fluorescent lights, the beating of the silence behind. So this is what death is really like, I think, what it becomes. Beyond the pain of loss, there is finally only this sense of absence. The night quiet. And the way that memories blur, running into one another in the dilution of time.

NOTES

CHAPTER ONE: RETROSPECTIVE

page 8, line 18   "Philip Guston: Carnegie Winner's Art Is Abstract and Symbolic," *Life*, May 27, 1946.

page 8, line 35   Emily Genauer, "Abstraction Takes an Emotional Tack," New York *World-Telegram*, July 13, 1948.

page 10, line 26   Saul Bellow, *Herzog*, Viking Press, New York, 1964, p. 140.

page 12, line 3   Philip Guston, unpublished notes, c. 1974.

page 12, line 11   Philip Guston, letter to Dore Ashton, August 25, 1974, courtesy Archives of American Art.

page 13, line 2   Ross Feld, essay in *Philip Guston*, catalogue of Retrospective at San Francisco Museum of Modern Art, Braziller, New York, 1980, p. 6.

page 13, line 14   Philip Guston, notes from annotated manuscript of Dore Ashton's critical study, *Yes, But . . .*, 1975.

page 13, line 24   Dore Ashton, *Yes, But . . .: A Critical Study of Philip Guston*, Viking Press, New York, 1976, p. 12. For these and countless other details, I am deeply indebted to Dore Ashton's study. I could not have reconstructed my father's career, particularly the early years, without this valuable book. As a work of careful and thoughtful scholarship, it is one of the very few of its kind where the artist himself has reviewed and corrected the entire manuscript.

page 14, line 18   Josephine Chalmers, from an interview with the author, 1987.

page 14, line 35   Reuben Kadish, from an interview with the author, 1987.

page 18, line 6   Herman Cherry, from an interview with the author, 1987.

page 18, line 32   Dore Ashton, *Yes, But . . .*, op. cit., p. 16.

page 19, line 26   Philip Guston, notes from manuscript of *Yes, But . . .*, 1975.

page 20, line 8   "On a Mexican Wall," *Time*, April 1, 1935.

page 21, line 24   Francis V. O'Connor, Introduction to *New Deal Art: California*, de Saisset Art Gallery and Museum, University of Santa Clara, 1976, p. 11.

page 24, line 34   Philip Guston, unpublished, 1978.

CHAPTER TWO: WOMEN ARE LEARNERS

page 27, line 33   Dore Ashton, *The New York School: A Cultural Reckoning*, Viking, New York, 1973, pp. 46–47; Oliver W. Larkin, *Art and Life in America*, New York, Rinehart and Company, 1948.

page 30, line 19   Dore Ashton, *The New York School*, op. cit., p. 57.

page 30, line 26   Harold Rosenberg, "Action Painting: Crisis and Distortion," *The Anxious Object*, University of Chicago Press, 1964, p. 39.

page 31, line 9   Philip Guston, as quoted in Dore Ashton, *Yes, But . . . : A Critical Study of Philip Guston*, Viking Press, New York, 1976, p. 40.

page 31, line 20   Ruth Green Harris, "Public Taste in Murals," *New York Times*, July 28, 1940.

page 32, line 7   Philip Guston, notes on annotated manuscript of *Yes, But . . . .*

page 32, line 15   Philip Guston, interview with Joseph S. Trovato, January 29, 1965. Courtesy of the Archives of American Art.

page 36, line 26   Philip Guston, as quoted in "Guston's Social Security Mural: Completed Despite War," *Art News*, March 1, 1943.

page 37, line 9   Stephen Greene, notes to the author.

page 38, line 4   Dore Ashton, *Yes, But . . .* , op. cit.

page 38, line 9   Philip Guston, unpublished interview by Karl Fortess, April 14, 1966, at Brandeis University, Waltham, Mass. Courtesy Archives of American Art.

page 43, line 25   Musa McKim, unpublished poem.

CHAPTER THREE: STERN CONDITIONS

page 47, line 19   Philip Guston, notes on annotated manuscript of *Yes, But . . .* , 1975.

page 48, line 37   Philip Guston, as quoted in Sam Hunter, *Modern American Painting and Sculpture*, Dell, New York, 1959, p. 159.

page 49, line 9   Philip Guston, unpublished interview by Karl Fortess, April 14, 1966, at Brandeis University, Waltham, Mass. Courtesy Archives of American Art.

page 49, line 26   Nathan Silver, *Lost New York*, Houghton Mifflin, Boston, 1967.

page 57, line 25   Robert Phelps and Rosemarie Beck, from an interview with the author, 1987.

page 58, line 34   Musa McKim, "The Lightning Bird," unpublished.

page 60, line 23   Dore Ashton, *Yes, But . . . : A Critical Study of Philip Guston*, Viking Press, New York, 1976, p. 92.

page 61, line 5   Mercedes Matter, from an interview with the author, 1987.

page 61, line 27   Morton Feldman, "Philip Guston: The Last Painter," *Art News Annual XXXI*, 1966.

page 61, line 34   Philip Guston, as quoted in Dore Ashton, *Yes, But . . .* , op. cit., p. 95.

page 62, line 25   Philip Guston, notes on annotated manuscript of *Yes, But . . .* , op. cit.

page 62, line 37   Harold Rosenberg, "The American Action Painters," *Art News*, vol. 51, no. 5, September 1952.

page 63, line 4   Philip Guston, as quoted in *12 Americans*, Dorothy C. Miller, editor, Museum of Modern Art, New York, 1956.

page 63, line 8   Philip Guston, as quoted in *Time*, January 7, 1952.

page 63, line 23   Bill Berkson, from an interview with the author, 1987.

page 63, line 31   Philip Guston, Fortess interview, op. cit.

page 64, line 9 Elaine de Kooning, from an interview with Robert Storr, 1985.

page 64, line 17 Dore Ashton, unpublished journal entry, December 20, 1955.

page 64, line 30 Philip Guston, as quoted in Jan Butterfield, "Philip Guston—A Very Anxious Fix," *Images and Issues,* Summer 1980.

page 65, line 22 Morton Feldman, from an interview with Robert Storr, 1985.

page 65, line 27 Elaine de Kooning, from an interview with the author, 1987.

page 66, line 9 Mercedes Matter interview, op. cit.

page 66, line 20 James Brooks, from an interview with Dorothy Seckler, June 10, 1965. Courtesy of Archives of American Art.

page 66, line 27 Herman Cherry, from an interview with the author, 1987.

page 67, line 6 For this insight I thank Magdalena Dabrowski, of the Museum of Modern Art.

page 67, line 13 Philip Guston, from Jan Butterfield interview, 1979, op. cit.

page 67, line 21 Philip Guston, from a lecture given at the University of Minnesota, March 1978.

page 68, line 13 Elaine de Kooning interview with the author, op. cit.

page 68, line 36 Herman Cherry interview, op. cit.

CHAPTER FOUR: SO MUCH PREPARATION

page 73, line 5 Franz Kafka, "The Eight Octavo Notebooks," from *Dearest Father,* translated by Ernst Kaiser and Eithne Wilkins, Schocken Books, New York, 1954, p. 50. (Original presumed to date from c. 1917.)

page 76, line 33 Philip Guston, from a question-and-answer session following a talk given at Boston University, 1966.

page 77, line 10 Stephen Greene, from an interview with Dore Ashton, c. 1975.

page 77, line 25 Philip Guston, unpublished interview by Karl Fortess, April 14, 1966, at Brandeis University, Waltham, Mass. Courtesy Archives of American Art.

page 78, line 3 Joseph Ablow, "Philip Guston: The Last Paintings," *Bostonia Magazine,* April–May 1986.

page 78, line 26 Herman Cherry, from an interview with the author, 1987.

page 78, line 38 Elaine de Kooning, from an interview with the author, 1987.

page 80, line 2 Carol Barsha, in correspondence with Musa Guston, 1980.

page 80, line 10 Steven Gorney, in correspondence with Musa Guston, 1980.

page 80, line 23 Grant Drumheller, in correspondence with Musa Guston, 1980, 1984.

page 81, line 24 Laureen Rueckner, in correspondence with Musa Guston, 1980.

page 82, line 34 Ibid.

page 83, line 9 Philip Guston, from a talk given at Harvard, 1977.

CHAPTER FIVE: IN THE STUDIO

page 88, line 31 Philip Guston, from Michael Blackwood's film *Philip Guston: A Life Lived, 1913–1980,* 1981.

page 90, line 31   Søren Kierkegaard, *Either/Or, A Fragment of Life*, translated by David F. Swenson and Lillian Marvin Swenson. Princeton University Press, 1944, p. 31. (Originally published in Copenhagen, 1843.)

page 91, line 24   Philip Guston, "Statement," *It Is*, No. 1, Spring 1958.

page 98, line 13   Albert Camus, *Selected Essays and Notebooks*, reference by Stephen Greene in his notes to Dore Ashton, 1975.

page 99, line 20   Philip Guston, unpublished interview by Karl Fortess, April 14, 1966, at Brandeis University, Waltham, Mass. Courtesy Archives of American Art.

page 102, line 6   Philip Guston, as quoted in Dore Ashton, *Yes, But . . . : A Critical Study of Philip Guston*, Viking Press, New York, 1976.

page 102, line 15   H. H. Arnason, *Philip Guston*, The Solomon R. Guggenheim Museum, New York, 1962.

page 102, line 19   Sam Hunter, *Philip Guston: Recent Paintings and Drawings*, The Jewish Museum, New York, 1966.

page 102, line 30   Hilton Kramer, quoted in Dore Ashton, *Yes, But . . .*, op. cit., p. 133.

page 103, line 3   Søren Kierkegaard, op. cit., p. 33.

page 103, line 8   *The Diaries of Franz Kafka: 1914–1923*, edited by Max Brod, Schocken Books, New York, 1949, p. 118.

page 103, line 14   Jean-Paul Sartre, *On Baudelaire*, translated by Martin Turnell, New Directions, New York, 1950, p. 31.

page 103, line 29   Harold Rosenberg, *The Anxious Object*, University of Chicago Press, 1964, pp. 14–15.

page 103, line 34   Søren Kierkegaard, op. cit., p. 24.

page 104, line 3   Philip Guston, letter to Dore Ashton, October 1974.

page 104, line 10   Harold Rosenberg, op. cit., p. 17.

page 104, line 25   Philip Guston, Fortess interview, op. cit.

page 104, line 32   Philip Guston, unpublished, 1967.

page 105, line 2   Søren Kierkegaard, op. cit., p. 23.

page 105, line 12   Philip Guston, "Faith, Hope and Impossibility," *Art News Annual XXXI*, 1966.

page 105, line 26   Philip Guston, from the draft of a letter to Dore Ashton, c. 1974.

CHAPTER SIX: SOME MUSIC

page 111, line 29   Musa McKim, unpublished, 1950s.

page 113, line 3   Stephen Green, interview with Robert Storr, 1985.

page 113, line 22   Mercedes Matter, interview with the author, 1987.

page 115, line 4   Musa McKim, unpublished, c. 1958.

page 125, line 17   Philip Roth, from an interview with the author, 1987.

page 129, line 35   Virginia Woolf, *A Room of One's Own*, Harcourt, Brace, New York, 1929, p. 45.

page 131, line 27   Robert Storr, *Philip Guston*, Abbeville Press, New York, 1986, p. 87.

page 136, line 7   Musa McKim, unpublished, c. 1966.

page 136, line 2   Ibid.

CHAPTER SEVEN: PAINTER'S FORMS

page 141, line 4   Evgeny Zamyatin, from *Literature and Revolution*, as quoted by Philip Guston in a letter to Dore Ashton, September 4, 1974. "I jumped out of my skin, as you can imagine, when I read this," my father said.

page 141, line 10   Philip Guston, *It Is*, No. 5, Spring 1960.

page 141, line 28   Philip Guston, as quoted in Dore Ashton, *Yes, But . . . : A Critical Study of Philip Guston*, Viking Press, New York, 1976, p. 154.

page 142, line 11   Philip Guston, undated letter to Bill Berkson, c. 1967.

page 147, line 17   Musa McKim, unpublished, 1950s.

page 148, line 14   Philip Guston, unpublished, 1970.

page 148, line 18   Philip Guston, as quoted in Bill Berkson, "The New Gustons," *Art News*, October 1970.

page 148, line 21   Philip Guston, unpublished.

page 149, line 2   Philip Guston, in "Philip Guston Talking," a lecture given at the University of Minnesota in March 1978, appears in *Philip Guston: The Late Works*, National Gallery of Victoria, Melbourne, Australia, 1984.

page 149, line 12   When Mark Rothko died, by his own hand, in 1970, his will provided for a nonprofit foundation that would handle his work. The members of the board of directors of the Rothko Foundation, his trusted friends, Frank Lloyd among them, engineered a scandalous bulk sale of his work through Marlborough Gallery for a fraction of the actual value of the paintings. A multimillion-dollar suit was brought against them by the Rothko children, which they eventually won, and a new set of directors was chosen.

page 150, line 3   Philip Guston, unpublished, c. 1977.

page 150, line 11   Ross Feld, essay in *Philip Guston*, catalogue of Retrospective Exhibition at San Francisco Museum of Modern Art, Braziller, New York, 1980, p. 23.

page 150, line 31   Harold Rosenberg, "The Game of Illusion: Pop and Gag," *The Anxious Object*, University of Chicago Press, 1964, p. 63.

page 151, line 7   Elaine de Kooning, from an interview with the author, July 1987.

page 151, line 36   Harold Rosenberg, op cit., p. 86.

page 152, line 13   Musa McKim, unpublished, 1970.

page 152, line 20   Ross Feld, op. cit., p. 23.

page 152, line 26   Philip Guston, letter to Bill Berkson, August 16, 1970.

page 152, line 34   Philip Guston, from a lecture given at the University of Minnesota in March 1978.

page 153, line 21   Norbert Lynton, "An Obverse Decorum," essay published in catalogue for *Philip Guston: Paintings 1969–80*, The Whitechapel Art Gallery, London, England, for an exhibition that traveled to the Stedelijk Museum, Amsterdam, and the Kunsthalle, Basel, 1982–83.

page 155, line 16   Hilton Kramer, "A Mandarin Pretending to Be a Stumblebum," *New York Times,* October 25, 1970.

page 156, line 13   Musa Jane Kadish, "A Personal Vendetta Against Guston?" *New York Times,* Sunday, December 6, 1970.

page 156, line 29   Philip Guston, from University of Minnesota lecture, 1978.

page 157, line 6   Philip Guston, as quoted in Jan Butterfield, "Philip Guston—A Very Anxious Fix," *Images and Issues,* Summer 1980.

page 157, line 33   Harold Rosenberg, "Liberation from Detachment," *The New Yorker,* November 7, 1970.

page 158, line 19   James Thrall Soby, *The Early Chirico,* Dodd, Mead, New York, 1941.

page 158, line 36   Philip Guston, letter to Dore Ashton, summer 1971.

page 159, line 17   Robert Storr, *Philip Guston,* Abbeville Press, New York, 1986, p. 66.

page 159, line 37   Philip Guston, as quoted in Mark Stevens, "A Talk with Philip Guston," *The New Republic,* March 15, 1980.

CHAPTER EIGHT: DRAWING ASIDE THE CURTAIN

page 168, line 34   Philip Guston, letter to Bill Berkson, October 21, 1972.

page 170, line 9   Philip Guston, letter to Bill Berkson, September 4, 1974.

page 170, line 14   Philip Guston, letter to Bill Berkson, March 25, 1974.

page 170, line 33   Philip Guston, unpublished.

page 171, line 14   Philip Guston, from University of Minnesota lecture, 1978.

page 171, line 28   Philip Guston, as quoted in Jerry Talmer, " 'Creation' Is for Beauty Parlors," New York *Post,* April 9, 1977.

page 172, line 4   Philip Guston, statement in *It Is,* No. 5, Spring 1960.

page 172, line 13   Philip Guston, as quoted in Jan Butterfield, "Philip Guston—A Very Anxious Fix," *Images and Issues,* Summer 1980.

page 172, line 24   Philip Guston, letter to Dore Ashton, October 1974.

page 172, line 29   Philip Guston, letter to Bill Berkson, March 17, 1975.

page 172, line 36   Philip Guston, letter to Dore Ashton, August 11, 1975.

page 173, line 10   Philip Guston, letter to Dore Ashton, August 25, 1974.

page 173, line 20   Isaac Babel, "The Story of My Dovecot," *The Collected Stories,* edited and translated by Walter Morison, New American Library, New York, 1960, pp. 262–63.

page 173, line 25   Ibid., Lionel Trilling, Introduction, p. 17.

page 173, line 30   Virginia Woolf, *The Common Reader,* Harcourt, Brace, New York, 1925, p. 59.

page 173, line 37   Philip Guston, unpublished, 1972.

page 176, line 13   Philip Guston, unpublished.

page 177, line 7   Philip Roth, from an interview with the author, 1987.

page 179, line 2   Musa McKim, "Honorarium," unpublished short story, 1976.

page 179, line 11   Philip Guston, letter to Bill Berkson, July 26, 1976.

page 179, line 22   Joseph Ablow, "Philip Guston: The Last Paintings," *Bostonia Magazine,* April–May 1986.

page 179, line 36 Philip Guston, letter to Bill Berkson, May 20, 1977.

page 180, line 5 Philip Guston, unpublished.

page 180, line 21 Philip Guston, letter to Bill Berkson, March 21, 1976.

page 180, line 29 Robert Storr, *Philip Guston*, Abbeville Press, New York, 1986, p. 95.

page 181, line 6 Clark Coolidge, from an interview with the author, 1987.

page 182, line 2 Philip Guston, unpublished.

page 182, line 21 Ross Feld, essay in *Philip Guston*, catalogue of Retrospective Exhibition at San Francisco Museum of Modern Art, Braziller, New York, 1980, p. 29.

CHAPTER TEN: OPENINGS

page 204, line 14 Philip Guston, from University of Minnesota lecture, 1978, appears in *Philip Guston: The Late Works*, National Gallery of Victoria, Melbourne, Australia, 1984.

page 204, line 20 Ibid.

page 204, line 24 Philip Guston, in Robert Storr, *Philip Guston*, Abbeville Press, New York, 1986, p. 98.

page 213, line 36 Philip Guston, in *Philip Guston: A Life Lived*, a film by Michael Blackwood, 1981.

page 214, line 16 *The Jessie Willcox Smith Mother Goose: A Careful and Full Selection of the Rhymes*, Dodd, Mead, New York, 1914, p. 102.

CHAPTER ELEVEN: IF THIS BE NOT I

page 223, line 24 Philip Guston, unpublished, 1978.

page 233, line 24 Philip Roth, *My Life as a Man*, Holt, Rinehart and Winston, New York, 1970.

page 235, line 9 Morton Feldman, essay in *Philip Guston: 1980, The Last Works*, catalogue for an exhibition organized by the Phillips Collection, Washington, D.C., 1981.

page 235, line 37 Stanley Kunitz, "Remembering Philip Guston," in *Next to Last Things*, Atlantic Monthly Press, Boston/New York, 1985.

page 237, line 2 Sheldon Kopp, *If You Meet the Buddha on the Road, Kill Him!* Science and Behavior Books, Palo Alto, California, 1972, p. 223.

page 238, line 25 T. S. Eliot, "East Coker," *Four Quartets*, Harcourt, Brace, New York, 1943, p. 32.

CHAPTER TWELVE: NIGHT STUDIO

page 243, line 21 Henry James, "The Lesson of the Master," as quoted in Cynthia Ozick's essay of the same name, in *Art and Ardor*, Alfred A. Knopf, New York, 1983, pp. 291–92.

page 241, line 35 Elizabeth Hardwick, "Thomas Mann at 100," in *Bartleby in Manhattan*, Vintage Books, New York, 1984, p. 181.

page 244, line 31 Cynthia Ozick, "Previsions of the Demise of the Dancing Dog," in *Art and Ardor*, op. cit., p. 281.

page 245, line 24 Philip Roth, from an interview with the author, 1987.

page 246, line 14 Virginia Woolf, *A Room of One's Own*, Harcourt, Brace, New York, 1929, p. 110.

A Note on the Type

The text of this book was set in Janson, a typeface thought to have been made by the Dutchman Anton Janson, who was a practicing type founder in Leipzig during the years 1668–1687. However, it has been conclusively demonstrated that these types are actually the work of Nicholas Kis (1650–1702), a Hungarian, who most probably learned his trade from the master Dutch type founder Dirk Voskens. The type is an example of the influential and sturdy Dutch types that prevailed in England up to the time William Caslon developed his own designs from them.

Composed by New England Typographic Service, Inc.,
Bloomfield, Connecticut
Printed and bound by The Murray Printing Company,
Westford, Massachusetts
Inserts prepared and printed by The Studley Press,
Dalton, Massachusetts
Designed by Iris Weinstein